WILDMEN, WOBBLIES & WHISTLE PUNKS

Northwest Reprints
Series Editor: Robert J. Frank

Other titles in the series:

WILDMEN, WOBBLIES & WHISTLE PUNKS

STEWART HOLBROOK'S LOWBROW NORTHWEST
Edited and Introduced by Brian Booth

Oregon State University Press
Corvallis, Oregon

For my family and for Dutch

The paper in this book meets the guidelines for permanence and durability of the Committee on Production Guidelines for Book Longevity of the Council on Library Resources and the minimum requirements of the American National Standard for Permanence of Paper for Printed Library Materials Z39.48-1984.

Library of Congress Cataloging-in-Publication Data
Holbrook, Stewart Hall, 1893-1964
     Wildmen, wobblies and whistle punks : Stewart Holbrook's Lowbrow Northwest / edited and introduced by Brian Booth.
          p. cm. -- (Northwest Reprints)
     Includes bibliographical references.
     ISBN 0-87071-367-1 (cloth)
     1. Northwest, Pacific--History. I. Booth, Brian.
II. Title. III. Series.
F851.H7 1992   92-19836
979.5--dc20   CIP

Contents

Stewart Holbrook's Lowbrow Northwest

An Introduction to Stewart Holbrook

Looking back more than a quarter of a century after his death, it is difficult to fully appreciate the impact that journalist and historian Stewart H. Holbrook once had on the Pacific Northwest, and the role he played in characterizing the region to the rest of the nation.

His death, in Portland, Oregon, at age 71 in 1964, was front-page news and resulted in editorial tributes throughout the West. The media, from the *New York Times* to the

Eugene *Register-Guard*, expressed its admiration for, and fascination with, the high-school dropout who emerged from the logging camps of New England and British Columbia to lecture at Harvard and become the "Lumberjack Boswell," the author of three dozen books, the Northwest's best-known storyteller, and one of the nation's most popular historians. He was also remembered as a "24-karat character," a raconteur and lively public speaker, a satirical painter, a leading forest conservationist, and a witty opponent of growth and development in the Pacific Northwest. Holbrook's friends were scattered from Madison Avenue to skidroads and included lumber executives and literary luminaries, but his fellow writer James Stevens said that his "true love was for the lowly of forest and stream, of mine and mill and railroad."

A tribute in the *Seattle Post-Intelligencer* was typical: "No one wrote of his adopted West with as much zest, and no contemporary historian better understood the American character." "The Northwest from Juan de Fuca to Klamath Lake lost its most ardent lover," wrote John McClelland, Jr., Washington editor and historian, adding that "we almost expect the trees themselves to bow their dark green tops when the last of him is carried to some hillside for burial."

In Portland, the *Oregonian's* editorial said:

> When Stewart Holbrook wrote about a Pacific Northwest logging camp you could fairly smell the smoke from the crooked stove pipe of the cookhouse. You could hear the sound of the iron on which the bull cook pounded the call to breakfast . . . . He made all his writing live through a rare gift for noting the unusual. The high and mighty received adequate, somewhat sardonic attention, but the often humorous, always human sidelights on lesser men gave him his distinctive, highly readable style . . . . He dug up the stories of unusual people and places outside the mainstream of regional life, without which our history would be comparatively dull reading.

From the time of his death and for years afterward, suggestions for an appropriate memorial to Holbrook were widely discussed. Statues and plaques were suggested. Some urged that Portland's new Forecourt Fountain be named after him and, when the consolidation of Portland and Multnomah County was being discussed, the *Oregon Journal* recommended that the combined metropolis be named "Holbrook." Historian Ellis Lucia argued against a man-made memorial, saying, "I lean toward a beautiful park or wayside or perhaps a memorial forest, any of which contains tall fine timber like that which brought Stewart to the Oregon country."

None of the suggestions to honor Holbrook came to pass. Today none of his books is in print in a cloth edition, and copies are difficult to locate in used-book stores. Indeed, his paintings are more sought after than his books. The journalists, writers, editors, historians and lumbermen who admired him have retired or died.

The resurgence of interest in the history of the West by academic historians has not revived interest in Holbrook or his works, even though he anticipated several of the themes of the "New Western History." How can scholars be expected to take seriously a historian who did not like footnotes and rarely used them, laced his works with wit and playfulness, and perhaps worst of all, wound up with books on the best-seller lists?

Schools and colleges, which today use bland history texts that are carefully written to avoid offending any group, have no use for an author who wrote fondly of loggers, recommended drinking as the "great civilizer," mocked modern art, and treated subjects from religion to the pioneers with irreverence.

Holbrook would have understood this neglect. He knew about the fickleness of fame, because he so often wrote about the men and women history has forgotten. In *Dreamers of the American Dream*, he wrote:

> The vagaries of posthumous fame are neither to be explained, nor excused. One can only accept them, and still wonder why this man or this woman was tossed to some peak of eminence, high or low, to remain as a symbol, reasonably secure and shining in the beautiful mellow light of history; while others are almost as forgotten as if they never lived.

Still, with the growing interest in nontraditional Western history and the recent "discovery" of the Pacific Northwest by television and film as a showcase for eccentrics, perhaps now is an appropriate time to introduce a new generation to Stewart Holbrook and his "lowbrow" writings on the Northwest. For if an important part of history is the telling of stories, Holbrook merits attention. He certainly knew how to tell stories that brought the past to life in what Harvard historian Simon Schama recently called "all its splendid messiness."

3

Much of Holbrook's writing on the Northwest is unconventional because, compared to most writers of history, Holbrook's life was unconventional. He did not attend a

university, he never received a fellowship or a grant, and he never held a teaching job to provide a steady income while he did the research for a book.

Holbrook was not an academic historian. He was a journalistic historian who wrote for a living, usually against deadlines. His articles supported him between books and had to appeal to magazine editors and their readers.

Holbrook wrote books on many subjects, but the Pacific Northwest, along with New England, was his special province. Holbrook's short pieces on the Northwest are based on his own research, travel and interviews. They grew out of his work as a logger, as an editor for a lumber industry newspaper, and as a journalist covering "forest fires, kidnappings and the better class of murders and other skullduggery." He was not interested in celebrating the conventional heroic view of the pioneers and missionaries of the West that prevailed during his lifetime. Instead, Holbrook's colorful Northwest writings probed unconventional areas not often covered in regional histories of his time: the lore of logging camps and the lives of loggers; low life and rough characters; Wobblies and other radicals; forgotten scandals and crimes, especially in small towns or

Holbrook with his younger brother Roland and their dog Donald in 1909

rural areas; forest fires, floods and other calamities; obscure folklore; and profiles of various reformers, do-gooders, scoundrels, schemers and dreamers who had a brief moment of fame or notoriety before slipping into oblivion. Holbrook's writings reflect his sympathy for and romanticizing of workers, underdogs, visionaries and fanatics, his interest in the humorous and the offbeat, and his penchant for puncturing myths and poking fun at stuffed shirts and hypocrites from all walks of life.

II

Appropriately enough, the only memorial to Stewart Holbrook today is a 33,000-acre tree farm established in 1965 in his native state of Vermont by International Paper Co. Holbrook either coined the term "tree farm" or was one of the first to use it, and after his logging days were over he became an early and leading advocate of reforestation and sustained-yield forestry.

Holbrook was a ninth-generation New Englander, born in Newport, Vermont, on August 12, 1893. He was named for his Scottish mother, Katie Holbrook, whose maiden name was Stewart. He liked to refer to his "old-line Yankee stock," and said his forebears were "the only ones that didn't come over on the Mayflower."

Newport was a town of 5,000 dominated by a sawmill. In *Holy Old Mackinaw* he wrote that:

> none of the boys in our town wanted to be cowboys or soldiers or policemen. To be a riverman and go down with the drive was the ambition of all of us. To "card" logs through white water, to steer a bateau down Fifteen Mile Falls, to break the log jams — these were the greatest things any man could hope to achieve. Even to pilot a locomotive on the Grand Trunk was as nothing. We wanted a peavey, a pair of calked boots and a fast moving stream full of logs.

Holbrook described his father, Jesse Holbrook, as a "restless promoter." The family moved frequently, and Holbrook attended four different high schools in Northern Vermont and New Hampshire. He also worked in logging camps that his father operated.

When Stewart was 18 he dropped out of Colebrook Academy in New Hampshire and moved with his family to Winnipeg, Manitoba. Rather than continuing with school, he became a cub reporter for the *Winnipeg Daily Telegram* and played semiprofessional baseball. Holbrook made extra money yodeling in a local nightspot and singing "illustrated songs."

He continued his theatrical career by joining the Harry St. Clair Stock Company, which toured Western Canada and Minnesota. Holbrook claimed the 71-year old St. Clair took

A formal pose, perhaps when Holbrook was singing in theaters

all the romantic leads, while young Stewart sold tickets, played the piano and appeared in various guises, including crotchety old men and "Dutch Hall, the German Tourist, Comedian and Yodeler." Another member of the company was William Pratt, who later achieved fame as Boris Karloff. Holbrook called it "the worst dramatic stock company an amused God ever permitted to roam," and said "we stayed a week in each town if they'd let us." A year after Holbrook joined the troupe, St. Clair vanished with the box office receipts, and Holbrook returned to New England, where he worked as a store clerk, held logging jobs, and sang in local theaters.

Holbrook as "the Man who Put the Yo in Yodel" in about 1913

With America's entry into World War I, Holbrook enlisted in the army and became a first sergeant with the 303rd Field Artillery. He was in combat action in France, but still had time to write, direct and act in musical comedies for the troops, including "Follies of Verdun" and "After the Ball Is Over." After the war, Holbrook worked again as a logger in New Hampshire, and participated in one of the last log drives on the Connecticut River.

Holbrook's life changed forever in 1920 when he found himself in Boston with some extra cash. He liked to tell how he bought a derby hat in the Jordan Marsh emporium, and purchased a round-trip ticket to British Columbia with the idea of returning East after seeing the big trees he had heard about. He found work in a logging camp along the

7

Fraser River and eventually cashed in his return ticket; for the next several years he worked as a log scaler, supervised crews of Chinese fallers and buckers, and held other jobs in remote logging camps, where he heard the legends and lore of logging from bunkhouse storytellers.

Holbrook "acquired very early the habit of reading" and was never without books in the woods. "Every time I went to town I returned to camp with $100 worth of secondhand books." One of his sources of reading material was Jackson Marks, a saw-filer in a camp 300 miles north of Vancouver served once a week by boat.

> Marks' personal library was shelved in the long boxes crosscut saws came in. Here I first met the monumental Gibbon, in six thumping volumes; and no less thorough Frazer's "The Golden Bough" in an even dozen works. I read Carlyle, Buckle, Darwin; and Adam Smith, John Stuart Mill, and Herbert Spencer; and took aboard a whole raft of "Brann the Iconoclast."

Holbrook said that he did not know how he began writing, but "as early as I could write at all I liked it; I was making up stories by the time I was eight years old." In the Canadian woods, he started submitting cartoons and articles as "Hols" Holbrook to the *British Columbia Lumberman*, other trade publications, and the old *Life* magazine. James Stevens said Holbrook "made just the craziest, most horrible cartoons imaginable, but the readers of the *B.C. Lumberman* loved them." Apparently, his first payment was for a satirical verse on army life purchased for $5 by Harold Ross, publisher of the *Home Sector*, and subsequently the famed editor of the *New Yorker*. Many years later when he was a *New Yorker* contributor, Holbrook made a point of saying that now the checks from Ross "were a little larger."

Eventually Holbrook was spending more time writing than logging. In 1923, after receipt of a $100 check from the *Century* magazine for an article on bull cooks in lumber camps, he nailed his derby "to a big stump deep in the British Columbian timber," moved to Portland ("because

Portland has the finest public library in the West"), and joined the staff of the *Four L Lumber News* published by the Loyal Legion of Loggers and Lumbermen (the 4L). As associate editor and later editor of the *Lumber News*, he traveled throughout the Pacific Northwest visiting timber operations, interviewing loggers, lumbermen and local characters, and picking up the material which he drew on for the rest of his career.

The *Lumber News* was published by an employers' organization, originally formed to fight the radical Industrial Workers of the World (I.W.W.), whose members were known as Wobblies. This provided the opportunity for Holbrook to get to know a number of Wobblies, and he eventually became a leading authority on the I.W.W., "the least inhibited labor union the United States has known." Holbrook always enjoyed Wobblies and other radicals. He said they were more interesting than the other side.

Holbrook said the *Lumber News* "was to literary quality what Billy Sunday was to theology." When he was not traveling or writing for the *Lumber News*, Holbrook continued his free-lance work and gradually developed a reputation as a prolific journalist whose articles appeared with regularity in *Century, Sunset, Saturday Evening Post* and other publications ranging from *American Forests* to detective pulps.

Money was always a problem for Holbrook in the 1920s, and his goal in writing was to be published and to be paid. He would undoubtedly have understood Robert Benchley's observation that a free-lance writer is a person who is paid per piece or per word or perhaps. He told a friend, ex-logger M. T. Dunten, that: "My philosophy of writing is that it is far more important to know *what* to write and *where* to send it, than is the writing per se. Literary quality is quite secondary." Holbrook once wrote Dunten that he had "fallen to the lowest rung of the ladder," explaining that he was writing continuity for Paul Bunyan stories being read over the radio in Seattle.

In 1923 James Stevens, who was working on a green-chain in a sawmill in Bend, Oregon, sent a letter to Henry L. Mencken describing life in Bend. Mencken had Stevens revise his letter and published it as *The Uplift on the Frontier* in his new monthly, *American Mercury*. Stevens's article referred to the 4L as "a petting party between the lumberman and his employees." Holbrook contacted Stevens to complain, the two became great friends and, at Stevens's urging, Holbrook submitted an article on the language of the I.W.W., which was published in the *American Mercury* in January 1926 as "Wobbly Talk."

Holbrook and Mencken had much in common, and they became good friends. They were both witty, irreverent, suspicious of authority, liked debunking do-gooders, and

Holbrook in Portland in 1931

cherished regional lore. Holbrook was soon a regular contributor to the spirited, skeptical publication, where he appeared along with such national figures as Theodore Dreiser, Upton Sinclair, Carl Sandburg, Sherwood Anderson, Sinclair Lewis, and his fellow Northwest writers Stevens and H. L. Davis, who were also his colleagues on the Paul Bunyan radio series. Holbrook later wrote that "to write for the *Merc* in the twenties and thirties meant that you had Arrived." He also said Mencken "is the most wonderful guy I ever worked with," and credited Mencken and *Century* editor Hewitt H. Howland for giving him his first encouragement. Holbrook recalled that Mencken's "great good humor was one of many reasons that kept us young and indigent writers working for the miserable *Mercury* checks, which, in my case at least, were for the oddest amounts—$70, $85, $90; and once when a check for $105 floored me and I accused him of conspicuous waste, he replied promptly that it was due to a clerical error and that I should 'keep the matter confidential.'"

In 1924 Holbrook married Katherine Stanton Gill. As Kay Holbrook, she worked as a program director for KOIN, a Portland radio station.

In 1928 Holbrook became a contributor to Portland's leading newspaper, the *Oregonian*. For the rest of his life, he wrote articles, columns, book reviews, features and editorials for the newspaper. Even though he was never on the payroll, he was so prolific that on occasion his contributions were published under different names. Once, during the Depression, the *Oregonian* decided to eliminate his $75 weekly column and his editorial writing services. To the agnostic Holbrook's great chagrin, his column was replaced with a Bible game featuring local ministers who wrote for free. When Holbrook was reinstated and paid at space rates, he got his revenge when an efficiency expert hired by the *Oregonian* determined that he had made more than the publisher the previous month.

Holbrook, in the center, visiting a Washington logging operation

Holbrook became a master at recycling his research and experiences. In typical fashion he sold an article on log pirates to the *Oregonian, American Forests* and *Lumber News*, and later used the same material in his books *Holy Old Mackinaw* and *Tall Timber.* Colorful individuals such as Bunco Kelly, Harry Tracy, Jigger Jones, Joshua Creffield, Big Bill Haywood and Harry Orchard appeared with regularity in his newspaper columns, magazine articles and books.

Holbrook was a fast writer and a workaholic. His letters show that he regularly "turned out 3,000 to 5,000 words a day" on his Underwood typewriter. Writing to Dunten one evening he ended by saying: "I've got to write 3,000 words about Automobiles before I go to bed tonight. Think of that—writing 3,000 words about horseless carriages—and pity him who has to do it."

His travels for *Lumber News* and his assignments from the *Oregonian* took him all over the region, and he became as familiar with places like Elsie, Duckabush, Pe Ell, Paisley,

Orofino, Pysht and Enumclaw as he was with Vancouver, Seattle and Portland. He said he eventually visited nearly every sawmill and logging camp in the Pacific Northwest and rode on 292 logging railroads.

Holbrook was a skilled interviewer and he had a knack for finding stories wherever he traveled. He drew on his own experiences, his voracious reading, and the interesting characters he found. He said that almost every village had "a character known locally as an eccentric . . . . He might call himself a Socialist, Anarchist, Single-Taxer, or perhaps Pantheist, Freethinker, Wobbly . . . even Democrat or Republican." They helped provide Holbrook with ideas, and the articles poured out. A visit to a carnival turned into "Carnival Queen," a 3,000-word article; a sympathetic story about a local communist created a stir in conservative Portland. He profiled Butch Cassidy, Lola Montez and Calamity Jane, among others. In addition to profiles and logging articles, he wrote about such varied regional topics as the rise of the Ku Klux Klan ("the Oregon Klan is a very liberal Klan," his radical friend Tom Burns told him), anti-Chinese riots, "Gay Dogs of Portland's Old Saloon Days," the colorful madams of the bordellos of the area's lusty past, and the dismal failure of Billy Sunday's revival meetings in Portland.

Holbrook even found inspiration in his own life. A robust drinker, Holbrook took his last drink of alcohol on May 11, 1934, after he started to see "queer animal life" in the form of long black eels and gigantic bats. This led to at least four articles on his drinking days published under pseudonyms and bearing such intriguing titles as "Lizards, Bats and Stomach Pumps," "The Fauna of Alcohol," "My Nineteen Years in the Sahara," and "I Had 'Em, Mister!"

He was indeed "a notable consumer of vinus, malted or spirited liquors," to use his phrase.

> For the last four years of my drinking days I consumed an average of one quart of hard stuff daily. . . . It was my custom to throw down a jolt of whiskey as soon as I got

out of bed, take another as soon as I got the fire in the furnace to going, a third just before I started shaving (needed to steady my hand), and a fourth when I sat down to what I laughingly called my breakfast.

At 10 a.m., rain or snow or shine, I had two stiff jolts at my office. At noon with some amiable help from a friend or two we put away either one or two pints of hard stuff. At about 3 p.m. I went to my 'leggers for two or three quick ones, and at 5 p.m. my number one bootlegger called for me and brought two pints. That is, two pints every day except Saturday. On Saturday, a good provider that I have always been, I had the lad bring me five or six pints.

Holbrook gave up drinking for the rest of his life, but considered himself a "retired drinker" and not a "reformed drinker." He disliked "reformed drinkers" because they had the disconcerting and uncomfortable habit of trying to reform people and were apt to call "for the prowl car at the first strains of *Sweet Adeline* floating up from the apartment below." Convinced that alcohol in "decent moderation is perhaps the greatest civilizer there is," he stocked his home with a "modest variety of potables," served drinks "with a lavish hand" to his guests, and preferred the company of those who enjoyed a drink.

Lucius Beebe mixes one with Holbrook at the Iron Horse Bar in Portland's Union Station in 1956

Throughout his career Holbrook was able to adapt his writing style to meet the requirements of a wide variety of magazines. They ranged from the *American Scholar* to the *American Legion Monthly,* and included such diverse publications as *Forestry Magazine, True, Esquire, Saturday Evening Post, House and Garden, Life, Charm, American Heritage,* the *Nation, New Republic, Coronet, New England Quarterly, McClains, Travel,* the *Yale Review, Colliers, Look, Ford Times, Weyerhaeuser Times, New York Times Magazine, Woman's Day,* the *New Yorker, Master Detective, Saga, Saturday Review of Literature, New York Herald Tribune Review of Books,* the *Woman, Startling Detective,* and on and on. For the pulps and detective magazines, he often wrote under such fictitious names as Porter B. Underwood, Marcus M. Clark, Rodger Pinkham and Ethan O. Allen.

In 1935 Holbrook was appointed State Editor for the *Oregon Guide,* part of the Works Project Administration's *American Guide Series,* and began supervising and editing the work of fifty Oregon writers. Holbrook called the *Oregon Guide* a "boondoggling project," but he said it "is giving me a dandy view of Oregon history. Even if my memory is poor I can't help but absorb a lot of Oregon history in the editing of some two million or more words on the subject."

III

Holbrook said that he had been waiting twenty years for someone to do a book about loggers. "No one would, so I did." He did extensive research, drew on his own experiences and the stories he heard in the woods, and traveled the "3,500 miles of the lumberjacks' trail." The result was

Holy Old Mackinaw: A Natural History of the American Lumberjack, published in 1938 when Holbrook was 44. The book portrayed the lumberjack as a unique type of pioneer cutting the "Big Clearing" from Maine to Washington. Holbrook called it a "wild and vulgar book, quite true to life." "It took me 20 years to learn this particular subject and the schooling began near the headwaters of the Androscoggin and wound up some 300 miles north of Vancouver, B.C." Professor Kenneth L. Holmes of Linfield College wrote:

> It is the history of logging in America written by one who had absorbed through the pores of his skin the ways, the words, and the winsomeness of the man of the woods. It is history, sociology, geography, economics—lots of things— all told in the words of a man who had lived with the subject for years and years.

Mackinaw was a great success. It went through seventeen printings, and was then revised for a new edition. It made the author a national figure. From this point on Holbrook was known as the "Lumberjack Boswell," and was the first person editors turned to for articles on logging and the Pacific Northwest.

Introduction

In 1939 Holbrook moved to Cambridge, Massachusetts, "a good place to work for a guy that might want to use reference books." He also said he needed to be close to magazine editors because "the kind of books I write will never support us." He became a close friend of historian and critic Bernard DeVoto, and was invited to lecture at Harvard and Boston University, where he spoke on "Hellions of the Hinterland" and "Non-stuffed Shirts in American History." He also spoke to groups throughout New England on such topics as "Redlights in the Timber, or What it Was That Made Lumberjacks Wild" and "Do Lumberjacks Have Tails?"

Between 1938 and 1942 Holbrook wrote five more books on diverse subjects: *Let Them Live*, a chronicle of industrial accidents; *Iron Brew*, a history of the steel industry; *Ethan Allen*, an irreverent study of Vermont's Revolutionary War hero; *Murder Out Yonder: An Informal Study of Certain Classic Crimes in Back-Country America*;* and *None More Courageous: American War Heroes of Today*, written in the early days of World War II. His versatility and popularity as a writer also led to his becoming a regular book reviewer for the *New York Herald Tribune.*

By 1940, Holbrook had formulated what he called his mission or purpose in life. He said his ambition as a writer was "to put into books the figures or portions of American history that I think have been largely ignored or badly treated." He said it would take another twenty years for him to "seek out these unsung heroes of the past" and write "a shelf of books about them." He called this material "the

---

* In *Murder Out Yonder*, Holbrook wrote that "My research has . . . convinced me that the most interesting crimes in the United States have been committed by persons with rural and backwoods, or at least small-town, backgrounds. I don't think this proves anything in particular, or if it does that it is very important; but it does amuse me when I hear city folk wonder, as I often do, what on earth the folks at the forks of the creek can find to talk about."

untapped lode of American history," and said his subjects were "lying fallow in the unlighted underground of our history." Holbrook told a *Boston Herald* interviewer in 1940, "My pet theory of history is that there ought to be a lowbrow or non-stuffed shirt history of the United States. I hope to write it someday."

Holbrook moved back to the Northwest in 1940 to take charge of the new "Keep Washington Green" program in Seattle. It was the first forest fire prevention program involving public participation. Under Holbrook's leadership it became a model that spread to other states. Holbrook headed the program in Washington for four summers, and "attended all the biggest and best forest fires in order to remind myself that the program isn't a total success."

Holbrook used these experiences and his knowledge of forest fires from his logging days in writing *Burning an Empire: The Study of American Forest Fires* (1943). In telling the stories of the great forest fires, Holbrook pointed out that lumbermen did not deserve all of the blame for devastating America's forests, and that to their guilt "must be added the far greater guilt of the settler, the homesteader, the pioneer, who used and abused fire right down to the

The now famous author in Boston in 1940

present day" to clear the land of timber. He wrote a friend that he expected to be "jumped all over by various pioneer associations" for his "thesis of Destruction by Pioneers." *Empire* was praised by both the timber industry and academic critics. W.D. Hagenstein, Executive Vice President of the Industrial Forestry Association, called it the "best piece ever written on the 300-year history of our failure to run smoke out of the woods . . . ." In 1989, forestry historian Robert E. Ficken wrote that:

> Because of the relatively sophisticated approach he brought to a complex phenomenon—forest fires, after all, were more than the simplistic product of the greed and stupidity of lumbermen—Holbrook deserves ranking as a pioneer of environmental history.

During the last twenty years of his life, Holbrook published a major work about every two years. To support the research on these books he continued to do free-lance writing, wrote seven books for young readers as part of publisher Bennett Cerf's *Landmark* series for Random House, edited anthologies and collections of photographs, usually on the Pacific Northwest (Lucius Beebe called them "Valentines in hard cover"), and wrote histories for forest product companies and other businesses. He even wrote advertising copy featuring timber industry topics for Simpson Logging Company and Bethlehem Pacific Coast Steel Corporation.

Holbrook was a diligent and thorough researcher. In *The Yankee Exodus*, the bibliography lists 215 works "which proved especially helpful." Lee Barker of Doubleday & Company said that Holbrook wrote "in such a lively and interesting way that readers were scarcely aware of the fact that they were absorbing a vast amount of accurate information."

Holbrook's significant books typically reflect his goal of celebrating unsung heroes of the past, and feature what journalist Walter Mattila called his irresistible desire to make light of any fanatic, be he religious, reformist, educational or whatnot. His "digs" at spellbinders in religion, politics and salesmanship sparkle through his most serious efforts as an author. He couldn't lay off. Yet his attitude toward the spellbinder was quite charitable—he liked a good show from anyone and was fond of nonconforming individuals—a Yankee intellectual taste.

Lost Men of American History (1946) profiled dozens of "mavericks, mal-contents, unorthodox thinkers—men and women who were go-ing against the wind and the tide," but who in Holbrook's view had not been given their just due. "Right or wrong, every last one of them had some influence in forming the character of the American people. It is of them I sing."

The Yankee Exo-dus (1950) described the Yankee immigra-tion from New Eng-land to the West and its contribution to the national experience. The *New York Times* found it "a treasure trove of Americana." It was so detailed with names that it reminded one reviewer of the Book of Genesis, but he added that "hardly a Yankee alive could look over the list without running across a relative or famil-iar name." Holbrook wrote that in the mid-twentieth century

Portland and Walla Walla probably display more of the characteristics of New England than any other [community]. Neither is given to wild "progress"; neither is easily excited; both have a leisurely gait which is generally considered to be due to one of two things— either a Yankee failing, or good New England common sense and decency.

In *The Age of The Moguls* (1953), he profiled the 19th-century tycoons who established the great American fortunes. While they "plundered and wasted," they "were also builders," Holbrook felt. He said they were

> tough-minded fellows, who fought their way encased in rhinoceros hides and filled the air with their mad bellowings and the cries of the wounded; while their determined womenfolk badgered them into erecting monstrous houses . . . . The men were as magnificent in

Holbrook at Bread Loaf in Vermont, 1957

their piratical wars as they were pathetic in their dude clothes, trying to eat with a *fork,* wondering how best to approach a chaise lounge. They were a motley crew, yet taken together they fashioned a savage and gaudy age as distinctively purple as that of imperial Rome, and infinitely more entertaining.

With keen foresight he ended *Moguls* by writing:

It is amusing to contemplate the possibility, years hence, that the very names of these semi-literate or at best unlearned moguls will survive and somehow carry the authentic flavor of art, letters, and scientific inquiry; and Americans of that day will be proud to look back on the New World Renaissance which came so astonishingly into being in so young a country as the United States. It *could* happen, for history is filled with paradox.

Dreamers of the American Dream (1957) told the story of dozens of other "dreamers, visionaries and prophets," including Oregon's Abigail Scott Duniway and the Wobblies. "Only a few of their names can be found in our schoolbooks," Holbrook said.

Fewer still stand in marble or bronze in our halls and parks. The mass of Americans knows little or nothing of them. Never mind. They dreamed nobly, and they acted. Taken all together, they were enormously effective in making the United States a better place to live than it otherwise would have been and is. They were a daft, earnest, honest, and all-but-incredible lot of men and women. I think of them as a sort of national conscience.

In *The Golden Age of Quackery* (1959), Holbrook combined his interest in forgotten history with colorful frauds of the past. He wrote about the glory days of patent medicine and such cures for hypochondriacs as Lydia E. Pinkham's Vegetable Compound, Galvanic Love Powders, Invalid's Friend and Hope, and Duffy's Pure Malt Whiskey, which was endorsed by "Distinguished Divines and Temperance Workers."

Holbrook's other major works were: *The Story of American Railroads* (1947), which allowed the author, who never drove a car, to do for railroads and railroaders what he had done for logging and loggers; *Little Annie Oakley & Other Rugged People* (1948), a collection of his irreverent profiles of Annie Oakley, the James Boys, Kit Carson, Calamity Jane and Buffalo Bill, among others; *The Far Corner: A Personal View of the Pacific Northwest* (1952), Holbrook's reminiscences of his years in the region; *The Columbia* (1956), a book on the Great River of the West prepared for the Rivers of America series; *The Rocky Mountain Revolution* (1956), which told of labor and management violence in the hard-rock mines of Idaho and Colorado, involving dynamiter Harry Orchard and the Western Federation of Miners; and *The Old Post Road: The Story of the Boston Post Road* (1962), which gave Holbrook the opportunity to point out that George Washington's diary was "impressive evidence not only of the punctiliousness with which he fulfilled his engagements, but also something of a guide to the taverns of the period, both good and otherwise."

Several of his works became best sellers, and *Moguls,* which sold over 200,000 copies, and *Dreamers* were purchased for the Book-of-the-Month Club. Holbrook had a loyal base of readers. "It is a very articulate audience, and if one of my books ever fails to bring some 2,000 letters within 90 days of publication, I shall feel I am slipping." His correspondence became so immense that, following in the tradition of Mencken, he had a postcard printed that read: "Dear Sir or Madam: You may be right at that. Sincerely, Stewart Holbrook." Another printed card was apparently intended for correspondents who took issue with Holbrook's portrayals of historic figures. It read: "But I shall use neither gilt nor whitewash. Nor tar. You may be right at that."

Holbrook's books were widely reviewed, and the reviewers for major newspapers and magazines often tried to be as colorful as Holbrook. He was called "the irreverent logger," "a word slinger of rare talents," "a fine writer with a positive genius for flavor," "a man of color and vitality," the "lowbrow historian," "a historian of American curiosa," "the historian of back-country America," and "a writer of bizarre episodes in American history."

Lloyd Lewis in the *New York Herald Tribune Weekly Book Review,* commenting on *Little Annie Oakley,* said:

> This is one of the rarities of modern publishing, a book that is even better read aloud than alone . . . It is written with the speed and conversational raciness of a man who forever has imagined himself in the presence of open mouthed listeners.

After his death, Lee Barker said:

> One reason why Stewart has been so enormously successful in presenting the stories of the robber barons, the dreamers and the lost men and women to the American public is because he approaches them neither as a muckraker nor as a eulogist. He doesn't attack them for being human beings with human foibles, nor does he forgive them their crimes. His position is always a sane and healthy one, and there is always a twinkle in the corner of his eye. This attitude, of course, is a true reflection of Stewart Holbrook himself, and it is one of the main reasons why his books will live for many, many years.

Academic publications usually ignored Holbrook, dismissed him as a "popular historian," or criticized his work as derivative. But even academics sometimes got carried away. Professor E. Douglas Branch of the University of Pittsburgh, writing in the *Saturday Review,* described *Holy Old Mackinaw* as

> substantial as a redwood bole, enlivening as a willow withe, and meaty as a Georgia pecan. It is recommended munching save for those on a proteinless diet.

Bernard DeVoto, another successful popular historian, saluted Holbrook's ability to make history lively and interesting, and asked his friend:

> Do you suppose that after we've taught historians that history can be interesting without putting anyone in danger of hell fire, we can then move on and repeat the instructions for the benefit of ethnologists? It would help, God how it would help.

IV

In 1943 Holbrook returned to Portland, where he lived the remainder of his life, although he took trips almost every year to the East and New England.

Katherine Holbrook died in 1947. The next year, Holbrook married Sibyl Walker, an Oregon native who was then working as a nurse in Boston. In a press release he prepared announcing the marriage, Holbrook, who often chided the "pioneer cult," noted that Sibyl was a "granddaughter of the well-known family of pioneers who settled Walker, Oregon, in covered wagon days." He told Sibyl that

Holbrook and Sibyl, as shown in their 1948 wedding announcement, outside their house at 2670 NW Lovejoy Street in Portland

Holbrook with Sybil and their daughters Bonnie and Sibyl in 1955

"the perfect house would be on top of the library next to the Post Office." Instead they lived in a stately colonial house on a dead-end street in the Northwest Portland hills, which reminded Holbrook of homes in his native Vermont. The house had an elevator and, from the upstairs "work shop" where he wrote, Holbrook had a view of downtown Portland and Mount Hood. Sibyl and Stewart adopted and raised two daughters.

From the end of World War II until his death in 1964, Holbrook was perhaps the best-known personality in the Pacific Northwest. The press covered his books, his travels, his views on current issues, and the famous people who came to Portland to visit the Holbrooks. One would have to turn to the very different Norman Mailer in the 1960s and 1970s in New York for a literary figure who was so omnipresent and highly visible in a community. Holbrook was everywhere, and his early acting experience and interviewing skills were no hindrance in keeping him in the public eye.

Introduction

Although he was only about five feet seven inches tall, Holbrook was not easy to miss. He wore a snazzy bow tie with his suits or blazers, and a bowler or a rumpled Stetson on his head, except at home when he put on his painter's French beret, which he said was a "sort of fake tam-o'-shanter." His tie, vest or blazer was often in the Stewart plaid pattern. He smoked Sweet Caporal cigarettes, or "coffin nails," as he called them, and carried a snoose can in his pocket because he liked a "parlor chew" of Copenhagen. Robert E. Mahaffay wrote that he had "eyes the color of thin blue smoke" and "when he walks, he somehow manages to give the impression, particularly from the rear, that he is clambering over logs." He liked bagpipe music, barbershop quartets, steaks and baked beans, preferred Sen-Sen to life savers, and was "helpless with mechanical things." At parties he liked to sing old Wobbly songs from the *Little Red Song Book.* Ellis Lucia wrote:

> He hated dogs and horses, and loathed the automobile, never learning to drive. He refused to fly; the railroad was by far the best form of transportation ever devised, the

Holbrook signing copies of American Railroads *in 1947*

27

way he went East most every summer. He never witnessed the Rose Festival Parade, although he was Grand Marshall of one. He quit going to movies, unless W. C. Fields was on the bill; and he never saw his own *Ethan Allen* on film, refusing to have even a credit line.

The publication of each significant new book was a major event, involving national publicity, tours, interviews, dozens of reviews, and crowded book signings in bookstores from the Pacific Northwest to New England. Book distributor Katharine McCanna remembers as many as 150 people lining up in the J.K. Gill's store in Portland for a Holbrook signing.

Holbrook was in great demand as a speaker and master of ceremonies for audiences ranging from chambers of commerce to college groups. One Portlander who heard him many times said his anecdotes "must have been as good as Will Rogers'." A friend who also observed him in many public appearances said he was "sort of a Groucho Marx." In describing a talk at the Woman's University Club in Seattle, a reporter wrote,

> you found a man who looked like a business executive or college professor, who spoke with a New England accent (you should hear him say "Harvard"), whose casual humor

Speaking at the Vermont Historical Society's annual meeting in 1954

convulsed you all the more because in the face of that quiet effortless voice you didn't feel you could laugh right out loud.

His books made him a figure of national stature as a historian. In 1950 the *Boston Sunday Herald* listed him as one of eight eminent historians from New England, placing Holbrook in the company of Samuel Eliot Morrison, Henry Adams, George Bancroft and Francis Parkman. Together with Bernard DeVoto, J. Frank Dobie and Arthur Schlesinger Jr., he was an original member of the editorial board of the History Book Club.

Holbrook was recognized as the nation's leading authority on logging history and language, and he carried on a crusade to prevent the misuse of words derived from early logging days. He wrote scathing letters correcting any publication that used the term "skid row" to describe the down-and-out section of a city. Holbrook said the correct term was "skid road," which originated in Seattle when logs were hauled through part of the town over a road of wooden skids to the water. Around this road grew up the saloons

Holbrook and William Faulkner at the Oregon coast in 1953

and various establishments catering to loggers and other itinerants, and the district became known as "The Skidroad." "Skid row is used only by those who know nothing of what they are talking or writing about," Holbrook chided.

In 1950 he was nominated by a board of "Representative Oregon Citizens" as one of the outstanding "100 Men of the Century" to be selected by the *Oregonian*, in observance of its centennial. However, the newspaper decided to eliminate all living persons from consideration, making the 57-year-old Holbrook ineligible. He later became the only author ever selected to serve as Grand Marshall of Portland's famed Rose Festival parade, joining such notables as Burl Ives, Merv Griffin, Lorne Green, Hank Aaron, Pat Boone, Jack Ramsay, Mitch Miller and Mickey Mouse.

Holbrook was good company, and lunches and dinners were the occasions for story telling with his wide circle of friends, ranging from bank presidents and lumbermen to journalists, longshoremen, and the radical Tom Burns, "Mayor of Burnside Street." He was the unofficial chairman of a group of Northwest writers, some with national

Holbrook and Sibyl at an Oregonian Christmas party in 1949

reputations, known as the Oregon Freelance Club, who met regularly at the Press Club and other spots in Portland in the late 1940s and 1950s. Members, in those pre-television days, were some of the leading contributors to national magazines such as the S*aturday Evening Post* and *Colliers*, and included Ernest Haycox, Ellis Lucia, Rod Lull, Peg Bracken, Don James, Evelyn Sibley Lampmann, Steve McNeil, John and Ward Hawkins, Richard and Maurine Neuberger, Robert Ormond Case, Bill and Eloise McGraw, Victoria Case, Thomas Thompson, Ardyth Kennelly, Walt Morey and Vivien Bretherton.

In 1945 Holbrook, as editor, selected the works of 38 Northwest writers, including 10 women, for inclusion in *Promised Land, A Collection of Northwest Writing*, the first significant anthology of writers from the region. "The book definitely adds to the recognized stature of Northwest literature," the *New York Times* review said. Holbrook wrote that the job of making an anthology was no easy task.

> It is hard on the eyes, irritating in many respects, and as
> aesthetically difficult and frustrating as being a lone judge
> in one of those so-called contests to choose, from among
> half a dozen devastating beauties, she who is to be
> crowned queen of the mighty Turnip Festival at, say,
> Drain, Oregon.

The Holbrook home became the literary social center of the Northwest. Each year the Holbrooks entertained thirty Portland booksellers at a sit-down dinner featuring baked beans, brown bread and apple pie. Lucius Beebe arrived by private rail car to visit Holbrook. Bennett Cerf, H. L. Mencken, William Faulkner, Robert Frost, Alfred Knopf, Irving Stone, Elizabeth Bowen, John Dos Passos, Wallace Stegner and Katherine Drinker Bowen came to Portland to visit, as did other editors, agents and publishers from the New York literary world. Holbrook often took his guests on well-publicized trips to Erickson's saloon, Jake's Famous Crawfish restaurant, the Timber-Topper restaurant, and other colorful spots with a past.

Holbrook's wit, irreverence and tongue-in-cheek attitude were a key part of his work and his personality, and helped account for his popularity. In 1992, his old friend Reginald "Dutch" Brummer, a youthful 95, would shake his head and chuckle as he recalled Holbrook's "hellish sense of humor."

•He claimed to have been so impressed in grammar school by the graphic anatomy charts showing the havoc that alcohol and tobacco could do to vital organs that he didn't start smoking until he was eight or drinking until he was eleven.

•He explained the popularity of his first book by noting that

> through an error of someone in the Cardinal's office, *Holy Old Mackinaw*—probably because of a part of its title—got into the list of 100 Best Books Recommended for Summer Reading by Cardinal Hayes. This all but wrecked the Cardinal, who died shortly thereafter.

•He often told how the community of Pluvius in the Coast Range in Washington got its name. Holbrook said its first resident named the town after the god of rain. "I've seen it rain right here in Pluvius for 362 days on end," the fellow recalled, and then added, "them other three days were damn cloudy."

•He said he received an irate letter from a sports fan who bought *Burning an Empire,* the book on forest fires. The fan wanted his money back because he thought it would be about the fitting end of a baseball umpire.

•He said that after his highly publicized appointment to head up the "Keep Washington Green" program, Seattle suffered its rainiest summer in decades, making Holbrook so unpopular he had to slink through alleys to avoid being seen when he visited the city.

•He claimed that loggers in the early days "were so well recognized as a distinct species" that, in reporting a steamboat accident on Puget Sound, a newspaper reported that "three men and a logger were drowned."

Holbrook admiring his favorite curmudgeon

•He scorned footnotes and rarely used them in his books. Instead he would use an occasional asterisk which would lead the reader to a typical Holbrook comment at the bottom of the page.*

•He formed a group to remove all Roman numerals and "V's" from inscriptions on public and private buildings, claiming they were affectations of "legends carved in marble."

•He started a huge hullabaloo in 1953 when he headed a committee to change Portland's name to Multnomah, contending that "we should prefer to live in a city uniquely named, rather than in one that calls for the addition of a qualifying state to make clear exactly where we live." He castigated Portland's founders for choosing a "shopworn" name shared by 22 other American cities and for "perpetrating the most notable opportunity in the United

---

* One of these asides in a chapter on Mormonism in *The Yankee Exodus* states: "It has always appeared ironic to me that conventional Christians attack the Book of Mormon for its miraculous discovery and translation. The miracle of the Book of Mormon pales beside that of the birth of the founder of Christianity. The antiquity of a miracle, apparently, is of the greatest importance."

States for misdirection of mail." The proposal drew fierce opposition and generated immense local, and even national, publicity before the City Council turned down the committee's request to put the issue on the ballot. Holbrook had the last word, saying that the proposal attracted more notice to Portland than any event in the past century except the Vanport Flood of 1948, which "was not the sort of notice that local boosters yearn for."

•He told reporters that on his death he didn't want a funeral or any involvement with an undertaker. He said his will provided funds for a party for his friends and for his body to be taken to the nearest medical school by a Bekins moving van.

Holbrook liked to challenge and expose various myths of history, but he was not averse to perpetuating myths that supported his themes. His colorful depiction of the rugged Pacific Northwest could prove disappointing to those who tried to follow in his footsteps. Lucius Beebe wrote that Holbrook took

> intense pleasure in the delusion that Portland, in proper fact as sedate a metropolis as its namesake in Maine, was a sink of vice and licentiousness recapitulating the Old West in a red light district of rich resources in sin. He once walked me from the Union Depot to the town's only bookstore through what he was pleased to call "Portland's Hell's Half Acre," an eminently dreary vicinage of warehouses and wholesale produce merchants. We were, in actual fact, accosted by a single blowsy and superannuated strumpet far gone in wine and Holbrook was happy as a kid with firecrackers. "There you see," he said leeringly, "anything goes in Portland. Widest open god-damned town since Dodge City!"

Holbrook's concerns about the problems that growth would bring the Pacific Northwest preceded by many years the similar concerns of Oregon Governor Tom McCall and today's environmental organizations. In 1948, Holbrook wrote about the arrival of the day in the Pacific Northwest when the population doubles, and triples, then doubles again; when roads and highways line all the valleys and reach for mountain peaks and back countries; when timber is grown to order in tree nurseries and set out in tree farms; when homes or mills or factories or auto courts dot every other acre, then the country out back of beyond, and the people of it, will have disappeared. They will disappear along with the stake-and-rider fences, the covered bridges, the corduroy roads, the homemade irrigation plants.

His concern resulted in the imaginary James G. Blaine Society (named after a now forgotten 19th-century Maine politician, Secretary of State and presidential candidate), devoted to discouraging economic development and growth in the Northwest. The movement started out in a tongue-in-cheek manner, with Holbrook suggesting "that perhaps the whole Northwest should be set aside as one great park before it is wholly overrun by foreign immigrants like myself." But it soon caught on, and in speeches and articles Holbrook contended that "the Pacific Northwest is the Promised Land and we need to protect it from the steadily mounting danger of overcrowding by the hordes of Goths and Vandals who have been touring our blessed region in increasing numbers." He said publicizing the region's "everlasting rain" was "our first line of defense" to discourage migration. Holbrook sent news clippings on record rainfalls and locals being bitten by rattlesnakes to out-of-state editors, mailed postcards of billowing smoke stacks saying "Greetings from Oregon," and told Eastern audiences that the Hanford nuclear facility would eventually sterilize every man in the Northwest. Visiting New York after the disastrous Vanport flood of 1948, he remarked that "they have them every year. This time it just happened to get in the papers."

While he was often kidding, he was serious about what he saw as the efforts of the chamber of commerce boosters and developers "to make Portland identical with all other imitations of civic futurity." While writing *The Far Corner*, he stopped work "to attend the obsequies of" old mansions and buildings, including "the magnificent old Hotel Portland," which were being replaced by "the ugly modern gold mines called parking lots."

Urban renewal was a particular horror. Holbrook said he found himself lying awake in the night wondering if "a gang of urban renewers" would "come to remove the two small hitching rings in the parking strip in front of my home."

Sybil encouraged Holbrook to take up painting as a form of relaxation, because he claimed to have no hobby other than writing and reading. He had drawn cartoons several decades before in British Columbia, and was able to quickly become proficient with oils. He started signing his works "Maholy Nagy," then "Calvin Otis," and finally "Mr. Otis," because it didn't take so much time to write.

Bearing such titles as "Someone Has Been Here Before Us Meriwether," "Return of the Farmer's Daughter," "The Man Is Here About the Wallpaper," "Truth Crushed to Earth at Third and Burnside," "Lydia E. Pinkham Enters Heaven (No. 2)," and "I Was With Custer, The Old Man Said," the

paintings resemble a sort of bizarre blending of Grandma Moses with Salvador Dali. Many of the works poked fun at what Holbrook called "the overly sentimental cult of the Western Pioneer." Initially Holbrook would not

Mr. Otis with some of his paintings

*Sibyl with Bennett
Cerf in the Holbrook
kitchen in front of a
mural by Mr. Otis*

sell the works; he bartered them to friends for such items as
a bushel of filberts, 20 pounds of wild rice, 12 cans of dog
repellant, and a lifetime supply of Vermont maple syrup.

Holbrook never publicly admitted that he was Mr. Otis.
He claimed he was a friend of Otis, a "frail, weak-eyed figure of shabby gentility" who lived and painted in the "Chaos
and Old Night" of the "rotting old mansion" that housed
the Portland Press Club, and then later moved to an abandoned root-house. Holbrook said he also allowed Mr. Otis
to paint in the work shop in the Holbrook home.

As the fame of Mr. Otis spread, the works were reviewed and reproduced. Holbrook said "I'm amazed . . .
now they're beginning to buy the damn things." Exhibitions
of the paintings of "the celebrated Mr. Otis, founder of the
Primitive-Moderne* School," were held in New York, New
England and Portland. The Portland Art Museum refused a
request to hold an exhibition, and so Portland's Central Library opened its doors to Mr. Otis, as did Erickson's saloon.
Works of Mr. Otis were acquired by admirers of Holbrook
and collectors from across the country.

---

*Holbrook said the final *"e"* in 'Primitive-Moderne" was imperative. "It
makes the word foreign, hence fashionable."

Mr. Otis in his studio

In 1958, Macmillan published a book of twenty-five color reproductions of paintings by Mr. Otis, with a long introduction by Holbrook describing his relationship with the unusual artist. In his introduction, Holbrook wrote that, after newspapers featured color reproductions of Otis's paintings,

> a woman who said she had been painting pictures for forty-six years and had been studying art appreciation ever since it was invented wrote direct to Otis saying among other things and in capitals that "YOU CAN'T PAINT ANY BETTER THAN PICASSO."

The publication of the *Mr. Otis* book provided a happy opportunity for making fun of the modern art world. Bennett Cerf said, "In Mr. Otis we obviously have another Van Gogh and he's got two ears." *American Heritage* wrote that "A new talent burst on the art world a few months ago, a talent which lies somewhere between Jackson Pollock and Gluyus

Williams, and within shouting distance of Maxfield Parrish."
The *Oregonian*'s critic acknowledged "that the artist is quite
right in placing himself in a school of painting occupied by
himself alone." Dinner parties at the Holbrook home now
often ended with the guests adjourning to the work room
where Holbrook donned his beret and smock and became
Mr. Otis.

V

In the early 1960s
Holbrook had several
strokes that restricted
his activities. During
this time he was re-
searching a one-
volume history of the
American Revolution,
and acting as the editor
for a series of books on
North American mili-
tary forts to be
published by Prentice-
Hall.

In 1963 Holbrook
suffered a major stroke
which severely limited the time he could work. He appeared
to be making a good recovery, though, and in August 1964
Sibyl and Stewart travelled to New England for a vacation
to visit Holbrook's former haunts and old friends in the
North Country of New Hampshire and Vermont. During his
stay in Colebrook, New Hampshire, he typed out his *Oregonian* feature articles in the domestic science room of the
Colebrook Academy he had attended over fifty years earlier. Shortly after their return to Portland, he was admitted
to Good Samaritan Hospital on September 2, 1964, for what

Holbrook's work room at the time of his death.

Sibyl called "a good rest." However, he went into a coma the next day and died from a cerebral vascular hemorrhage.

A simple memorial service was held in Portland in the Unitarian Church. His friend Dr. Richard Steiner gave a brief, eloquent tribute, which some said Holbrook helped write, and then a solitary bagpiper clad in a Stewart tartan kilt walked up the aisle and back out the church, piping all the while.

Brian Booth

Death and Times of a Prophet

On what date a shaft of divine light transformed Franz Edmund Creffield from an obscure rural evangelist into Prophet Joshua the Second in all his glory is not known. Neither is the exact spot where the visitation took place. But the time is certain. It was 1903, and the neighborhood of the miracle was Corvallis, Oregon.

Troubles follow in the wake of a prophet as naturally as water runs downhill. If the prophet has a set of Old Testament whiskers and a chronic case of satyriasis, then the troubles are sure to be multiplied and likewise interesting.

This particular backwoods Joshua had both the whiskers and the affliction. And when he raised his voice in holy anger, as he did on one remembered occasion, the vast city of San Francisco shook horribly in the grip of an Act of God, then went down, writhing and smoking, in one of the greatest disasters within the memory of living men.

Driving up the lush green Willamette Valley from Portland to Corvallis, one scarcely wonders that this land once produced a veritable prophet. It is amazing there have not been more of them. Here was the Promised Land where the creaking covered wagons came to rest at the far end of the Oregon Trail; where the immigrants shouted "Glory to God!" and drove their stakes, naming their settlements Amity, Sweet Home, Salem, Aurora, and Corvallis—which last is said to mean "heart of the valley." Here along the many creeks is beaver-dam soil, richer than the delta of the Nile. Vegetables grow as large as the pictures on the seed packages. Enormous prunes and the finest walnuts on earth hang heavy on the trees. Vetch and clover grow thick and big enough to stop the wheels of powered farm machinery. The climate is damp and mild. Seldom is there more than a trace of snow.

Here and there along the ninety miles the highway plunges into groves of Douglas fir, tall and mighty before Lewis and Clark and the Hudson's Bay Company came. To the east rises the backbone of Oregon, the majestic peaks of the Cascades, and on the west are the Coast Range mountains, faintly hung with mist and with haze in season—brooding, black, faraway hills to make a prophet out of almost any man.

In the heart of this valley is Corvallis, seat of Oregon State College, a spick-and-span town in 1941 that holds court for Benton County; sells things to farmers; makes considerable lumber; has a daily paper, a radio station, and a library of 130,000 volumes including "a 15th century antiphony composed of Gregorian chants in Flemish, hand-printed and illuminated on parchment, and bound in calf over the original board covers."

Corvallis is sedate enough today, as serene as any campus town in the land. It has, in fact, been sedate throughout most of its three-quarters of a century. Only during the days of Joshua the Second, when signs and portents were on every hand, did Corvallian blood run hot and fast.

II

Unheralded, Franz Edmund Creffield made his first appearance in the Corvallis of 1902 in the form and style of a Salvation Army worker. He was thirty-five years old, smooth-shaven, short of stature, and had large brown eyes. He retained a slight but noticeable accent from his native Germany.

A few months later, or early in 1903, he either left or was discharged from the religious group, and seems to have disappeared for a time. It was likely during this obscure period that the great light beat upon him and he talked with God somewhere in the tall forests that edged close to the town. In any case, he was soon back in Corvallis.

In 1903 no man could be a true prophet who did not have a beard, and when Creffield emerged from the timber he was wearing an astonishing growth. It was of the veritable Moses type, flowing down over his chest and spreading to left and right, unruly, wild, burgeoning like everything in the Willamette Valley, while over his shoulders tumbled falls of unkempt hair. Both beard and hair were of a reddish, golden brown.

He was Edmund Creffield no longer, but Joshua the Second—sole prophet and for a short period sole communicant of the Church of the Bride of Christ. Even the tone of his voice had changed. It no longer had the supplication, the winning humbleness, of street and field evangels. It now boomed like muffled thunder and in it, many came to think, was the authority of Jehovah.

It must have been that the Corvallis of the time, in spite of its several churches, was lacking somewhat in spiritual life, at least so far as the women were concerned. In those days, of course, there were no movies, no serial radio dramas, no bridge clubs to entertain and thus protect the dim minds of vapid females; so it is conceivable that time in Corvallis, as in any other American town, often seemed interminable to those who live chiefly to kill time.

And it is conceivable, too, in view of the record, that this brand-new Joshua possessed a magnetic if not a downright hypnotic personality. Within a month he had a sizable cult of converts. It was all done so quietly that even the town fathers, who fancied they knew almost everything that went on locally, were wholly unaware of the great harvest of souls that was going forward.

The first meetings were held openly in the homes of converts, of whom at least six were men. At this period the prophet seems to have had no particular message other than that the ways of the world were all wrong and should be changed. One by one the male converts dropped away, leaving Joshua and a stooge known as Brother Brooks to carry on with the increasing flock of girls and women.

If you think that the apostasy of the few men was discouraging to the prophet, then you don't know how an

Oregon Joshua works when he gets going Full Gospel style. The meetings in the homes of converts were continued; but they now were held in the afternoons, when menfolk were away.

There must have been a female Judas in the flock, for it was presently whispered around town that never before had there been seen such manifest workings of the Spirit as Joshua Creffield brought about. Pulling down all the blinds of the meeting place—so this she-Judas reported—Joshua began a chant, swaying to its rhythm, waving his arms, and calling upon what he addressed rather familiarly as the Full Spirit to descend upon the meeting.

The girls and women soon began to sway. They chanted; they moaned; they "spoke in tongues" and cried aloud while the prophet seemed to gain in stature and his normally calm eyes sank deep into his head, where they glowed like two pits of fire. The swaying and the chanting went on.

Suddenly, like a thunderbolt, the prophet's voice boomed out: "Vile clothes, begone!" The whiskered fellow then disrobed and, without urging on his part, many of the women present did likewise. There was nothing coy about it, no sense of shame. They threw off their peekaboo waists, their skirts, and their multitude of petticoats; they tore wildly at their whalebone corsets, meanwhile moaning like all get-out.

"Roll, ye sinners, roll!" thundered Joshua; and roll they did, some in chemises, some without, all over the bare floor, with Joshua and Brother Brooks rolling happily among them.

Either at this or at a subsequent meeting Joshua began to expound the canons of his sect. He had already announced that he and his followers were members of the Church of the Bride of Christ. Now he let it be known that the Lord had commanded him to select from among his followers she who was to become the Mother of a Second Christ.

It soon became apparent to the faithful that Joshua was going about his quest for a second Mother in a thorough and searching manner, which manner was obviously of the empirical school. Several married women left the sect at this point, taking their daughters with them. But many remained, and new females appeared at every meeting. So many came, in fact, that Joshua and Brother Brooks felt the need for more room.

On Kiger Island, in the near-by river, the prophet and his stooge, with girls and women helping, built a large wigwam of poles covered with boughs. The boughs were interwoven cleverly and tightly, and the entrance was closed with a door curtain. It is recalled that one of the most willing workers was a beautiful and young ash-blonde girl, Esther Mitchell.

Their hands torn and covered with the pitch of Douglas fir (*Pseudotsuga taxifolia)* but with their eyes shining with the light of Gospel, girls of fourteen and women of fifty-five toiled on the pretty wooded island. Some brought small tents that were set up, and small wigwams also were built. Throughout the summer of 1903 meetings were held on the island almost every afternoon, and the vast workings of the Spirit could be heard on either shore of the mainland.

With cooler weather and heavy rains, the island retreat was not a happy place to roll in the altogether. A new and suitable spot was soon found in the residence of O. P. Hunt, in Corvallis. Mr. Hunt was a respected citizen, member of a pioneer family, and Corvallians were shocked one day in early fall to see a large sign over the door of his house.

"Positively No Admittance, Except on God's Business," said the sign, and a smaller one attached to the gate repeated the warning. Now things began to happen in quiet Corvallis. A reporter of the local *Times* viewed the premises and wrote:

> Certain caprices of religious fanaticism have been manifested at the house that are so unusual as to suggest a condition bordering insanity. Walks about the house have been torn away. Much of the furniture of the house has been reduced to ashes in a bonfire held last night in the

yard, on the theory that God wills it. The shrubbery and
fruit trees and all the flowers have been digged up and
destroyed. Kitchen utensils have been beaten to pieces
and buried . . . It is reported that house cats and dogs have
been cremated.

Joshua and Brother Brooks were taken to the courthouse
for a sanity hearing. Joshua sneered at the proceedings, and
told Deputy Sheriff Henderson not to "talk that way to God's
anointed." The men were found sane, but officers advised
them to leave town. Brother Brooks said nothing. Joshua
merely laughed quietly as he went out the courthouse door.

In the meantime Mr. Hunt—but apparently not his
womenfolk—had discovered that he wanted no more of
Joshua and his sect. In the meantime, too, prints of a photograph that had been taken many weeks before began to
circulate in Corvallis. The name of the Unbeliever who took
this picture has been lost to history, but his little Brownie
camera had a good lens. The picture was what today would
be termed a candid-camera shot, and it was taken during
one of the spiritual orgies of the cult on Kiger Island. The
film was small but as clear as crystal, and the picture was
as candid as could well be imagined. It showed Joshua, quite
naked, amid nothing less than a bevy of naked and local
matrons and girls, some of them standing, some rolling in
the lush wild grass. Several were easily identified. The film,
it is said, was soon worn out in making prints.

No movie ever made created such a furor as this two
inches of silent, static film. There was an immediate up-
roar, as enraged fathers and injured husbands had their kids
and wives packed off to the state hospital and to the home
for wayward girls. Some fifteen of Joshua's sect were at once
taken out of circulation, while others got warnings to which
they paid little if any heed.

Then, on the coolish evening of January 4, 1904, a band
of silent men called at the house where Joshua and Brother
Brooks had quarters. None of the men were masked, nor
was there any attempt at concealment of the affair, and

nearly all of the mob were citizens of high standing. Without a word this band took the two long-haired boys to the edge of town, where a pot of tar was heating over an open fire. They were made to strip, then given a coat of tar and feathers, and told to keep out of Corvallis.

III

Brother Brooks was never again seen in town after the party at the tarpot. It was different with Joshua. Mrs. Hunt and her young daughter, Maude, searched for and found the feathered prophet hiding miserably in the woods. They brought him to their home. The sticky coat was removed, and a few days later Joshua dropped his Biblical name long enough to marry Miss Maude Hunt. The marriage proved something of a local sensation, for it isn't often that the daughter of a respected pioneer family ties up with a man who has just had tar and feathers scraped off his hide. The marriage, too, doubtless eased the minds of many Corvallis males; they could well believe that now the prophet's search for a second Mother was done.

But the search *wasn't* done. Leaving his new wife at the home of her parents in Corvallis, Joshua went to Portland to commune with a married woman who had been a follower in the palmy days of the Kiger Island colony. She and the prophet were presently taken *in flagrante delicto* by her husband, who swore out a warrant in which he called the prophet's holy search by the vulgar name of adultery.

Police had been waiting for something tangible like this to work on. But now they couldn't find the prophet, and to stimulate the search for him O. P. Hunt, the prophet's own father-in-law, offered a reward of $150 for his arrest. Maude Hunt Creffield secured a divorce. Things looked dark for Joshua the Second.

Nearly three months thus passed with the prophet supposedly at large. Then, one day in June, young Roy, adopted son of O. P. Hunt, made a startling discovery. Crawling under the Hunt home in search of a tin can to carry worms on a fishing trip, the youngster was frightened near out of his wits when he suddenly found himself looking into the great, blazing eyes of a bearded man.

Backing out of the hole as fast as he could, the lad ran screaming to his foster father. Mr. Hunt came and peered into the hole, then called police.

The cops came and hauled the prophet from his den under the house. He was, as one of the officers remarked thirty years after, a sight to behold. Naked as to clothes, and dirty as a hog, the prophet was hairy all over as a water spaniel, and most wonderfully endowed by Mother Nature withal. His beard grew down to his stomach and was bushy as a clump of black alder. But he was as thin as a fence rail. He was weak, too, and could scarcely stand.

"You're Creffield, ain't you?" asked a doubtful cop, no doubt recalling folk tales of surviving specimens of *Pithecanthropus erectus.*

"I am Joshua." The voice that came from the long beard was weak, yet obviously the voice of a prophet.

It was a weird tale that the officers and Mr. Hunt pieced together. For more than two months the prophet had lived day and night in his lair under the home of his ex-father-in-law, unsuspected by menfolk of the house. He had existed on jars of fruit and scraps of food that Mrs. Hunt and other faithful (who were admitted to the secret) could smuggle to him. He had thrown away all his clothes before he entered the den. The only covering he had when taken out was a ragged and filthy quilt.

Creffield was put on trial before Judge Sears in Multnomah County court in Portland. He readily admitted what the court charged were improper relations with the former Corvallis matron, but he said that such things were not at all improper in a man of God such as he. "Christ," he said in the usual manner of mountebanks, "broke the Sabbath day and the Jews put Him to death. I've broken your laws, and you will undoubtedly do the same to me. Like Christ, however, I will rise again and ye all shall suffer."

The jury was made up of forthright men. In twelve minutes, or about the time it took them to go to the jury room and back, they brought in a verdict. It was "Guilty." Judge Sears asked Creffield if he had anything to say before sentence was pronounced. He did. He had a lot to say. In a rambling yet fervid harangue, during which he misquoted considerable Scripture and called the saints to witness, he told the court and the jury that he forgave them, for they knew not what they did.

"Two years in state's prison," said Judge Sears, a man of few words.

"God bless you," replied the prophet, and impious deputies laid hands on him and whisked him away to Salem. He was dressed in at the pen as Number 4941 on September 16, 1904.

IV

Fifteen months later the prophet was released. The warden, of course, couldn't know what a baggage of trouble and tragedy he was turning loose. His beard gone, his hair cut close, Joshua left the scene of his triumphs and trials, going at once to Los Angeles, then as now a lodestone for prophets of all kinds. He didn't stay long, but was soon in San Francisco. How he lived during this period of exile is not known, but one should consider that no prophet has ever starved in California.

Very soon Corvallis learned that Joshua was writing letters to seventeen-year-old Esther Mitchell, she who had attended the prophet's meetings on Kiger Island. He wrote her that God had at last made it clear to him—that Esther and no other was to become the second Mother. This had been revealed to him in a message direct from Heaven. What young Esther replied is not known, but events that were soon to pile up would indicate she was favorable to the message. The prophet also sent a letter from San Francisco to Mr. Hunt, his former father-in-law at Corvallis.

God has resurrected me [wrote Joshua]. I have now got my
foot on your neck. God has restored me to my own. I will
return to Oregon and gather together all of my followers.
Place no obstruction in my way, or God will smite you.
Joshua II.

That was clear enough. And from San Francisco, too,
the prophet wrote his ex-wife, Maude Hunt, then living in
Seattle with a brother and a sister-in-law, Mr. and Mrs. Frank
Hunt. Maude replied that she would re-marry Joshua if he
would come to the Puget Sound metropolis.

The prophet, now in full beard again and ready for
anything, came north, stopping neither at Corvallis nor in
Oregon but going direct to Seattle. He and Maude were
married by an orthodox minister. And now he made plans
for a triumphant return to the state that had used him so
shabbily. He would, he vowed, go to a primeval spot that
he knew on the Oregon coast and there establish a colony
for the faithful, a true Garden of Eden in which the flock
could live in a manner best suited to them and their beliefs,
free from the profane gaze of scoffers.

It would take a little cash, obviously, to purchase this
Eden, which he had visited, and he suggested that Mr. and
Mrs. Frank Hunt dispose of their Seattle property and buy
the land for the glory of God.

So hypnotic was this bearded man with the startling
eyes that the Hunts did just that. They sold their Seattle
house and bought the strip of land in question. It was south
of Waldport, Oregon, fronting the Pacific, and in 1906 was
a very remote place indeed. The Hunts and Maude were to
go to the spot as an advance party. Joshua would in the
meantime sound the call to the faithful, telling them that
they would remain away from Eden at their own peril.

"Peril?" asked Frank Hunt, who was not yet fully ap-
prised of the powers of a genuine prophet.

"Peril, yes," replied Joshua, and added, "Brother Hunt,
I have called down the wrath of an angry God on these
modern Sodoms of Seattle, of Portland, of San Francisco, of

Corvallis itself. Have no fear, Brother Hunt. My faithful will return to the fold—all of them. They will leave all behind them—their scoffing fathers, their brothers, their husbands—and come to our Eden." And then he let go an awful curse.

"A curse, O God, on San Francisco, on Portland, on Corvallis, on Seattle."

This tremendous curse was loosed on the morning of April 17,1906, just as the Eden advance party got aboard a train at Seattle on the way to Newport, Oregon, nearest railroad station to the Garden.

Next day, the eighteenth, Joshua again laid foot on Oregon soil. He avoided Corvallis, where he would have had to change cars, by getting off the train at Airlie and being taken in a livery-stable rig to Wren, twelve miles west of Corvallis, where he boarded the train for Newport. He was met at the depot by his wife and the two Hunts, who were all but speechless and who told him in awed tones of telegraphic dispatches that day reporting the total destruction of San Francisco by earthquake and fire.

Joshua smiled, probably smugly. "I knew it," he said quietly, "I knew that God would respond. The other cities of the plain will be next. We must rouse the faithful before it is too late."

And rouse they did. When a man with a big long beard has friends who can shake a big city to pieces, well, it is time to pay heed. And Joshua had sent the word through the mails to Corvallis. Within twenty-four hours trainmen on the Corvallis & Eastern Railroad wondered at all of the traffic, all of it female, heading for the end of the line at Newport. There were middle-aged women with babies, middle-aged women with grown daughters, middle-aged women alone, and young girls who, it turned out, had run away from home. Most of all, trainmen were struck with and remembered the slim beauty of fair-haired Esther Mitchell, soon to be in headlines throughout the West.

There were two trains daily out of Corvallis, and for the next several days every train brought a few more girls and women. All had to be ferried across Yaquina Bay, thence on foot or in buggy to the Garden of Joshua.

The cynical folk around Waldport put no stock in the prophet, not even after the terrifying results of his great curse became known. Waldport was openly hostile. But ninety miles east, back in troubled Corvallis, Joshua's trumpet call had sounded loud and clear. Young girls in their teens started for school and disappeared. Husbands returned home at evening to find their wives gone, at least one of them carrying a six-week-old babe with her. Still another husband found a note pinned to a pillow in his home. It told him his wife had heard the call.

Down in the Garden, Joshua was receiving more revelations. One message told that Corvallis itself was to be the next sinful city to be destroyed. Another directed all members of the cult to burn their clothing and to wear a sort of "holy" wrapper. A big fire was set going and into it screaming, moaning women and girls heaved all their vile finery, and forthwith dressed themselves in the wrappers that Joshua provided. And the prophet's search for the second Mother went on wonderfully well. . . Praise Joshua and great day in the morning!

Living conditions in the Garden were pretty bad. Lean-to and wigwam huts were made. Everyone slept on the ground. Food was cooked over open fires and was plain. Between forty and fifty girls and women and the two men made up the colony.

By April 26 at least one man in Corvallis had learned the whereabouts of Joshua. This man's young daughter had disappeared and investigation showed she had walked most of the way to Newport, then down the coast road to the Garden. The youngster, all alone, had done more than eighty miles of the trip on foot. Her father, one of Corvallis' highly respected citizens, set out to find her.

This man meant business. At Newport he paused long enough to purchase a thirty-two-caliber revolver and a box of cartridges. Going down to the water front to get transportation across Yaquina Bay, he barely missed the ferry which was just pulling away from the dock. On the ferryboat he saw the bearded prophet amid a group of wrappered females. Without more ado this man pulled his gun and aimed it at Joshua, while the women screamed. But the gun only clicked—clicked five times in a row.

Out on the ferryboat Joshua smiled gently at the puny attempts of mere man to kill him. "See," he told his women. "You see. No man can kill Joshua." And the women were certain they had witnessed another example of the prophet's power.

Not so the man on the dock. "It was the god-damn fool who sold me them cartridges and gun," he complained to friends. "The gun is center-fire, and the cartridges rim-fire. That's why that — is still alive."

But the men of seething Corvallis, now thoroughly aroused, were getting ready to lay the prophet low. Singly and in twos and threes they took train to Newport. Armed with rifles and revolvers, they crossed on the ferry and went to Waldport. Here they learned that Joshua must have been forewarned. He was last seen heading for Newport, alone, and had no doubt hidden in the woods to let the several posses pass.

This information was hurriedly telephoned to Corvallis. In that town was George Mitchell, twenty-one-year-old brother of Esther. Taking a revolver, he went to Albany— thinking he might catch the prophet there waiting for a train to Portland. Mitchell learned he was too late. The prophet was already gone. With him was his wife, Maude, and the two had bought tickets to Seattle. Young Mitchell had to remain overnight in Albany for another train. He arrived in Seattle on the morning of May 7, 1906.

Whether or not Mitchell knew where in Seattle to look for the prophet has never been clear. What is clear as daylight is this.

About eight o'clock on this May morning Joshua Creffield and his wife, now both dressed in orthodox fashion but the prophet in full beard, left the cheap rooming house where they had taken lodgings and walked down Second Avenue. At Cherry Street they turned and walked to First Avenue. In front of Quick's Drugstore was a weighing machine. The prophet's wife stepped onto the machine, while Joshua stood looking into the store window.

Young Mitchell had sighted the couple. He stepped quickly up behind the man, placed the muzzle of his revolver at the prophet's left ear, and fired. Joshua the Second slumped quietly down to the sidewalk.

The small and wiry woman turned and screamed. She flew at Mitchell like a cat and tried to take the gun from his hands. Mitchell retained the gun but made no attempt to escape. In a moment Maude left him and bent over her husband, whose blood was now running in a stream across the sidewalk. The prophet had died without moving, without even a shudder.

Mitchell stood idly, holding the gun in his hands. Without a word he handed it to a policeman who had hurried from a near-by corner.

Mrs. Creffield at first was frantic, but she calmed. "This man," she told the surprised cop, pointing to the figure on the sidewalk, "this man is my husband, Joshua the prophet. He will arise in three days and walk."

"Sure, sure," said the officer, who was used to all kinds of people. He called the wagon and an ambulance.

At the police station George Mitchell was calm, even happy. He asked for a telegraph blank and sent a message to O. P. Hunt at Corvallis, who, it will be remembered, was again the prophet's father-in-law. "I got my man," read the wire, "and I am in jail here."

In spite of protests of the widow and of Mr. and Mrs. Frank Hunt, who had hurried from Eden to Seattle, the body of the late prophet was turned over to the Bonney-Watson undertakers. These kindly men stuffed cotton into the hole in the prophet's ear, and laid him away tenderly in Lakeview

Cemetery on May 9. Only the widow and Bonney-Watson employees were at the grave. No services were held.

That was how they laid Joshua the Second away in the ground. But his work was far from done.

V

As King County (Seattle) prepared to prosecute George Mitchell for the murder of Edmund Creffield, all eyes turned to the Puget Sound city where the trial would be held; and the late prophet's Garden of Eden, three hundred miles to the south, was forgotten. Things were going badly there. On May 15, a week after the shooting, George Hodges, timber cruiser of Salado, Oregon, had been looking over some fine old Douglas fir not far from Waldport on the coast. It was a cold, windy day. When he emerged from the timber onto the beach he saw something that liked to have caused him to swallow the *Climax* he was working on.

Hodges couldn't know, of course, that he was in Garden of Eden country, and he brushed his eyes when he saw five women and young girls, one of them with a baby in arms and all dressed in outlandish wrappers, camped on the beach. One look told him they were starving. Their cheeks were pinched and some were too weak to stand. They were grouped around a frayed and torn old tent and they told the startled timber cruiser that they were followers of Joshua, the prophet who recently had destroyed San Francisco.

Hodges was a man who read the papers. He began to get the drift of what he had stumbled into. And where was this Joshua, he asked. The women said that Joshua had gone north to Queen Charlotte Islands, off the north coast of British Columbia, where he was seeking out a new Garden of Eden for his followers.

"But this prophet of yours, he is dead," Hodges told the women. "He was shot and killed in Seattle a week ago."

The women laughed crazily at that one. Joshua dead? He could not be killed. They had seen a man try it with a revolver. You couldn't kill Joshua.

Convinced that the bedraggled women were completely out of their heads, and learning that they had had nothing to eat in two weeks except a few crabs and mussels, Hodges left them what provisions he carried in his pack and went to Newport. He then telephoned authorities at Corvallis, giving them, in true landlooker style, the line, range, and section of the Garden of Eden. Expeditions of brothers, husbands, and fathers set out at once to bring their womenfolk home.

Up in Seattle the trial of George Mitchell was getting under way. It brought out some sensational stuff and it would have made front pages all over the country had it not been for Harry Thaw, concurrently on trial in New York City for slaying Stanford White. The revelations concerning the late and lusty prophet Joshua, as brought out by Mitchell's defense counsel, made the Thaw case a Dorcas Society meeting in comparison.

William D. Gardner, superintendent of the Oregon Boys and Girls Aid Society, testified that "a large number of young girls" had been sent to his institution from Corvallis by their parents; that most of these girls had confessed to "criminal relations" with the prophet, but were really not criminal at all because the prophet was searching for the Mother of a Second Christ. Certain practices of the prophet had been particularly revolting and would have made a chapter or two for Herr Doktor Krafft-Ebing.

"Creffield was a degenerate of the worst sort," shouted John Manning, district attorney of Portland, in a letter to Kenneth MacKintosh, who was prosecuting Mitchell, and added, "He practiced unspeakable brutalities on ignorant and unsophisticated girls."

A Corvallis citizen testified that Esther Mitchell, sister of the defendant, had been sent to the Boys and Girls Aid home to get her away from Joshua. When released, she immediately took up with the prophet again. "She is obsessed," concluded the witness.

Esther herself attended the trial of her brother. Day after day she sat there, and spectators remarked on her lack of emotion—or was it something else?—as she watched and listened with a dead-calm face.

Another witness told of a broken home due to Joshua. His daughter, he said, had left Oregon State College in the last term of her fourth year because Joshua had told her that all learning was the work of the Devil. "She even destroyed the graduation dress she had been working on all winter," this witness said. The mother also was obsessed. She had destroyed all the family dishes except the plain white crockery; further, when he wanted something to eat, the witness said, he had to get it himself. All this was Joshua's doings.

Evidence to be given on several days of the trial was such that the court was cleared of spectators. "No such testimony has ever been given in a King County court," the Seattle *Post-Intelligencer* observed.

George Mitchell conducted himself with quiet dignity. He was the hero throughout the trial. A large delegation came from Corvallis, including Mr. O. P. Hunt, the late prophet's father-in-law, who attempted to give bail for Mitchell and who was a stanch supporter of the youth during the trial. Women heaped flowers on the defendant every day until the judge ordered that this should stop, so far as the courtroom was concerned.

Mitchell's statement was simple. "I came here to kill this man because he ruined my two sisters. I have completed my work." He seemed the happiest person in the room.

From the first it was clear that the Messrs. Silas M. Shipley and W. H. Morris, counsel for Mitchell, were attempting to indicate justifiable homicide as well as temporary insanity, which latter was just then coming into popularity as a defense in criminal trials. Nobody, one could guess, was surprised when the jury, out an hour, returned a verdict of not guilty. George Mitchell was all but mobbed by friends and well-wishers. It was noticed, though, that his handsome, sad-faced sister, Esther, left the courtroom without going near him.

The trial ended on July 10. Two days later George Mitchell and brothers Fred and Perry went to Seattle's King Street station to take the four-thirty afternoon train to Oregon. The waiting room was crowded with summer tourists and with perhaps seventy or eighty persons who had come to Seattle from Corvallis purposely for Mitchell's trial. It was a jolly gathering.

Fred Mitchell spied Esther standing near a pillar in the big depot, nonchalant and aloof. Another man recalls seeing her there. A jaunty new sailor hat sat on her ash-blonde head. Her skirt was a bit short, coming almost to the tops of her shoes. Around her throat was a white satin ribbon, done in a big bow, its ends streaming down over a white shirtwaist. She carried a light coat over one arm.

Fred left his two brothers and went to Esther, asking her if she wasn't going to bid good-by to George. The slim girl assented with a nod. She and Fred joined the others. She took George by the hand but did not respond to his greeting, and the four Mitchells walked toward the gate of the train shed. The station announcer was now calling the train for Portland and way points.

And now the silent girl moved quickly as a panther. Reaching her right hand under the coat on her arm, she brought out a small pearl-handled revolver—just the sort a woman would buy. In a move so quick that Fred Mitchell had no time to think or act, she placed the gun's muzzle behind George's left ear and pulled the trigger. George sank to the marble floor without a word.

In the noisy, crowded station the gunshot made little impression, but Patrolman John T. Mason had seen the move. He took the smoking gun from Esther and placed her under arrest. The man on the floor was already dead.

At the Seattle police station Esther remained calm and dry-eyed. She said the killing had been a matter of course. Her brother had killed God in the form of Joshua Creffield, hadn't he? Well, that is why she had killed her brother. Shot him in the same place he had shot Joshua, she pointed out.

It took no questioning at all by police to learn that Esther and Maude Creffield, the prophet's widow, had planned to kill George Mitchell should he be freed by the court. Detectives were sent to bring Maude to the station. The stories of the two women agreed in everything: Maude had bought the gun; it was decided after some discussion that Esther should do the killing. She loaded the gun herself and put it in the bosom of her shirtwaist. Maude had objected, saying that perspiration might prevent the gun from firing. Esther then wrapped the gun in a handkerchief and put it in her waist. She would have done the shooting on the day the trial ended, she said, but no opportunity had presented itself. It was the same on the day after the trial. She knew her brothers were to leave town on the following day. She was at the station, waiting.

This new sensation fairly rocked both Seattle and distant Corvallis. When a girl who had been chosen to be the Mother of a Second Christ picks a crowded railroad station to kill her own brother—well, the Harry Thaw case was moved off page one for a few days.

Both Esther and Mrs. Creffield were held. Tried on a charge of murder, Esther was found not guilty because of unsound mind. She was committed to the Washington State Asylum. Maude Creffield was being held in the county jail for disposition, but she took care of the matter herself. One morning the matron, a Mrs. Kelly, found the young woman still in her bunk, quite dead. An autopsy revealed much strychnine in her stomach.

Three years later Esther Mitchell was released from the asylum. Two days afterward a thin and tragically beautiful girl came into the editorial offices of the *Morning Oregonian* at Portland and asked Miss Amanda Otto, secretary to Editor Harvey Scott, if she knew where George Mitchell was buried. Miss Otto immediately recognized the girl as Esther Mitchell, and replied that she would see if she could find the information. She left the room a moment. When she returned, Esther was gone.

Some weeks later the unfortunate girl—she was only twenty years old—died at the home of friends not far from Waldport, scene of the late Joshua's erstwhile Garden of Eden.

VI

Memories of the Creffield-Mitchell cases are scattered over three hundred miles of the Pacific Northwest. Railroadmen in Seattle recalled the exact spot where George Mitchell stood when he was shot. At Corvallis middle-aged and elderly people sometimes gaze with mixed emotions at Kiger Island. Old-time court attachés at Portland remember how different, and how sad, the prophet Joshua looked once his beard and long hair were cut by the jailhouse barber. And now and again some visitor to Waldport will ask to know the exact spot of Joshua's Garden of Eden.

Murder Out Yonder (1941)

For additional information on Joshua Creffield, see Chapter 11 of *Murder Out Yonder.*

Daylight in the Swamp

The tradition of the American lumberjack is an ancient one, as industrial antiquity goes in the United States. It began more than three hundred years ago, some say in 1631, when colonists set up the first sawmill in America in what is now South Berwick, Maine, and fed it with the great white pines, a classic species whose graceful outline was soon to appear on flags, provincial coats of arms, even on shillings.

It was here in the New England timber, too, that certain customs and practices originated which were to follow the loggers across the continent. For instance, an early timber baron was Sir William Pepperell, who, says an old memoir, appeared at his log landings along the Saco River "attired in a coat of scarlet cloth." This is the earliest record of brilliant garb worn in connection with logging, and one likes to think it was from Sir William that the lumberjack took his liking for red, whether of sash, shirt, or honest woolen underwear.

There was also the attempt of the Crown to prevent the loggers from cutting every tree that grew. The Royal Navy wanted the best trees saved for masts, but the attempt to reserve them was futile. Neither the royal taboo mark of the Broad Arrow on the finest timber nor penalties as severe as those against heresy could stop the red-shirted boys from cutting everything that stood in their way. Their persistence survived down to our own time.

Meanwhile, the isolation of logging camps, combined with an occupation so dangerous to life as to remove all but the toughest and most alert, conspired to produce a unique race of men whose dedicated goal was to let daylight into the swamp and thus, as they saw it, permit the advance of civilization. For generations the customary getting-up cry in camp was "Daylight in the swamp—all out!"

When the Yankee loggers had cleared the white pines, the main body of them moved to join their kind in New York and Pennsylvania, where more pine and then the spruce and the hemlock went down before them like so much wheat in a storm. They did not stop. Before the Civil War they were letting daylight into the swamps around Saginaw Bay in Michigan, and when they had mowed their way across that state they tied into Wisconsin. Here in the lake states they began to discard the slow oxen in favor of horses; their steam-driven sawmills meantime were growing in size and speed and responding to native ingenuity. When cold weather froze the log ponds, they no longer sat around waiting for spring: some genius ran a steampipe into the frozen pond, thawed it, and sawed boards all winter. They discarded the old circular saw and replaced it with a bright, thin band of glittering teeth that wailed like a banshee as it made boards to build Midwestern cities and sawdust piles so high they could be seen decades later. In both mills and woods they bent every effort to get more speed—speed to cut the timber which they believed would last a hundred years, if not forever.

The Michigan and Wisconsin timber did not last forever, so the boys tore into Minnesota like locusts, and like locusts took all before them. What they did not cut they and the settlers managed to set afire, creating some of the most horrible disasters imaginable. The timber line receded, and before long the lumberjacks began to notice signs in hotels and saloons that read "No Calked Boots Allowed Here." Civilization had caught up with them. As they peered forth from the middle of billions of stumps, the boys could see it was time to move again. There was always more timber west, just over the hump.

Perhaps a quarter of the migrating lumberjacks of the lake states moved into the southern pine region, but the main army moved west. A few stopped in Montana. More went on into Idaho. Still more of them crossed the Cascade Range and came down the Columbia, the Snohomish, and the Skagit, tossing from the windows of the steamcars the now-emptied bottles and snuffboxes they had bought in Duluth, in Chippewa Falls, in Muskegon, in Saginaw. They were cutting the Big Swath, the Big Clearing, and now, although they didn't know it, they were in their last stronghold. Their backs were to the mountains, their faces to the sea.

Here they were in the largest forests of big timber they had ever seen. There are two distinct forests. East of the Cascade Range the woods are dominated by the ponderosa pine (western yellow), standing up to 200 feet on the best sites and running to six feet in diameter. Between the Cascades and the sea is the Douglas fir, standing up to 325 feet, with diameters up to fifteen feet. In the fir region also are large stands of western red cedar of enormous girth; and in coastal strips called the rain forest are stands of Sitka spruce and west coast hemlock. (The latter, for many years rarely considered worth cutting, has come into its own with the rise of the pulp and paper industry.)

Along with the loggers, even if most historians have rather prudishly ignored it, came a notable migration of fancy women from the old sawdust towns. They had seen altogether too much daylight in the swamps of the lake states; and now the more enterprising among them went out and bought new bonnets with sweeping feathers and one-way tickets to Spokane or Portland or Seattle.

In Montana and Idaho and in eastern Oregon and Washington, the loggers continued to use horses, but west of the Cascades, it was found, the timber was much too big for such temperamental animals. What was needed here was a lot of power and a slow, steady pull, so the west-side loggers reverted to the primordial force of the eastern pineries—oxen—only here they were called bulls. Sleds would not do to handle the big sticks. There was seldom snow enough for sledding anyway, and there were few streams deep and wide enough for good river driving. But the boys were adaptable—they invented the skid road.

The skid road was the western loggers' first and greatest contribution to the technology of the woods. A path was cleared in the forest. At suitable intervals trees were felled across the path, cut free of limbs, then half-buried in the soft ground. These were the skids that made a skid road, a sort of track to keep moving logs from hanging up on rocks or miring in mud.

It was crude, yet effective. They hitched the bulls to the logs—five or six, maybe ten yokes of them, in charge of the bullwhacker, or teamster, who was perhaps the all-time master of profanity, and the big sticks, held in tandem by hooks, were pulled over the skids. It was something to see, this skid-road logging. First, you heard the clank of chains and the loud, clear call of the bullwhacker's voice echoing down a forest road that was like a deep green canyon, so tall and thick stood the Douglas fir. Then the powerful line of red and black and spotted white would swing by with measured tread, the teamster, sacred goadstick over his shoulder, walking beside the team, petting and cursing them by turns. Back of the bulls walked the skid greaser, daubing thick oil on the skids, which smoked from friction. And then came the huge logs themselves, sliding along with a dignified roll.

Bull-team logging was drama. Small boys in Oregon and Washington, late in the last century, wanted to be bullwhackers when they grew up. More than a few authentic timber barons started to make their piles by whacking their own bulls down a skid road. Even the term "skid road" survives long after the last bull team has disappeared. In modern usage it refers to that district of western towns which, says the big Webster quite correctly, is "the part of a town frequented by loggers."

Use of the word in this sense originated seventy-odd years ago in Seattle, where Henry Yesler's pioneer skid road ran through the settlement from the timbered hills to the mill on tidewater. It was natural that hotels and saloons and other dives seeking logger trade should have been established along the skid road, and in good time the entire neighborhood became known as The Skidroad, a logical and useful term that quickly spread to all Far Western towns. Of recent years an abominable corruption has appeared, "skid row," whose use is confined to the glib who wish to appear sophisticated but patently don't know what they are talking about.

Bull-team technique developed one serious fault, best described by the maxim that any operator who attempted to haul logs more than one mile to a sawmill, or to water where they could be floated, was heading straight for bankruptcy. What was more, that mile must be a downhill haul, or at least level. Such a limit could not last long in a country where operators could lift their eager eyes to see billions of feet of fine timber all over the foothills, the valleys, even the mountains up to, say, the 4,000-foot level.

It is the history of technology that it advances according to need; and it was an inventive logger, John Dolbeer of Humboldt Bay, California, who in 1881 devised the rig that was to drive the bull teams from the woods. Dolbeer's invention, which he patented in 1882, was a new kind of donkey engine with a single cylinder, a vertical boiler, and a horizontal engine with a drum, or capstan. Though other men were simultaneously experimenting with steam in the Douglas-fir forest, they left no clear record, and the Dolbeer became the machine that supplanted the ox. By the early nineties Dolbeers were operating in Oregon and Washington.

The Dolbeer brought ground-lead logging: By means of a cable pulled by the turning capstan, the logs were led along the ground to a "yard." Once a turn was in, a line horse hauled the cable back into the timber. The animals became very knowing, needing scarcely any guidance at all. A man listed on the payroll as "sniper" prepared the felled logs for easy yarding by rounding their head-ends with an axe. "Choker men" put wire slip loops called chokers around the logs, then hitched the chokers to the main line from the donkey engine. On a high stump stood the signal boy. When the yarding crew's boss yelled "Hi!" the boy dipped his flag, or waved an arm, and the engineer put on the steam.

Ground-lead logging brought speed and volume. Throughout the nineties and well into this century, the donkeys grew in size and power to meet the increased production of the mills. By the turn of the century the influx of eastern operators and their men was getting into full swing in the Northwest. Camps grew from an average of perhaps 20 to more than 200 men each. Railroads were being laid to haul the logs from camp to mill, or to tidewater.

Rail logging had been made feasible by perfection of a geared locomotive credited in large part to Ephraim Shay, a Michigan logger as bearded as Moses and something of a prophet himself. A Shay engine could negotiate grades and curves that would have defeated a rod locomotive. This was sufficient. Old Shay's name went honorably into logging history.

Then, one inspired day, some unidentified logger in a hurry figured out a method to improve the ground-lead system. What he did was to hang a block or pulley high up in a big tree. Thus was the high-lead born. Through the block ran the main line from the donkey engine. A log could now be yarded with its head end in the air, riding free above the stumps and underbrush. The line horse was supplanted by an extra drum on the donkey, the haulback, which returned the main line to the woods after each turn more quickly than a horse could turn around. The high-lead speeded production almost beyond knowing. It also brought into being the most spectacular occupation in the timber, or perhaps anywhere—that of the high-rigger or high-climber.

With sharp steel spurs on his legs, a safety belt around his waist, and an axe and saw dangling from a rope beneath, this steeple jack of the woods hitches himself up a tall fir, limbing as he goes. At somewhere around 150 feet from the ground he straps himself in place and saws off the treetop.

Hanging there against the sky, he must work carefully lest he cut his belt and crash to his death on the circle of stumps below. When the great top starts to lean, then to fall, the high-climber must brace himself well. The trunk vibrates wickedly in wide arcs. For an instant, top and man are little more than a blur. Down goes the top, tons of it, to crash on the forest floor and send echoes up the canyon.

The topped trunk is now a spar tree—an anchor for subsequent high-lead operations. It is guyed all around with steel cables. Then the high-lead block, weighing some 1,800 pounds, is hoisted to the top and secured. The main line is run through the block and its end taken into the woods by the haulback. When a turn of logs has been hooked to the main line, the signalboy, now called a "whistle-punk," gives the go-ahead. The huge donkey engine snorts noise and steam and sparks; then, rearing up like some prehistoric monster from the underbrush, comes an imposing sight—a log six feet in diameter, forty feet long. It is yanked swiftly, one end dragging, surging, the head end clear, to the donkey where it is unhooked by the "chaser," and the rigging sent flying back into the timber.

High-lead logging almost doubled production. It also brought a notable increase in the accident rate, which was already far too high. With timber sailing through the air, rather than moving with moderate speed over the ground, there was an infinitely greater chance for a man to be hit—and harder. Added to this natural hazard was the yarding bonus offered by many logging operators. The boss, the "bull of the woods," set a footage quota, usually high rather than otherwise, for the crew. If they managed to yard more than this figure, every man got a dollar or so added to his wages that day. It was the timber-country version of the industrial speed-up. If it doubled production, it also doubled accidents; and it may well have tripled discontent.

Discontent among the loggers did not originate in the Northwest. There had been strikes, chiefly against the twelve-hour day then in force, back in Michigan. There had been protests over low wages and poor working conditions in Wisconsin and Minnesota. Yet labor unions failed to get a real foothold. Only the shingle weavers of the Far West cedar mills had managed to keep alive an organization of any effectiveness, and it had nothing to do with loggers.

It was often said of loggers—and they believed it themselves—that their isolation and the nature of their work made them individualists unfit to band together against the boss. And the babel of tongues characteristic of logging camps from the eighties onward was no help. But now, in the first decade of the new century, came a new union, the Industrial Workers of the World, led by Big Bill Haywood, an ebullient, one-eyed hard-rock miner who had also worked in the woods. He had just become labor's hero in a sensational trial in Idaho in which he was acquitted of a murder charge. Advocating a dictatorship of the proletariat, the I. W. W., or "wobblies," as they were called, were shrewd enough to go after membership by promising loggers higher wages, better food, the eight-hour day, safe working conditions, and almost anything else which organizers could think up to bring the boys running to get the Little Red Card denoting I. W. W. membership.

The wobblies were less a labor union than a religion. They staged strikes, first in Portland, later in the Willapa and Grays Harbor logging camps, then in Seattle, Spokane, and Everett. When they couldn't pull a strike on the job, it was their delight to get themselves arrested for speaking on the streets; then they would shout that they were making a "free speech fight," meanwhile sending word out over the remarkable wobbly grapevine for the boys to rally in number. They came in number, too, commonly on freight trains, to fill town and city jails to overflowing and make bedlam for days and nights on end. Among their organizers was a woman, Elizabeth Gurley Flynn—young, handsome, a flaming red tie at her throat—possessed of enough eloquence to send skid-road males hurrying to get their membership cards in the nearest wobbly hall.

Though the I. W. W. never troubled to consolidate its gains in the manner of conventional unions, it did put the fear of God, or possibly of Marx, into the lumber barons. Violence broke out sporadically in the camps and the sawmill centers—not just the violence of clubs and stones and brass knuckles but of guns in the hands of desperate and determined men who were playing for keeps.

Neither unions nor laws nor the slow national decline in the per capita consumption of lumber could put a stop to the steady progress of logging technology. Steam had inspired uncounted inventors to experiment with power machinery. In steep country, counterbalance incline railroads appeared. A primeval steam saw for felling timber, a forerunner of today's gas-driven chainsaw, was built and tried. A noted woods boss, C. C. (Whitewater) McLean, left his name secure in the industry by inventing the McLean loading boom. Some genius around Puget Sound came up with a truly fearsome combination of steam, wheels, and lines he called a Walking Dudley. Other men were already playing with the idea of a tall yet portable steel mast to perform the duties of a spar tree. And at least two brave fellows rolled into the timber aboard a monstrous overland steam engine they hoped would replace both a yarding donkey *and* a locomotive. It didn't.

Then, on a day heavy with portent—unmarked in history, it may have been in 1911, or even 1913—somebody went into the woods with a homemade truck operated by an internal-combustion engine, loaded it with logs, and drove it away to the sawmill on a road made of planks laid end to end. Here was a warning of things to come. Steam was to be driven slowly yet relentlessly from the woods by gasoline and diesel oil. A great thundering era was ending.

But not yet. There were still 3,400 miles of standard-gauge logging tracks in Oregon and Washington—over half the total in seven western states and the province of British Columbia—in 1929, a peak year when almost twelve billion board feet of timber went to the sawmills of the two states, most of it by rail. It was hauled by more than 600 steam locomotives, of which 400 were geared engines made by Lima-Shay, Climax, and Heisler; the rest were engines from Baldwin, Porter, American, and Vulcan.

Back in the early 1920s, I used to know gray old loggers, shaggy-headed and grown dim of eye, who would sit on the deacon seat, of an evening in camp, and damn the "modern" methods, by which they meant steam logging, and weep for the days when noble bull teams lurched down the skid roads, bellowing and grunting, while the bullwhacker cried aloud in protest to a Deity who had made such miserable oxen. In *that* great time, it seemed, men had been men, with hair not only on their chests but on their faces too. My own generation, according to these veterans, was a group of sheared weaklings dependent on machinery, coddled in camp with company mattresses, even sheets; with *white* crockery, not tin plates on the cookhouse table; with pretty female waitresses; with shower baths and electric lights; with mail and newspapers daily, or almost daily.

I realized, of course, that all this was merely a lament of ancient men for their youth, a youth gone now into the mists where ghostly bull teams walked a rotted skid road. Thus it is with me, thirty years later, when memory gives me pause to reflect on how little has survived of that so-called modern era I knew only yesterday. That era did not come to an end with a bang. Eras seldom do. But the logging railroad and the steam donkey had, by 1955, virtually disappeared in the Oregon and Washington timber. A few Shays work in West Virginia, but in general this locomotive is now an antique, drowsing with cast-iron generals in a park—a park past which highway trucks loaded with logs streak at dizzying speeds.

It makes my generation men out of Genesis; we can remember, for instance, when western loggers used snuff, not cigarettes. We can recall when loggers would eat hay, if you sprinkled a little whiskey on it. Above all, we can remember when logging was done by single men who lived in logging camps at the end of a railroad through the woods. Today, even the camps are passing, and loggers are young married men who prefer to live with their families in communities on the highway, to drive to and from the logging works in their own cars.

There is, however, one change in the industry which no man, no matter how beset with nostalgia, can fail to welcome. It is this: Every logging outfit worthy of the name— at least in the Pacific Northwest—has on its payroll from one to one hundred graduates of accredited forestry schools. Thirty years ago, the few foresters seen in the logging woods were exotics who had no more standing than a botanist. Loggers referred to them as bug-chasers, as pismire super-intendents. No longer. Industrial foresters today advise cutting practices to be followed and are responsible for the care and protection of company lands—from which one crop has been harvested and another crop from ten to fifty feet tall is growing.

Such lands used to bear the timber baron's mark of Cain when he was Public Enemy Number Two, if not Number One, his devastated acres strewn with debris, ready for burning again and again. Today these lands are tree farms, registered as such and expensively cherished. Timber is a crop. Forests are everlasting. Such is the theory now held by major loggers and lumbermen all over the country, and the theory has largely turned to practice.

Now that both logging camp and logging railroad are on their way to join the bull teams and the skid roads, I imagine that few of today's loggers, by now thoroughly and, I trust, happily domesticated, regret their passing. Yet, here and there may be an old-timer with a stubborn atavistic streak who, when the melancholy is upon him, will suddenly recall a dawn, back when the world was new, when all of us were young and handsome, when all phonographs played "Margie" and "Dardanella," and the wireless was not yet quite radio.

It was a magic time filled with dreams, even at the far end of a logging railroad in a logging camp, where the sun came over the mountain to slant in whirling mists, while the bull cook beat the daylights out of the camp gong, and two hundred single young men came stomping down the camp walk, their calks clicking rhythmically on the planks, heading for an incredible breakfast, then a thundering ride behind the rolling Shay to where the spar tree rose high above the round stuff lying among the stumps far below.

Such was my "modern" time. I thought then that it was a thumping great and wildly wonderful, if tragically heedless, era in the timber. Thirty years later I know it was.

American Heritage (1958)

For recent histories of the forest products industry in the Northwest, see Thomas R. Cox, *Mills and Markets: History of the Pacific Coast Lumber Industry*, University of Washington Press (1974); Robert E. Ficken,*The Forested Land: A History of Lumbering in Western Washington*, University of Washington Press (1987); Ellis Lucia, *The Big Woods: Logging and Lumbering—From Bull Teams to Helicopters in the Pacific Northwest*, Doubleday (1975); and William G. Robbins, *Hard Times In Paradise: Coos Bay, Oregon 1850-1986*, University of Washington Press (1988).

The Affair at Copperfield

The ugly blot on the map of Oregon that was Copperfield no longer exists. It was removed by Miss Fern Hobbs, who was twenty-five years old and weighed exactly 104 pounds when fully dressed and wearing her gold pince-nez.

The Copperfield affair was one of those happy combinations that no newspaper can resist, and no reader either. For a period of several days Miss Hobbs and Copperfield were known and discussed all over North and South America, in the British Isles, Holland, France, Germany, and in the Antipodes. It seems only reasonable to assume they were discussed also in Mongolia and in Madagascar.

There was no copper in Copperfield. The town grew suddenly up among the rocks and sagebrush of a grim, narrow canyon of the valley of the Snake River on Oregon's eastern border. That was in 1909. It had one purpose; namely, to cater to the uninhibited appetites of more than two thousand men who were engaged on two nearby construction projects, the one a railroad tunnel, the other a power plant. The town was near the far end of a tortuous sixty-mile branch that left the Union Pacific's mainline at Huntington. A mixed train came and went three times weekly.

Within a month from the day the first stake was driven, Copperfield had blossomed like some evil flower of the desert into a long street of false-front buildings which contained saloons, gambling joints, a big dance hall, and several places of easy or no virtue. There were also a couple of general stores, a tiny railroad station, and warehouses.

For three years or so the town thoroughly enjoyed vice and debauchery undisturbed by any sort of law, city, county, state, or federal. Remote from all other communities, and so situated as to discourage visitors from "outside," it grew fat in the manner of parasites. It was anything but dull. Gang battles between the two construction crews took on epic proportions. These were fought mostly with rocks and beer bottles, and thus resulted in many casualties, though few deaths. Drunken men lay on occasion strung out like railroad ties, both in the snow and in the dust under the blistering sun.

There were no arrests, ever. Copperfield bragged that it had no peace officer and no jail. The county seat and sheriff were at Baker, 150 miles by railroad.

Then, early in 1913, the construction jobs began to peter out. Fewer men were employed. Competition for the remaining trade became stiff. The saloonkeepers began feuding. One night the joint operated by a Montenegrin named Martin Knezevich burned to the ground. He and his wife narrowly escaped cremation. Pretty soon another saloonkeeper, William Wiegand, discovered his place to be on fire, and found the blaze to have been carefully prepared with oil-soaked kindling.

Then, rather suddenly, the faction to which Wiegand belonged decided to incorporate Copperfield as a city; and in a dubious election H. A. Stewart, saloonkeeper, was named mayor, his partner Tony Warner made councilman, along with William Wiegand. Just to fill out the ticket, Wiegand's bartender and handyman, one Charles Kuntz, was made third councilman. The first official act was to issue city liquor licenses to all saloons except that of Martin Knezevich.

Mr. Knezevich then made the grave error of appealing to the county prosecutor in distant Baker. The prosecutor made his weary way to Copperfield, remained between trains, then returned to his base. He said that Copperfield was so filled with wrangling and threats he could in no manner get at the bottom of the trouble.

Mr. Knezevich, a glutton for trouble, next appealed for protection to the county sheriff, who was Ed Rand, six feet six, and well over two hundred pounds. Sheriff Rand dutifully went to take a look at Copperfield, and so back to his office. He reported he could make neither head nor tail of Copperfield's troubles.

The new saloon of Mr. Knezevich again caught fire, and was saved from total destruction only by the quick work of the proprietor and his friends.

Such was the condition of affairs in mid-1913. At about this time Governor Oswald West, in Salem, the state capital, 450 miles across the mountains from Copperfield, began to hear of Copperfield and its troubles. Letters from ranchwomen complained that their sons were being debauched in the hellholes of the Gomorrah on the Snake. Presently, the governor received a petition signed by some fifty actual citizens of Copperfield, including the teacher of its only school, asking that the State of Oregon step in to do what needed doing, and which Baker County authorities had refused to do.

Governor West notified Baker County authorities to clean up Copperfield. They advised the governor that Copperfield was a city with its own government. West replied that Copperfield had no government, that it was being run by and for a collection of underworld characters. He named Christmas day as the deadline; if the place had not been cleaned up by then, the state would take steps.

Copperfield celebrated Christmas in its usual style, which was to say, in drinking, fighting, gambling, and whoring.

Os West was, and is, a man of his word. He was by all odds the most brilliant governor Oregon ever had. He was also a Democrat in a commonly Republican state, a militant Dry in a Wet state. Although absolutely incorruptible, he was a shrewd politician with an extraordinarily fine sense of drama as a part of the fitness of things.

So now, on the first day of 1914, he called his private secretary, Miss Fern Hobbs, and told her to prepare resignations for the signatures of the city officials of Copperfield.

He also dictated to her a proclamation of martial law. Then he instructed her to board a train for eastern Oregon, and proceed to Copperfield. In order to save time, he suggested, she might wire ahead to the mayor, saying she wished to meet with officials and citizens at the city hall immediately on her arrival.

"At the meeting," the governor went on, "you will call upon city officials who are in the saloon business for their resignations. If they refuse, you are to declare martial law, disarm everybody in town, close the saloons, and ship all liquor, bar fixtures, and gambling equipment out of Copperfield."

Miss Hobbs got aboard the train. With her, and in civilian clothes, were Lieutenant-Colonel B. K. Lawson and five soldiers of the Oregon National Guard, and Frank Snodgrass, chief of the penitentiary guards. All seven men were veterans of the Philippine Insurrection. All were large, rugged, and bold fellows.

With Miss Hobbs and her delegation on the way, Governor West called the press. He had just dispatched his secretary, he said, to clean up the mess of Copperfield. He pointed out that though Sheriff Ed Rand of Baker County was six feet six and weighed over two hundred pounds, he had admitted he wasn't big enough to handle Copperfield. "My secretary Miss Hobbs," the governor thoughtfully added, "is five feet three and weighs 104 pounds." The papers and the wire services got the idea, and at once shared it with their readers.

The news even reached Copperfield, and Mayor Stewart of that city replied with what he considered fine humor. "We are decorating the city with ribbons," he told the Associated Press, "and will try to have some flowers for Miss Hobbs."

Informed of this sparkling repartee, Governor West remarked that he thought flowers appropriate. Weren't they traditional at funerals?

While these amenities were being exchanged, Miss Hobbs and the Guards rolled on over the Cascades, then into the desert country of eastern Oregon. Years later, when I asked what her thoughts had been while heading for Copperfield, she admitted to a few qualms at the outcome; but apparently it never occurred to her to be frightened.

Miss Hobbs is obviously a self-reliant person anyway, and she had made her own way since high school. Born of New England parents on a Nebraska ranch, she had come to Oregon in 1904. While acting as governess in the family of a Portland banker, she had learned stenography. While working as secretary to the president of a title guarantee company, she studied law. In 1913 she was admitted to the Oregon bar. Governor West hired her as chief stenographer, and soon made her his private secretary.

And here she was on the way to what an Oregon clergyman had just termed "the poisonous toadstool of the badlands," a description, commented Governor West, of pure whitewash and arrant flattery.

On the bitterly cold morning of January 2, Miss Hobbs and guard changed from the Union Pacific's mainliner to the creaking mixed train for Copperfield. Four hours later the train wheezed into the stark white canyon, coming to a stop in front of a board shanty labeled Copperfield. Massed around the depot and strung out along the single street was the entire population. Three saloonkeepers and a bartender, comprising the mayor and city council, gave cheery if cynical welcome to Miss Fern Hobbs as she stepped down from the coach.

Miss Hobbs, demure enough in any garb, was dressed in a modish blue suit, and wore a muff and neckpiece of black lynx. She had on black shoes, and a black hat with two Nile-green feathers set rakishly at one side. Which was very good reporting for a male of the Associated Press. She carried a businesslike briefcase. Her grave blue eyes looked out from behind gold-rimmed glasses. She was escorted forthwith to the barn of a dance hall and took her place on the platform. The place was soon crowded with the citizenry, a good many of whom were patently wearing holsters under their jackets. Colonel Lawson and two Guardsmen stood at the back of the hall beside the one door.

This was one occasion when the speaker of the day really needed no introduction from the toastmaster; Miss Hobbs came directly to the point. She opened the meeting by saying that it was the governor of Oregon's hope that Copperfield officials would resign at once. One who was there recalls that she spoke clearly and precisely, unhurried, with neither undue aggressiveness nor apology in her tone. When she had finished, she passed the prepared resignations to the four saloonkeeper-officials.

Those gentlemen considered the documents briefly, then each rose, one after another, to say he had no intention of resigning.

The crowd grew tense. Miss Hobbs looked out over the audience of several hundred, which included a few women. There was no booing; there were no smart cracks or remarks. Only silence. At the door, Colonel Lawson held his breath, wondering. This was the moment when the situation could turn into a bloody riot.

Miss Hobbs stood for a long minute as though transfixed. Then she took the proclamation of martial law from her briefcase. She called to Colonel Lawson. He came forward. He read the message to the still silent audience. Then he placed the mayor and the three councilmen under arrest.

"You will now disperse in an orderly manner," Colonel Lawson announced in closing the meeting.

Both citizens and their officials seemed stunned. Lawson had another message for them. "Attention" he called in the booming tones fit for a colonel. "As you leave the hall you will turn over your revolvers and other weapons to my men at the door."

One after another the citizens of Copperfield meekly passed their many revolvers and a few long knives to the Guardsmen at the door, who piled them in an anteroom. There were more than 170 revolvers turned in.

As they filed outside, weaponless, Copperfield citizens found more bad news. The Guardsmen had been busy. Every saloon and gambling house on the street now had a bold and official *Do Not Enter* sign tacked to its closed door.

The mixed train was at the depot, ready for the return trip to civilization. Colonel Lawson escorted Miss Hobbs to the coach, which she boarded and waved her goodbye. As they pulled out of deathly silent Copperfield, the twilight of approaching night touched the stark canyon, and Miss Fern Hobbs suddenly recalled some verses in the Fifth Reader of her schooldays, and wondered if curfew really had rung in Copperfield that night.

Miss Hobbs returned to spend the night in Baker, county seat, where she reported by wire to Governor West. Colonel Lawson and men continued the process of instilling virtue and sobriety in Copperfield.

The attorneys of Copperfield's embattled saloonkeepers were getting busy in Baker; and now the telegraph instrument in the little depot began clicking out threats of lawsuits, injunctions, and other legal hocus-pocus. Colonel Lawson ignored them, and stationed a guard to prevent the sending or receiving of messages. Two other Guardsmen, rifle at shoulder, patroled the street after dark, keeping an eye on the closed joints. But nobody attempted to enter the posted premises. Copperfield's badmen seemed to have lost heart.

After dark, however, there was a moment of excitement near the depot. The guard at the telegraph office heard a noise and saw two shadowy figures leap aboard a speeder, which began to snort and chatter. Before it could get under way, the guard took into custody Councilmen Wiegand and Warner, who had had the idea of breaking arrest. They were confined in the depot.

But Copperfield was really stunned at its first meeting with the law. The citizens remained indoors throughout the night, and drinkless, too. It must have been a desolating experience. And although Colonel Lawson and men had no further trouble, next day brought ten additional National

Guardsmen to the scene, sent by the governor as an added precaution. They went to work rolling barrels of liquor and beer to the depot, where they were loaded into a commandeered boxcar, along with cases of wet goods and an imposing collection of faro tables, "twenty-one" tables, birdcage games, roulette wheels, cards, chips, and dice.

Meanwhile, Colonel Lawson staged a meeting in the dance hall to form a provisional government, and appointed Sam Grim, a carpenter, mayor.

Despite threats of lawsuits, Colonel Lawson shipped all of Copperfield's liquor and gambling devices to Baker, where they were placed under state bond in a warehouse. Then he and his men returned to the state capital, where Miss Fern Hobbs had already resumed her usual duties in the governor's office.

Miss Hobbs was also being startled at what can happen when the hot glaring rays of limelight are focused on a prim and genuinely retiring soul. The Copperfield incident got a tremendous press, in Oregon, in the United States, in the Western Hemisphere, and in foreign parts.

In provincial New York City, for instance, and for three days running, the Copperfield affair crowded the Becker-Rosenthal case for front-page position. In far-off Salem, Oregon, Miss Hobbs received wires from the *World, Journal,* and *Times,* asking for "I was there" stories, all of which she ignored.

The *Literary Digest* devoted pages of comment to the affair. The organized Dry forces in all parts of the United States sent messages to Miss Hobbs, referring to her variously as a modern Jeanne d'Arc, as a latter-day Carry Nation, or at the least a womanly knight on a white charger, banner unfurled, a challenge to the forces of evil. Even a part of the press saw her in relation to mythical or historic women of the ages. The Brooklyn *Eagle* ran quite a temperature, comparing Fern Hobbs to "Jael the Kenite woman," to "Zenobia defying the army of Aurelian," and to "the great Catherine of Russia in all her glory."

Miss Hobbs's mail was flooded with homemade poems written in her honor by total strangers; and laced with letters from other total strangers asking her hand in marriage.

In Oregon a group of militant suffragettes erupted and started a boom of Hobbs for Governor.

Vaudeville agents in Chicago and New York offered her contracts to appear on the circuits they represented. A San Francisco impresario wanted to star her in a stage play.

The trade press of the liquor industry banged away with much heavy-handed satire.

In England, the Copperfield story escaped all bounds. One read that Miss Hobbs took off for the hellish place in command of a full battery of field artillery, plus machine gunners, in a special train; that she snapped commands to her troops, and had them unlimber and train the heavy pieces on the doomed city.

On the heels of the daily press, magazines in the United States carried articles on the subject.

The alumni secretary of Massachusetts State College, Division of Agriculture, at Amherst, suddenly showed great interest in locating Miss Hobbs's father, J. A. Hobbs, an alumnus who had apparently dropped from sight. Mr. Hobbs was now the father of a famous daughter.

As to Copperfield, it was dying by the moment after January 2, 1914. I believe it was killed no less by Governor West, Miss Hobbs, and the Oregon National Guardsmen than it was by shame and ridicule. It scarcely breathed or moved an eyelid after the raid. It had surrendered without a shot. Its vaunted lawlessness had turned to meekness within two hours, or between Miss Hobbs's arrival and departure.

Copperfield was dead, and it disappeared altogether a few months later when fire, again of unknown origin, destroyed a block or two of the jerry-built structures. No saloon ever reopened. Citizens drifted away. The doors of the few remaining buildings fell from their hinges. Windows were broken, or removed. Curious coyotes dodged in and out of the old joints, while owls went in the windows to perch and sound their melancholy notes.

The railroad depot was closed. Copperfield for a time was a flagstop, then wholly ignored. Sagebrush grew up and over and through the rotting plank walks. The everlasting winds blew, and sand covered and at last buried deep the last remnants of Copperfield.

Ex-governor Os West is my neighbor in Portland. I often talk with him. He is as alert and as energetic as most men of forty, and though he pretends to be retired, his occasional letters to Oregon newspapers are the joy of editors and readers who like sharp and sometimes blistering comment on local and state affairs.

I often see Miss Hobbs, who lives in Portland in a modest home as neat and tidy as the Curfew of Copperfield herself. She still weighs 104 pounds. Her eyes are clear and blue behind her glasses. There is not a gray hair in her trim head. She lives as quietly as she has always lived, except for those dreadful few days so long ago when duty required otherwise. I doubt that the Copperfield affair had the least effect on her as a person or on her career. She practiced law in Portland, and later became secretary to the business manager of a local daily, from which occupation she not long since retired.

The subject of Copperfield bores her. She had much rather talk of her two years with the Red Cross in World War I, in France, and with the American Army of Occupation in Germany. *That*, she says, and her eyes light up, was a real adventure. One gathers that she considers the affair at Copperfield to have been a deplorable incident.

The Far Corner (1952)

Cargoes of Maidens

When young Asa Mercer arrived early in 1861 at the new port of Seattle in Washington Territory, he found a region occupied largely, so far as white people were concerned, by young and unmarried males. Conditions were no better than they had been two years before, when Charles Prosch, the observant editor of the *Puget Sound Herald* in Steilacoom, had remarked plaintively there were in his little village alone some fifty bachelors, all of whom, he vowed, were "eager to put their necks in the matrimonial noose."

The ratio of men to women, regardless of marital status, was estimated at 9 to 1, and virtually all females of fourteen and over already were married. This was due chiefly to stipulations in the Land Donation Act which gave 320 acres to each man, another 320 acres to his wife. Being like all pioneers hungry for land, the males of Puget Sound were avid to marry almost any white woman who was, as the saying went, between six and sixty. More than one child as young as thirteen had been given as wife, with parental blessing, to a man of forty or more.

The few white women arriving in Washington Territory of the fifties and sixties were mostly married, wives of the loggers and sawmill workers whom the firm of Pope & Talbot was importing under contract from East Machias, Maine, to operate its camps and mills at Port Gamble, commonly called Teekalet Mills, on Puget Sound.

Thus, the lack of unmarried females was much on Editor Prosch's mind. He had brought the subject to public notice first in 1858. A year later he reverted to it, brooding in an editorial entitled "The Scarcity of White Women" that at least two-thirds of the three thousand voters in the territory wanted to get married, right then. The editor did not approve of Indian-white marriage. "Half-breeds," said he in print, "carrying in their veins the blood of men now historic are known to all pioneers." But he thought the products of mixed marriages did not add luster to either line, and perhaps he knew what he was talking about.

Editor Prosch's brooding at last resulted in a meeting. On a Tuesday evening in February of 1860, the bachelors of Steilacoom rallied in the Delin & Shorey Building to discuss their deplorable condition. They admitted that their "only chance for a realization of the benefits and early attainments of matrimonial alliances depends on the arrival in our midst of a number of the fair sex from the Atlantic states," and sought "to devise ways and means to secure this much-needed and desirable emigration to our shore."

All these noble words, however, were as the sound of the wind in the tall firs that hemmed Steilacoom on three sides. Nothing came of them. Then, almost a year after the abortive meeting, Asa S. Mercer arrived in the near-by and newer settlement of Seattle. He came from Illinois. A student of Franklin College, Wilmington, Ohio, he was good-looking, of attractive manners and, as it turned out, had no lack of confidence in his own abilities. It seems certain, too, that he possessed more imagination than any other unmarried male in Washington Territory, for he practically alone did something about the dreary condition of Puget Sound bachelors.

Judge Thomas Mercer, who was already an old and respected pioneer, got his younger brother a job helping to clear a site for the University of Washington, and Asa went on to work as a carpenter on the lone building. In the autumn of 1862 he became the first president of the university, teaching a small class, the only class, of students.

Judge Mercer, like Editor Prosch, often spoke of the lack of decent white women and proposed, only half jocosely, that territorial funds should be used to bring a party of young women "of unblemished character" to Puget Sound. The idea took fire in the mind of young Asa, who may well himself have felt the mating urge. In any case, he went to Governor William Pickering and talked the matter over. The governor was most favorable to the plan but said, doubtless with truth, there was no money in the territorial treasury.

Asa Mercer was patently a dreamer of wondrous dreams and possessed of all the faults common to dreamers. But he was also a man of action. He promptly went about Seattle in a private crusade to raise money and seems to have had little trouble getting donations from young male citizens. Then he took ship to Boston.

Near Boston was the industrial town of Lowell, a Yankee textile heaven where the morals of female mill operatives were carefully guarded and guaranteed. Mercer went there at once, to find the town in abject depression. Its population of 40,000 depended almost wholly on the cotton mills. Little cotton was to be had from the embattled South. More than a thousand female operatives were out of work. It looked to Asa Mercer, who certainly wasn't interested in the war that was raging, as if Lowell were the spot God had chosen for him.

He lost no time. He engaged Mechanics' Hall and called a meeting for the purpose of telling "girls and young women who are war orphans" about the attractions of Washington Territory. There was a good turnout. One who was present, a young girl named Flora Pearson, said that Mercer pictured in glowing terms the "wonderful financial advantage that without doubt would accrue to any and all young ladies of good character" who would leave New England with him for the delights of Puget Sound and Washington Territory. The subject of possible matrimony was carefully not mentioned, but Mercer bore down heavily on the astonishingly good pay the girls could earn teaching school.

Charming and eloquent as he was, Mercer must have lacked what high-powered sales people term "the ability to close with the prospect": only eleven young women of the large gathering "found courage to leave their friends and make a journey of seven thousand miles into a wilderness."

He was somewhat disappointed in the results. Right after the meeting, he related in later years, a "large number of the audience" had come forward and expressed a desire to see Puget Sound. But all except the eleven stanch girls soon "lost courage."

With Mercer in charge, the eleven Yankee and Irish girls took ship in New York in March of 1864 and crossed the Isthmus of Panama; so on to San Francisco, where the barge *Torrent* took them to Port Gamble, to be transferred to still another ship. In this they arrived at Seattle about midnight, May 16, 1864, and even at that hour were given a royal reception. One who was present recalled that the welcoming males, which is to say a majority of Seattle's population, looked something like grizzlies in store clothes—which may, of course, have been a piece of smug condescension. But they meant business, these single young men of Puget Sound. Ten of the girls were soon wives. The other young woman died, unmarried.

As for Asa Mercer, he became a local hero and prophet at almost the same moment his cargo of virgins set foot on the Seattle dock. The appreciative voters of Puget Sound elected him, seemingly on the strength of his importations, without an opposing vote, to a seat in the upper house of the territorial legislature. The *Puget Sound Gazette* praised him without stint. Fellow legislators were honored to shake his hand. His name was known in Olympia, in Steilacoom, Nisqually, Port Gamble, Port Townsend. He basked in celebrity, which can be just as dazzling in a backwoods settlement as in a metropolis.

As young Asa Mercer basked in this happy and disturbing new light, which had made an obscurity into a personage overnight, he dreamed up a bigger and better importation of females, a stupendous cargo of five hundred, perhaps seven hundred, war orphans, "daughters of those brave, heroic sons of liberty," of whom Mercer was patently not one. It could be made an event of the first magnitude, one of national significance. Much good would be accomplished for all concerned—female war orphans and widows would be removed from their woeful condition in New England and become happy housewives on Puget Sound. Puget Sound would gain even more. Its bachelors would no longer spend their nights in Madame Damnable's place on the water front, but would go to work at the production of children and the support of families. The infusion of the blood of old New England stock, into the cosmopolitan and perhaps doubtful stream common to frontier settlements would make for solidity of character. The well known New England Conscience would temper and refine the careless ways of adventurous men. Aye, and Asa Mercer would be a bigger man than before.

Being a celebrity is all very well, but it pays no bills. In March of 1865, just before he left again for the East to carry out his tremendous plan, Mercer drew up a contract which was not publicized but was circulated among those who might be interested. There were a number of such. The contract read as follows:

> I, Asa Mercer, of Seattle, Washington Territory, hereby agree to bring a suitable wife, of good moral character and reputation from the East to Seattle on or before September 1865, for each of the parties whose signatures are hereunto attached, they first paying me or my agent the sum of three hundred dollars, with which to pay the passage of said ladies from the East and to compensate me for my trouble.

If poor Asa could have known the troubles he was to undergo on this expedition, then three times three hundred dollars per maiden would not have begun to compensate him. But he didn't know; and, being an optimist of the highest power, he wouldn't have believed the difficulties ahead, even if an authentic Sibyl had warned him. How many of the single men of Puget Sound signed the $300 contract is not known.

Asa Mercer, bubbling over with enthusiasm for his great project, arrived in New York City just in time to buy a newspaper announcing the assassination of President Lincoln. This tragedy was not only bad for the United States, but bad for Mercer as well; for, having sat on Lincoln's knee as a boy in Illinois, he had counted on the President to help him. Lincoln, he was sure, would be glad to give him a government ship for transporting "war orphans and widows" to Puget Sound.

This was the first blow. More were to come, with discouraging regularity.

But Mercer was resilient in the face of his first tragedy. He bounded up to Boston, where he had no trouble getting an audience with Governor John A. Andrew. His Excellency professed to be much taken with Mercer's idea, and he knew the man, the very man, to help. This turned out to be Edward Everett Hale. What help, if any, the author of "The Man Without a Country" gave Mercer, I can't learn. I imagine Hale quickly introduced the young man to somebody else, for no matter how worthy the scheme, the very idea of moving several hundred unattached girls to a wild and little known part of the West unquestionably struck conservative people as of doubtful propriety. And, too, there was the danger of public ridicule. Prominent men must be careful.

But Mercer was doing very well with the recruiting part of his project. He ranged from Maryland into New Hampshire, talking up his idea. On July 23 he wrote to the *Puget Sound Gazette* from Lowell, Massachusetts—apparently his stronghold—that he would sail from New York City "with upwards of 300 war orphans" and asked that Seattle be ready to give them a fine welcome. The *Gazette* and all Puget Sound were delighted. The paper ran the communication and sent marked copies to brother editors in all parts of the territory.

But still Mercer had no ship. He went to Washington, and after weeks of a sort of chain-introduction, being shunted from one catchpoll to another, he at last got the ear of General U. S. Grant. Now Grant had soldiered in the Oregon country before the war, and understood thoroughly what Mercer meant when he said the great need on Puget Sound was for single women of good character. As soon as he had heard the young man's story, the first hero in the United States went into action. "Mercer," said he, "sit down and read the morning paper until my return. I am going over to the White House to meet the President and his cabinet and will bring your matter to a head one way or the other."

Mercer was understandingly pleased, even elated. After weeks of the Washington treatment, he had at last found the man who would act.

Half an hour later Grant returned, and as he entered the room he spoke briskly to his aide: "Captain Crosby, make out an order for a steamship, coaled and manned, with capacity to carry five hundred women from New York to Seattle, for A. S. Mercer. I will sign it." Sign it he did, and sent the delirious young man of Puget Sound on his way to Montgomery Cunningham Meigs, quartermaster general of the Army, who like Grant was a man of quick decision "No," said Meigs as soon as he had read Grant's note. "I will not accept this order." He remarked that the order was illegal, as probably it was.

But though Meigs was extremely watchful of government property he was not adverse to selling surplus goods. He told Mercer he would sell him a fine ship of 1,600 tons for $80,000, in cash; it would be a bargain, too, for the steamship *Continental* had cost $240,000 to build just two years before, and was in excellent shape. The price might as well have been one million dollars. Mercer possessed the price of little more than a lifeboat. He told General Meigs he would think it over. Then he went to New York to think.

Now an amazing thing happened. While Mercer was glooming in his room in the Merchants' Hotel a card was brought from a caller in the lobby. The visitor was Ben Holladay, a man of many parts who had made considerable money supplying food to troops in the Mexican War and more recently had been doing very well with freighting and government mail contracts in the West. He had also organized a ship line. He was looking for more ships—cheap. Mercer was astonished that a big man of affairs, nationally known, should look him up. He had the magnate shown to his room.

In later years Mercer came to realize what a lamb he must have seemed to Ben Holladay, one of the shrewdest and most ruthless operators in the United States. But Holladay could be genial, and now he told Mercer he would advance the money to purchase the *Continental*—for Holladay, of course—and said he would be happy to carry the war orphans to Seattle "at a nominal sum."

While this wasn't exactly the way Mercer had envisioned the outcome of the expedition, still it seemed the only way. He met later with Holladay and that sharp trader's attorneys, who drew up a contract. This instrument said Holladay should have the ship at the price offered to Mercer, and that the ship would transport "500 passengers at a minimum price" to the Pacific coast. Whether or not Mercer read the contract, I do not know. If he did, it did not mean anything to him. He signed it, proud to collaborate with the great Holladay. The first part of the deal went through.

Now that the ship was ready—as Mercer thought—he sent out his call for the war orphans to assemble in New York, ready for the voyage to the promised land. Just then, according to Mercer, the New York *Herald* got wind of the project and promptly came out with a story strongly intimating that the five hundred female orphans were being shipped to Seattle for the express purpose of becoming inmates of Puget Sound brothels—a fate, allegedly, worse than death. The *Herald,* said Mercer, also termed Puget Sound males a pack of lecherous louts.

The Massachusetts legislature had also been discussing the migration of women from Lowell, and an official committee had made its report, saying, among other things:

In the polygamous realm of Brigham Young, it seems that the numbers of male and female were nearly equal, and this, too, when the chief magnates of the so-called latter day saints have harems which are but little inferior to that of a Mahometan Shah of Persia . . . . There are, or were, Massachusetts women in those same households of abomination; and it is painful to believe that the class from which they went would be the first to offer candidates for emigration to Oregon [*sic*] and other parts of the remote West.

The implications of that report are obvious and may well have reached the ears of the maidens. But Mercer always claimed it was the New York *Herald*'s remarks which had the most effect. In any case, the results were immediate and lamentable. "More than two thirds of the ladies wrote me," Mercer recalled wistfully in later years, "and inclosed clippings of the *Herald* story." They also inclosed their resignations from this proposed voyage into a land of venery. The *Continental*'s passenger list dwindled.

One can appreciate the feelings of Asa Mercer, the great dreamer from Puget Sound, to see his public-spirited project turned into a monstrous scheme of commercialized lechery. It was a blow to fell the stoutest. Consider these innocent and alluring maidens—one could almost see them arriving at Seattle. One could see also those profligate characters with which all Puget Sound was infested, slavering, pawing dirt, avid to lay their obscene hands on these tender flowers from the land of the arbutus. Was Christian New England to supply women whose lips dropped as an honeycomb, and whose mouths were smoother than oil? . . . Was Yankeeland to be the source of the kiss that had poison and was as a pernicious drug?

To make matters worse, indescribably worse, the report of the Massachusetts legislative committee spelled Mercer's name "Mercier," thus making him a Frenchman and hence almost automatically a procurer of the most subtle and dangerous sort. It was easy to see, even at a distance of three thousand miles, the wicked gleam and glow of red lights along the Seattle waterfront . . . .

It was, surely, a blow to fell the stoutest. And now Mercer, the great procurer, suddenly thought of his contract with Ben Holladay. With an armful of the letters and clippings received from the girls who did not wish to engage in the profession of trollop, thus indicating why he could not now carry out the 500-passenger stipulation of the contract, the naïve young man went to the prince of commerce for understanding and sympathy. Holladay had his faults, but they did not include the shedding of crocodile tears. He displayed a modicum of sympathy, accompanied by a brisk, businesslike notice that, though it was too bad about the cancellations, a contract was a contract: Mr. Mercer certainly would understand that he would have to charge "regular rates" for the lesser number of passengers. Dizzy from one blow after another, and virtually penniless, Mr. Mercer went away with a new understanding of the manner in which business was carried on in his native country by experts.

The faithful were already gathering at a New York dock, ready for the voyage to Puget Sound—and possible perdition—and they numbered something less than one hundred female war orphans and widows. The total passenger list, including several married couples and a reporter from the New York *Times,* totaled two hundred. Mercer thought that others might be on the way, but Mr. Holladay could wait no longer; they must be off.

The passengers found the ex-troopship in anything but shipshape order. Little had been done to improve it since it had carried its last contingent of soldiers—men who are not ordinarily careful of United States property. Nor had Mercer done anything about assignment of quarters. Nobody knew where he or she was to sleep. Angry men and weeping girls sought everywhere aboard to find the man responsible, but he could not be located. Thus, on January 6, 1866, the steamship *Continental* pulled out of New York harbor in a state of wild chaos, with Mercer safely hidden in an obscure coal bunker. He emerged, somewhat later, to find himself not the most popular person on deck.

Flora Pearson, whose two older sisters had gone to Seattle in the first Mercer expedition, was on the second, and kept her eyes open. She reported the vessel was in such terrible shape that tidy New England girls went to work scrubbing the decks and walls. The food was a disgrace— so bad, indeed, that Mr. Mercer himself started taking his meals at the captain's table, where the provender was of the finest. Not for long, though. The sharp tongues of Yankee maidens quickly brought him to book and to share with them the Spartan fare Ben Holladay thought good enough for New England war orphans. And for the next ninety-odd days Mercer relished the salt beef and tea steeped in salt water which appears to have been the basic ration; that is, except for one period of two weeks when parboiled—not baked—beans were the main course.

There was one good meal during the entire trip, and that was when one of the Yankee girls somehow prevailed on the ship's cook to permit her in the galley, where she made and baked a rousing-fine batch of gingerbread. Then, back to the salt beef. But the sparse diet probably was the reason that no case of seasickness was reported.

An artist for *Harper's Weekly* depicted life aboard the *Continental* as ideal. He drew handsome sketches showing hundreds of young and beautiful girls in the "grand salon" of the old trooper—playing the organ, singing, writing letters, or improving their minds with literature. The heading above the pictures said, "Emigration to Washington Territory of Four Hundred Women on the Steamer *Continental*." The brief text termed Mr. Mercer "The Moses of the Exodus from New England" and said he had induced "about 750 to enter the expedition, but that many had returned to their homes"—probably with a clipping from the New York *Herald* in hand, their virginity still intact.

Ninety-six days brought the ship to San Francisco, where the newspapers had a wonderful time with the party, which by then was reputed to number seven hundred beauties. All hands had to go ashore, for Ben Holladay had other plans for his new vessel. A number of the girls never took ship again but disappeared into the life of California. "What inducements some of them found to remain in California," remarked the tart Flora Pearson, "I do not pretend to say." I can imagine Flora sniffed. But perhaps the deserters suspected that Mercer had got to the end of his rope, that he would be unable to take the party to Puget Sound. If so, they were not without reason. Mercer was all but penniless. He couldn't have bought himself passage to Seattle, to say nothing of his brood of maidens. But there was his friend, good Governor Pickering of Washington Territory. Just before Mercer had left Seattle, Pickering came to him and said, in the grand freehanded manner suitable to pioneers, to count on him, Pickering, should Mercer need financial aid.

Mercer did need aid, and so with the last two dollars to his name he went to the telegraph office in San Francisco and dispatched a wire to Pickering. It was simple, and clear: "Send two thousand dollars quick to get party to Seattle." Then he sat back to wait for good old Governor Pickering, a friend to count on in any emergency. Next day the telegraph company notified him they had a message for him. He could have it by paying the $7.50 charge. Puzzled and worried, Mercer went to the telegraph office manager to explain he was without a cent. But the message, said he brightly, contained two thousand dollars; and if the company would let him have it, he would of course pay the collect charge.

The manager, I can imagine, wearily eyed Mercer, then let him have the telegram. It was from good old Governor Pickering of Washington Territory—one hundred windy, gorgeous words of congratulations on the "success" of the expedition, and not one word about money.

Well, there he was—still a thousand miles from snug harbor, with no money, no ship, no credit, a pack of irritated females waiting for the next move, and not with patience. But many a lumber schooner plied between California and Puget Sound. Somehow Mercer had enough spirit left to talk several schooner captains into taking portions of his feminine cargo to Seattle, and there they finally arrived, not in one exuberant and overpowering party, but in batches of half a dozen or more. It was a pale ending to such a dream as Mercer's had been; nor was the popularity of the business enhanced by the fact that the Puget Sounders, then as now hospitable people, had taken Mercer at his word and had prepared a truly gigantic welcome for the seven hundred maidens, or the four hundred, or the three hundred, whichever they turned out to be. Instead, the welcome had to be cut down to size, to fit less than a hundred persons who, moreover, arrived at odd times and in small parties over a period of days.

But the Mercer girls began to fulfill their destiny as soon as they landed. On May 27, Sarah Robison married David H. Webster. On July 15, Mercer himself took as wife one of his charges, the charming Miss Annie Stephens. Other marriages followed in quick succession.

Asa Mercer did not remain in Seattle, or even Washington Territory, but removed to the Middle West, where he lived and died. Estimates of his character have varied. Clarence Bagley, the Seattle historian, believed that his great trouble was his proneness to take whatever he urgently hoped for as certain of accomplishment, which, in view of the record, seems fair appraisal. He was also careless. Large sums of money had been put into his hands when he went east the second time. These sums were given to him by relatives and friends for various and specific purposes and had nothing to do with getting a bride or with the emigration scheme in any way. Mercer diverted most or all of this money into his great dream, and could never pay it back. Bagley remarked that he "broke up several of his best friends and financially crippled others." He was also "made the subject of ugly charges by many of those whom he had injured. But that he used these monies for his personal benefit no one claimed."

After commenting on Mercer's contract with the unnamed Puget Sound bachelors, Bagley remarks that, though he "did not lose sight of the financial profit that might be obtained" from his scheme, "his every action, his whole attitude toward those who had entrusted themselves to his guidance and care was that of a chivalrous, pure-minded American gentleman."

Bagley also thought that Mercer had done both the Yankee maidens and Washington Territory a good turn. The immigrants themselves received "far-reaching and beneficial effects," and they "proved a blessing to every community from the Cowlitz River northward to the Canadian line."

The Yankee Exodus (1950)

See Roger Conant, *Mercer's Belles: The Journal of a Reporter*, edited by Lenna A. Deutsch, University of Washington Press (1966), for the annotated journal of a *New York Times* reporter who accompanied the 1866 Mercer immigration. It also contains a bibliography of writings on Mercer's voyages.

Anarchists at Home

One of the great glories of the Puget Sound country is the serene tide-washed community of Home. This community is fading now with a graceful nostalgic air, but it still retains many of the spiritual vestiges of what was once America's sole anarchist colony—in its heyday one of the most celebrated or notorious spots in the United States. Home is never mentioned by the booster organizations, and even the evangelical churches have given it up as a Sodom fit only for the fires of the Pit.

The place lies on the pretty shores of Joe's Bay, an arm of the Sound, and is approximately 2,530 miles (as few if any crows have flown it) west of Roxbury, Massachusetts, site of Brook Farm, the short-lived and tremendously unsuccessful attempt of Yankees to found a colony in the manner laid down by M. Fourier. There is almost no intellectual connection between the two communities, and although I know of Brook Farm only by the vast literature that has been coming out about it for a hundred years past, I have spent considerable time at Home, right in the bosom of anarchist families, and I should rather have lived there than at Brook Farm. I also think it long past time that Home Colony was called to the attention of the many Americans who never heard of it.

I doubt that the Brook Farmers had a great deal of enjoyment. There was constant bickering over the division of tasks, there was much worry over getting the substantial contributions of cash needed to support the fancy play-farmers, and the nearest thing to excitement was old Bronson Alcott's heaving in for a free meal and delivering himself of a few Orphic Sayings. It was all very daring, and quite dull. Read the Brook Farmers' own accounts, if you doubt me.

Life at Home Colony was assuredly never dull. Never. Home accepted no contributions or advice from anybody. It did not labor under the many inhibitions that plagued the Brook Farmers. In fact, Home had no inhibitions whatever, and several times it made headlines that would have shocked and stunned the pale maidens of both sexes who inhabited Brook Farm. To the good people of Tacoma and Seattle who remember it, Home was and largely is a place of smoking bombs of the Johann Most variety, and of unspeakable orgies unequalled since the times of Messalina. Yet for half a century it has successfully fended attacks by incendiary and murderous mobs, by the courts, by private detectives, Secret Service agents, and United States marshals. Jay Fox, so far as I know the sole surviving anarchist in the United States, who has lived at Home for forty years, says it has been a sort of Wild West Brook Farm, with overtones of Oneida Community and Nauvoo.

Home grew out of the failure of a socialist community called Glennis, in 1896. Fed up with the internal battles which seem to bedevil all socialist communities and also with the lazy parasites who always attach themselves to "cooperative commonwealths" three disillusioned members of Glennis, situated near Tacoma, built a boat with their own hands and struck out to cruise Puget Sound, seeking a likely spot to pitch an out-and-out anarchist paradise. These founding fathers were George Allen, University of Toronto, class of '85, O. A. Verity and F. F. Odell. They soon found a primeval spot that looked pretty good—and still does. Towering Douglas fir grew down to the beach. Ducks swarmed in the bay. Clams held conventions there. Bees worked on the fireweed. No man lived here, or for miles. There were no roads. Twenty-six acres could be had from a bloated capitalist for $2.50 an acre.

The three men mustered a total of five dollars to make a down payment. Then Allen went to teaching school, while the others worked at anything handy to earn money for the move. In the spring of 1897 the Allen, Verity and Odell families, wives and children, voyaged to Joe's Bay and began pioneering. They tore into the gigantic trees with ax and saw, and quickly made cabins in which to live until they could build frame houses. They also formed the Compact, which was called the Mutual Home Colony Association.

There was nothing of socialism in this group. The Association was as near pure anarchism as the laws of the land would permit, and its sole reason for being was "to obtain land and to promote better social and moral conditions." It did not even attempt to define anarchism, although Founders Allen, Verity and Odell considered anarchism—no matter what Bakunin or Kropotkin or Josiah Warren said—as a society so imbued with decency and honesty that no laws were required to regulate its members.

Each member paid into the Association a sum equal to the cost of the land he or she was to occupy, not more than two acres to a member. The land remained the property of the Association, but the member could occupy it indefinitely simply by paying such taxes as were imposed by the Enemy, which in this case was the State of Washington in the style and form of Pierce County. Any improvements, such as barns and houses, were personal property and could be sold or mortgaged.

Like the thoroughgoing fanatics they were, the Home colonists, as soon as they got shelter over their heads, started a paper, the *New Era*, which from the start intimated that the Association had no interest whatever in the personal lives of its members. "The love principle of our being," said an early hand-set editorial, "is a natural one, and to deny it expression is to deny nature." This was clear enough, and the implied sanction of casual relationships between men and women was in time to bring an assortment of cranks, malcontents and plain Don Juans. But the early settlers were too busy with recalcitrant stumps to worry very much about the love principle in their being, for if there is anything to hold old Adam in bounds it is the science and art of removing stumps of *Pseudotsuga taxifolia*. Before their homes were finished, the busy colonists had whacked up Liberty Hall, a sort of meeting place and school, where Founder Allen was the first teacher.

Within six months half a dozen new families had been added to the original three, and along came Charles Govan, a wandering printer, who proposed a new paper which should take the colony's message to the far corners of the earth where mankind still lived either in savagery or, worse, under imposition of State and Capital. Govan also induced James F. Morton to leave the staff of *Free Society*, a noted anarchist sheet of San Francisco, and come to Home. Morton (Harvard, 1892, and Phi Beta Kappa) was later to become a noted Single Taxer, but he was pure anarchist when he arrived at Home, and there he and Govan brought out the new paper under a masthead that was sheer genius: *Discontent, Mother of Progress.*

This paper was presently to be notorious from one end of the country to the other, but its early issues were read mostly by other radical editors and by persons who were predisposed to what *Discontent* said was anarchism anyway. There appears, from a close reading of the yellowing files, to have been more about sex in *Discontent* than about economics. A leading article dealt with "The Rights of Woman in Sexual Relations" which, it appeared, were many and interesting. Another piece asked "Is 'Sin' forgivable?" It seemed that it was. The early issues also looked at Home with a realistic eye, stating that hard work was necessary to clear the thickly timbered land, and warning intending settlers to make inquiries before coming, lest they be disappointed. There was no balm in the anarchist Gilead, simply hard work and FREEDOM (to use their typographical emphasis). *Discontent* went on to say there was nothing of socialist cooperation about Home. Everything was on a purely voluntary basis. These ex-socialists were determined they should be free of the easy-riders who had hamstrung and wrecked Glennis and nearly all other cooperative communities.

It wasn't long before *Discontent*, hand-set and hand-printed among the stumps that were still smoking, began to attract attention. Emma Goldman went to Home to lecture in Liberty Hall in June of 1899. New families arrived from San Francisco, from Virginia, from Michigan. A tract of sixty-four acres adjoining the original colony was made available at reasonable rates. A Tacoma boat line put Joe's Bay on its list of ports of call. The colonists, proud as sin, built a floating wharf and a neat shelter.

From Portland, Oregon, where they had got into trouble editing the *Firebrand*, which the courts held to be "obscene and otherwise unmailable," came Henry Addis and Abner J. Pope. A venerable man, bearded like a prophet of old, Pope called himself a Quaker-Spiritualist-Anarchist, which was quite an order but which he took easily in stride. He was soon lecturing in Liberty Hall. Addis contributed to *Discontent* a series of articles in which he came out flat-footedly for Free Love, with uppercase letters. Although the Addis articles were a bit later to get the colony into a dreadful stew, the period of 1897-1900 was on the whole active and peaceful, a very idyll of community pioneering in the backwoods. The population rose to one hundred. Deer flitted in and out of the clearings. Roosters greeted the dawn from the interminable stumps. Communist bees gathered honey for the anarchists. The hens laid famously.

Founder Allen came to have thirty pupils in his school, and he sat them down on a windfelled fir and taught them that natural laws were the only laws worth minding. He gave them Mill, Huxley, Darwin, Josiah Warren and those parts of Henry Thoreau dealing with the necessity for civil disobedience. Four who attended Allen's school have said that truancy was never known.

Presently there began a second trek of new settlers, several coming from foreign parts. Among them was Lewis Haiman, a Jewish barber from Lithuania, who married an American gentile, took two acres at Home and built a house. He also opened a shop which, he said in an announcement, he hoped would keep Homeites from looking like the cartoon conceptions of anarchists. Dances, masquerades and picnics were a part of the social life. Lectures were its meat and drink. Liberty Hall was open to all who had something to say, or only thought they did—the subject mattering not. Reconverted socialists arrived from the defunct Ruskin Colony in Tennessee, and from the Cooperative Brotherhood Colony at Burley, Washington. The Home Colony Library was organized. *Discontent's* announcement columns began to fill up with notices of periodicals named *Freedom* (London), *Free Society* (San Francisco), and the Boston *Investigator*, founded by the celebrated Abner Kneeland, whose trial Henry S. Commager has considered in an interesting historical monograph.

II

The first shadow to fall on the industrious and intellectual pioneering colony of Home was an occurrence in far-away Buffalo, New York, where on September 6, 1901, President William McKinley fell under a bullet fired by a witless youth, Leon Czolgosz, who said he was an anarchist. A wave of hysteria swept the nation. Socialist speakers and halls were set upon by mobs. Any soapboxer on the curb was labeled "anarchist" and was either mobbed or arrested. And then, somebody in Tacoma, Washington, recalled that only twenty miles away was a whole pack of wild men and women, a veritable nest of vipers, who had never denied being anarchists.

McKinley died on September 14. On that day an anti-anarchist meeting was held in Tacoma, and a Loyal League formed by members of the Grand Army of the Republic. They chartered a steamboat, collected firearms and incendiary materials and prepared, three hundred strong, to invade Home and put it to the torch, with murder as a possible incidental.

Not everybody in Tacoma lost his head. Ed Lorenz, skipper of a steamboat which called at Home, knew the colonists there to be sober and industrious people. He went to the mob's leaders and said so eloquently. So did the Rev. J. F. Doescher, pastor of the German Evangelical Church in Tacoma, who had visited Home and had found the people, in spite of their agnosticism, which he deplored, to be honest and kindly folk. These two heroic men stopped what might well have been a forerunner of the melancholy tragedies perpetrated in later years in near-by Everett and Centralia.

Thus was Home saved surely from the torch. But its troubles were just beginning. Someone had sent copies of *Discontent* to Federal authorities and demanded it be barred from the mails. Post office experts in belles-lettres looked over the Home paper and were horrified to discover that it had come out whole hog against marriage, terming it "the lowest form of prostitution" and adding, for good measure, that "free mating in cities of the United States is on the increase and the ecclesiastics cannot seem to halt it." There was even a trace of gloating in the article, which was one of those contributed by Henry Addis, who was not even a member of the Home Colony.

So, packing a gun on each hip and wondering what size of bombs he should have to dodge, a United States marshal went over to Home to arrest *Discontent*'s editors and contributors. Hearing that the Law was on the way, the colonists met him at the Home wharf with a delegation of welcome, including pretty little flower girls, took him to one of the homes for an excellent anarchist supper, then made him the guest of honor at a whopping big dance in Liberty Hall. The astonished officer put away his guns and thoroughly enjoyed himself, remaining overnight. In the morning he returned to Tacoma with his prisoners, and re-ported that he had never met more agreeable people than in Home, or had a better time.

The *Discontent*'s staff stood trial and were freed by an understanding judge, who ordered the jury to sign a directed verdict of acquittal. It was a clear victory for Home Colony, but a year later it lost its post office, by order from

Washington, and Home folks have since, and to this day, had to get their mail at Lakebay, two miles distant. Another blow quickly followed the loss of the post office: *Discontent*, which Federal authorities held to have been the mother of altogether too much progress, was forbidden the mails.

The rumpus had another and more cheerful result. It called national attention to Home, putting it briefly if luridly on the front pages of big-city newspapers, and Home went into a boom. Henry Dadisman, well-to-do farmer, arrived and bought two hundred acres next to the Association land, which he threw open to settlers at cost. A Minnesota widow came, built a fine farmhouse, and settled down. Families came from Indiana, and during the 1902-1907 period, more Russian Jews arrived to take up colony or Dadisman land. A new Liberty Hall, much larger than the first, was built; and a co-op store, still flourishing, was opened.

When *Discontent* was barred from the mails, Editor Morton merely changed the masthead to read the *Demonstrator*, and kept the editorial policy intact. In the light of Home's new notoriety there started a flow and ebb of eccentrics that has made the place one of the most interesting spots on all Puget Sound. This period at Home, indeed, deserves the serious attention of some scholar who is interested in the manner in which old and new radical theories permeated the utmost reaches of the United States at the beginning of this century. Here was a tiny community, set in the deep woods in the northwestern corner of the Republic, as remote from the intellectual centers as possible, and reached by an awkward boat trip, or by mere mud trails. Yet Home's Liberty Hall shook and shimmered with virtually every intellectual breeze one could name, while the colonists listened to and often argued with a continuous congress of cranks and prophets.

III

From Chicago to Home came somewhat moth-eaten agents for Koreshanity, the otherwise forgotten philosophy-religion founded in 1886 by Dr. Cyrus R. Teed, to reveal the True Faith to Homeites and incidentally, as part of their belief, to prove that the earth is a hollow ball and that we live on its inside, the quickest way to China being straight up into what we call the atmosphere.

Then came Professor Thompson, no first name, perhaps the mogul of all individualists, who walked down the Home gangplank one afternoon displaying a magnificent beard but the dress and other garments of a woman. Professor Thompson was male enough; brawny and tough, he immediately went to work chopping wood. That night he gave a rousing lecture on the need, if the world were to make any progress, for all to wear women's clothing. It was more aesthetic and comfortable, he maintained.

From California came the then celebrated Lois Waisbrooker, author of a strange book entitled *My Century Plant*, a work that revealed how to free the world from "the disease of Sex." She liked Home, took an acre, and settled down in company with Mattie D. Penhallow, a noted radical of the day, to get out a very odd sheet called *Clothed with the Sun*. I regret much that I have failed to find a copy of this periodical. Old-timers of Home inform me it was a humdinger, even for anarchists, and reported all of the facts of life in no mealy-mouthed manner. It didn't last long. The post office department took one look at it, and presently a whole delegation of United States marshals swarmed into the colony like locusts and carted off the two maidens, one of whom was indicted, convicted and fined. It was one more case of "unmailable matter."

The place was now rolling high. Home and its odd residents and visitors were good for a story in almost any newspaper and periodical in the country. College professors came to see and write learned pieces. *The Independent*, a national magazine of wide circulation, sent a man to Home, who reported favorably on the place and remarked it was the most sensibly managed of any community attempt he knew. It had 170 adult members. Work was exchanged at the rate of fifteen cents an hour, although no cash changed hands. The co-op store was doing well. So were the Home logging operators.

After her conviction in the *Clothed with the Sun* affair, Miss Waisbrooker returned to Home and promptly started getting out another sheet, this time called *Foundation Principles*. I haven't been able to get the faintest idea what it was about, but Jay Fox, who can be ribald at times, told me he thought it was "the same old subject, Adam and Eve."

Elbert Hubbard, no slouch himself as a community man, made the trip to Home from East Aurora, New York, to stay several days and to lecture nightly in Liberty Hall. Colonists found him heart and soul in sympathy with the colony, and later he spoke good words for it in a characteristically graceful and inaccurate piece in the *Philistine*. Emma Goldman, famous now since McKinley's death, came to Home a second time. Moses Harmon, the old-time crusader for almost any unpopular cause, and editor of *Lucifer*, which advocated the use of contraceptives, came to recuperate at Home from his several incarcerations in the prisons of Illinois and Kansas.

Meanwhile, children had been born in Home of legally married couples, and their very given names reflect the faith of their radical parents. Listen to the roll: Albert Parsons Grosse, William Morris Grosse, William Morris Snellenberg, Emma Goldman Falkoff, and Eugene Debs August. There was also Radium LaVene, who has told me that the Homeites, like many others, were much taken with the news of the discovery of radium and felt it would be a good name. Radium LaVene's brother was first named Revolt LaVene, but a bit later became Francisco Ferrer LaVene, honoring the Italian school-reform martyr. These boys and girls, now grown, recall a welcome visitor to Home in Dr. Ben Reitman, who used to gather them around a fire on the beach to tell them ghost stories, then to show how the seemingly supernatural always had a rational solution. Harry Kemp came too, to get material for his *Tramping on Life* and his poems.

Big Bill Haywood, fresh from his acquittal in the Steuenberg murder case, came to Home to spend several weeks, and of course to speak in Liberty Hall.

What a yeasting it was, the boiling and bubbling at Home! Spiritualists came, and one remained to set up in business. A school in Esperanto was opened. Exponents of various food fads came and went, among them one Dr. Hazzard, an eloquent female who spoke to such effect that John Buchi, Swiss butcher at Home, wished "a Got damn on all der wegitarians." Local enthusiasts started a Class in Hatha-Yoga, another in straight theosophy. Russellites came to report the imminent end of things, which was all right with the anarchists. Pantheists, Freethinkers of all shades, Monists, Mormon missionaries—they all came, and Home gave them all a hearing. One Homeite, Laura Wood, set up housekeeping in an Indian wigwam; another, Joe Kapella, went to live in a tree for several months. It all must have been quite wonderful. Brook Farm had nothing like it.

IV

The great activity at Home Colony did not go unnoticed around the Sound, and stories of horrible sex orgies became current and popular with orthodox Washingtonians. Much of the talk stemmed from articles in the uninhibited *Demonstrator*, as untrammeled as a yearling Durham bull put to pasture in May. It seldom appeared without a few remarks on something very similar to free love. The colony itself never held any canons regarding the desirability or undesirability of free love. That there were domestic arrangements in certain homes of Home which had not received the benefit of either church or state was of common knowledge, but they were neither sanctioned nor condemned.

Meanwhile the Philistines were gathering their forces. Their next attack occurred in 1910, and is still referred to as the Great Nude Bathing Case. The colony had by then split into two factions over the subject of landholding. This was settled, amicably on the whole, and each member was given a deed to his two acres. The Association was dissolved, although Liberty Hall and the co-op store were continued as community enterprises. The store, indeed, may have been a factor in attracting to the colony a number of farmers who liked the low prices at the Home co-op but had no sympathy for Home's live-and-let-live policy. In any case, it was from these latecomers that a complaint came to the county authorities, naming names and charging that certain Home anarchists were bathing in the nude, men and women together.

The charges were true enough. The simple Russians who had come to Home many years before brought their samovars with them, and also their custom of nude bathing. It had been going on at Home for a decade, without scandal. But now, because of the Philistines, one man and four women were arrested and found guilty on charges of indecent exposure. The trials made front page news in almost all sections of the country. Home was again in the papers.

At this time Home had a new paper, the *Agitator*, edited by the aforementioned Jay Fox, a radical who dated back to the Haymarket Bomb in Chicago. Fox had long been an agitator and organizer of left wing labor groups. He still carried in one shoulder a bullet that had been fired in the McCormick Harvester strike in Chicago in 1886, and he had been active in the I.W.W. and in the rambunctious shingle-weavers' union in the Northwest woods. He was also an able journalist, and now he came out with a sizzling editorial, "The Nudes and the Prudes," in which he more than suggested that all lovers of liberty should ostracize the persons who had brought the charges of indecent exposure. Editor Fox was hauled off to jail and charged with "encouraging or advocating disrespect for law." The prosecution naturally brought "anarchy" into the case and played up Home's reputation in a successful effort to convict

Fox, who was sentenced to two months in Pierce County Jail. On appeal, the state supreme court upheld the verdict.

Now the wobblies, the I.W.W., and other radical groups the country over took up the case and made it into a national *cause célèbre* in all liberal circles. The Free Speech League, forerunner of the Civil Liberties Union and headed by such well known persons as Leonard Abbott, Brand Whitlock and Lincoln Steffens, joined the battle. Dances and rallies for the "Jay Fox Free Speech Fight" were held from Boston to Portland, Oregon, and money raised for an appeal to the United States Supreme Court, which found the verdict proper. Fox gave himself up and went to jail for six weeks. Then he was given an unconditional pardon by Governor Lister of Washington. He returned to Home and resumed publishing the *Agitator.*

Next came the McNamara case. One night in October of 1910, the building of the Los Angeles *Times* was wrecked by an explosion that took twenty-one lives and was followed by the sensational confessions of the two McNamara brothers. Also implicated was one David Caplan, and a vast man hunt was set in motion to find him. Presently at Home there appeared a tall, suave and handsome book agent who was peddling one of those sets of home encyclopedias (170,000 pages, beautifully illustrated, fine bindings) without which no home, not even an anarchist's home, could be said to be complete. The tall agent circulated around Home for several days. Mrs. Lewis Haiman recalls that when she went to the door, and kept the man safely on the outside, he appeared to be far more interested in peering over her shoulder to see who was inside, than in selling his array of the world's knowledge. He was, of course, the famous William J. Burns, the detective, looking for the missing Caplan. Fugitive Caplan was taken later, though not at Home, and given ten years. In Burns's memoirs, published not long before his death in 1932, the detective devotes several pages to his days as a book agent in Home.

During World War I, Home was infested by marshals and secret agents of the United States government, some with false whiskers, some plain, but all of Home's citizens managed to keep out of their clutches. In the more recent war, so quiet had Home been for two decades, it was never under suspicion.

Today Home is, as it must always have been, a charming place in which to live. The last of the Founding Fathers, George Allen, died in 1944, well into his eighties. Dead, too, is Tom Geeves, the patriarch of Home, as whiskered as any legendary Nihilist, who had wandered ashore from a British ship, circa 1910, and for no doctrinaire reasons, but simply because he liked the place, had taken abode in an old shack at Home. There he lived to be almost one hundred and nine years of age.

The younger generation of Home, for the most part university graduates, have gone away and married. Many are in California where each year a Home picnic, staged by Radium LaVene, now a Los Angeles businessman, draws up to a hundred old Homeites and their children.

Jay Fox, perhaps the last of the veritable anarchists, genial and mellow at seventy-seven, lives on in Home and is writing his memoirs, while his wife, Cora, spends her talented spare time hand-painting and glazing chinaware of such beauty that it is sought after by the wives and daughters of Seattle and Tacoma capitalists.

The outlander visiting Home is sure to find it pleasant, both physically and socially. The Home Colony tradition is still strong. These are well-read people. When you come across two-acre farmers conversant with Mill and Bentham and Marx and Dewey and Emerson and Thoreau, as well as with poultry feed and beehives, you know you are in no orthodox rural community. There are Homeites today who teach art and music. There is much professional interest in and practice of crafts, especially of weaving. Bees, hens and ferns are the chief sources of agricultural income.

Over all is a feeling, not of revolution, but rather of a lack of interest in political movements. It would not be fair, however, to include Jay Fox in this placidity. The fires of Revolution still burn in the old anarchist, perhaps the last of his kind, and he is happy when William Z. Foster, more in direct touch with the world, comes to visit him, as he does occasionally, and tells him how goes the battle with the minions of Capital.

The American Scholar (1946)

The Wildest Man of the West

In the Grays Harbor County court house at Montesano, in western Washington, a small bronze plaque lists the names of six men and relates with sinister brevity that they met their death in futile attempts to take the celebrated outlaw John Turnow. This is the only tangible reminder of the most crafty and dangerous man ever to roam the timbered reaches of the Pacific Northwest and by far the strangest outlaw I know of.

Through some incomprehensible literary freak, Turnow has never been the subject of a paper-backed biography of the Harry Tracy-Jesse James school, and the dime-novel trade thus lost a sure-fire perennial. Hence Turnow's renown is purely local where it has flourished mightily for three decades and is in no danger of dimming. Barrel-stove historians of the logging camps, some of whom saw Turnow in the flesh and others of whom were in at his death, keep the story alive and enhance it with the embroidery characteristic of folk tales. When winter gloom settles down over the still vast forests of the Olympic Peninsula of western Washington and stiff gales make logging operations dangerous, young loggers who have been brought up on Tarzan and Superman sit on camp deacon seats and listen with awed respect to stories of the life and times of a human animal who combined in actuality many of the qualities of their comic-strip heroes. In his own region, Turnow has long since become a folk character comparable to the mythical Paul Bunyan. And with some reason. The bare facts about Turnow were enough to build a mountain of legend.

What might be called the public life of John Turnow began on September 3, 1911, an otherwise pleasant enough autumn day in the wild Grays Harbor country of western Washington. A reddish sun beat down through the blue smoke haze of settlers' clearing fires. Here and there in the vast wilderness the toot and stutter of a logger's donkey engine could be heard. Blows of firewood drifted like snow in the air and got into the sourdough of the few trappers and prospectors in the region. Mostly, though, the region was untracked, without roads or trails, and silent except for the occasional bickering of jays and the report of some lone hunter's rifle.

On that particular September afternoon two rifle shots occurred, close together. If they were heard, no one paid them heed or gave thought to the matter until it was learned that the Bauer twins, John and Will, had not returned from a bear hunt along the Satsop river. A few days later, Deputy Sheriff Colin McKenzie, one of a large searching party, found the two bodies tucked away under some brush, side by side, on the upper reaches of the Satsop. Each had been shot once, and that through the forehead.

John Turnow was at once suspected of the double murder, strange enough when you knew that Turnow was blood uncle to the twins, but not so strange if you knew about Turnow. This man was thirty-two years old in 1911. Born of a pioneer and respected family on the Turnow homestead near Satsop village, John had never, people said, been quite right in the head. From the time he began to walk he had been most peculiar. Didn't care for human companionship at all. Wanted to be alone, especially alone in the woods. By the time he was ten John was going into the timber along the Satsop and Wynooche rivers and staying all night, sometimes for several days. His family tried to curb the youth's wildness, and his response was to stay away for a month. He told his parents that he found birds and animals better companions than men. He liked to listen to what he termed the talk of crows and jays, he said, and he also heard beautiful music, "like that of organs and harps" in the winds that sifted through the tall fir and hemlock.

On his lone trips into the woods young Turnow never carried any food. Got all the food he wanted from wild things, he said—roots, birds, animals. He always carried a rifle and when he was twelve he could drill a Copenhagen snuffbox at a hundred yards. At home he was moody. He did chores and other farm work under duress. He would not play with other children, not even with his brothers and sisters. I imagine he was what today would be called a retarded child.

So his parents finally sent John to a private sanitarium in Vancouver, Washington. Here he proved so hard to handle that he had to be removed and was then committed to an institution in Salem, Oregon. Though he was watched rather closely, one morning late in 1909 nurses found his bed empty. It hadn't been slept in.

Turnow left no connecting trail, but within a few weeks of his escape from Salem—which is nearly two hundred miles from the Satsop—trappers reported seeing him some twenty-five miles up the Satsop river. Turnow told two of these woodsmen that he would never be locked up again. He asked them to take a message out to his folks. "You tell them," he said in his short gruff way, "and you tell everybody else that none of them had better come after me. I'll kill anyone who does. These are my woods. I want to be alone."

For almost two years Turnow lived on in the woods undisturbed, listening to those harps in the hemlocks, those arbor vitae organs, and communing with owls and cougars, a deranged and unlettered Thoreau without brains. His father died and word of it was taken to his son by a trapper who was on friendly or at least on speaking terms with him. John said he wouldn't go to the funeral, and he didn't; nor did he go a bit later when his mother died. The estate was left to the six Turnow children and John's share, some $1,700, was put in a Montesano bank and John notified by the friendly trapper. "I don't want no money," said John. He stayed on in the woods.

Such was the status of Turnow on that September day when his nephews, the Bauer twins, were found dead. It was surmised that the twins had been sighted by Turnow and that he may have thought they were searching for him, to take him back to the hated sanitarium. And Turnow, as was later to become very evident, was a man of direct action.

II

A huge man hunt followed immediately on discovery of the murdered twins. Some two hundred men ranged the Satsop and Wynooche watersheds for forty miles north and south, then spread east and west from Puget Sound to the Pacific. Here and there they found where the wild fellow had made camp, but not once was he sighted although the hunt was kept up sporadically throughout the winter of 1911-1912.

Meanwhile, the usual alarms occurred: Turnow was reported to be near Port Angeles. An unknown had killed a cow near Shelton. Another unknown who, by the size of his monstrous tracks in the snow, must have been huge, was said to be in the neighborhood of Hama Hama, on Hood Canal. Any or all of these reports may have been true. Turnow was now a man six feet two inches tall and he weighed around 195 pounds, all of it bone and muscle. He knew the woods of all western Washington as other people know their living rooms—and indeed these woods were John Tumow's living room. He traveled through the timber, hunters said, swiftly and with no more noise than the soft whish of an owl. And after a fresh fall of snow, at a time when the posses were thick and numerous, he left no tracks at all, leaving one to suppose that he holed up for weeks on end like a bear; or, as some said, he took to the trees.

In fact, one Emil Swanson, a log bucker of stout back and of no imagination whatever, came into a camp one night in a condition bordering on hysteria. Not until he had downed a lusty slug of high-power lemon extract in hot water could he compose himself sufficiently to say what was the matter. When he had been about to fell a big fir, he vowed, "some kind big animal look like man," swung out on a high branch of the tree, grabbed the limb of another tree and went sailing off to be lost in the gloom of the towering timber. "Bay Yesus," said Emil, "aye vork here no more." He got his time and went to town.

The search for Turnow ebbed and flowed throughout the winter. Then, on March 2, 1912, word came out with a prospector that Turnow had made camp at a bend of the river far up the Satsop known as the Oxbow. Colin McKenzie, the deputy sheriff who found the Bauer twins, and A. V. Elmer, deputy game warden, started in to the Oxbow country to get Turnow. They did not return.

Thirteen days later a searching party found the bodies of the two missing men. Each had been drilled once through the forehead, and an attempt made to bury them in a shallow trench dug in the form of a T. Most of the dead men's clothing had been removed. Their rifles and ammunition were gone.

The hunt for Turnow now engaged the authorities of three counties. Rewards for the man, dead or alive, totaled $5,000, and hundreds of citizens joined the hunt. Not since the time of Harry Tracy and Dave Merrill had a man hunt of such proportions been on. The searchers used caution, too, for they knew they were pitted against a half-human animal who not only was deranged but who knew almost every acre of the large territory he had chosen for his home.

The usual alarms again occurred; the Wild Man of the Olympics, as the press now called him, was reported seen simultaneously in widely separated places. Loggers at the Simpson camps, nearly in the center of the region most favored by Turnow, took pains not to be found strolling quietly and alone through the woods. Southwest Washington, and in fact a good part of the Olympic Peninsula, had the Turnow jitters.

If you didn't know the country of John Turnow you might think it odd that more than twelve hundred men, most of them expert woodsmen, failed so much as to get sight of the wild man in a year's time of hunting. But Turnow had the craftiness of a cougar, and his domain was wide and wild. In 1912 it was pretty much virgin timber, not pines of parklike aspect, but a dense jungle of tall fir and cedar and spruce and hemlock, growing close together and with their bases set in vines and underbrush of almost tropical lushness.

Somewhere in that savage country the wild man spent the winter of 1912-1913, seen by no one. Not a track of his was found. Spring came on and the manhunt continued without abating. On April 16, 1913, almost two years after the murder of the Bauer twins, and more than a year after the killing of McKenzie and Elmer, Deputy Giles Quimby sighted a small wickiup, or rude shelter of bark, in a natural clearing by a tiny lake, perhaps a mile from the scene of the last two killings.

With Quimby were two trappers, Louis Blair and Charles Lathrop, who had turned man hunters with the $5,000 reward in mind. The three men were certain they had stumbled onto a hiding place of the wild man. But was Turnow there, in the hut?

They withdrew to a safe distance to consider the matter; and after a brief council of war decided to approach the hut from three directions. They began the advance, slowly, cautiously, and as quietly, or almost as quietly, as a cougar stalking a deer their rifles cocked. It wasn't, however, quiet enough . . .

Deputy Quimby was moving ahead a few feet at a time, picking his every step and halting now and then to listen. He heard nothing at all until a blast of gunfire suddenly shattered the wooded silence. At the same instant he heard the crashing of brush and looked to see Louis Blair tumble headlong, blood gushing horribly from what had been his face.

Quimby's gun was at his shoulder. For a flash he saw a great head and an ugly bearded face pop out from behind a fir. Quimby fired. The head disappeared. Quimby knew the head belonged to John Turnow—but had he hit it with his shot? Quimby couldn't know—for a few moments. He listened, straining every sense to penetrate the deathly silence. Then came another shattering blast. Charles Lathrop threw up his arms, gave one agonized cry and went tumbling to the ground. Again the ugly head and face peered from behind the fir tree. Quimby fired instantly, again and again, until his gun was empty. He crouched down to reload. He knew he was alone now with the wild man.

With his rifle once more ready, Quimby peered around the tree he was using for protection. He saw that his tree had been chipped by bullets and knew then that Turnow had also been shooting at him, though Quimby had been too busy to notice. He looked at the tree where Turnow was hiding and could see that it had been chipped by his own bullets. But, and it was rather important to know, had one of his bullets hit Turnow?

Deputy Quimby couldn't know. He pondered. All was silent in and around the glade. That is, silent except for the worried sniffing of two hounds belonging to Blair and Lathrop. Quimby could hear the animals whining in wonder at the sudden smell and aspect of Death. But of Blair or Lathrop or Turnow, Quimby could hear nothing. For probably five minutes, which Quimby later declared to have seemed an age, the deputy listened. Then, as quietly as he could he made his slow way through the timber and away from the lake. It had been an ambuscade, and for all he knew it might be one now. When he had got a hundred yards or so from the spot Quimby stopped to listen again. The mournful baying of the two hounds, still contemplating their late masters, was all he could hear. He now put on all speed and hurried to Camp 5 of the Simpson Logging Company, four miles distant. Here he found High Sheriff Matthews with a large posse. He led them back to the sinister little lake.

All was quiet. The posse spread out, then converged slowly toward the wickiup. Presently came a shout. "Here's the son of a bitch," a deputy called. "And he's dead, by

God." At about the same time other posse members found the bodies of the two trappers. Each had been shot once, fair between the eyes.

III

John Turnow hadn't been shot through the head, but he was just as dead as the six men he had killed. There he was, the wild fellow, sprawled on his back, his big old-fashioned repeating rifle across his chest and clutched in his two hands. He was a sight that men who saw him vividly remember today, more than thirty years after. The huge wild man with great matted beard and long hair, dressed in ragged garments made chiefly from gunny sacking, laid fold upon fold and filled with fir needles. On his feet was the only conventional bit of clothing he possessed, a pair of comparatively new calked boots, later identified as having belonged to the late Colin McKenzie, one of Turnow's victims.

In the little hut by the lake the posse found $6.65 in silver, a small knife, a pair of scissors and more gunny sacking of the sort the wild man had used to make his clothing. Not in the hut or anywhere else in the vicinity could the posse find so much as a scrap of food.

Reconstructing the brief, deadly battle, it was thought that Turnow, who had been accustomed to meeting *pairs* of men in the woods, and killing them, had not at first suspected the presence of a third man. It was a bullet from Quimby's gun which killed the outlaw.

Horses were brought in and Turnow and his last two victims taken out to Montesano, where an undertaker said he had never before seen the like of Turnow—all of the big man was bone and muscle. His shoulders, so the mortician reported, were like those of a gorilla; the palms of his hands were like leather. From this report, perhaps, and the added fact that it had never been possible to trail Thurnow—either in snow or on bare ground—plus the experience of Emil Swanson, he who saw the strange thing among the treetops, grew up the story, still widely believed, that the wild man often traveled through the trees, two hundred feet above the ground, like a gigantic ape. Perhaps he did. In any case, he went straight into legend, and there he remains today, half man, half ape, the Wild Man of the Olympics, intimate of bear, cougar, owls and buzzards, an unlettered, witless Thoreau who wanted to be alone and worked hard to that purpose.

The American Mercury (1943)

Fire in the Bush

For more than a week we had been speculating on the sky that appeared above the mountain across the inlet from camp. Varying in hue from a deep gray in the early morning to a feverish red at night, it got grayer and redder as the week passed. Old-timers among the loggers said "she was a dirty sky." The grizzled scaler allowed it was as dirty a sky as he had seen in forty years.

Each morning the sun had risen like a ball of fire, only to be completely hidden along toward noon as a smoky slate-colored haze fell slowly over everything. Occasionally, when the wind was from the south, stray flecks of burned-out embers floated in the air. One evening they had fallen thick as thistle-blows. When picked up and pinched between the fingers they were like black white powder, ashes.

All day Tuesday a sense of uneasiness pervaded camp. It had been muggy in the afternoon when we were yarding and loading the big fir logs; not a breeze had stirred. The sweat ran in great salty drops from our chins and noses as we struggled with the heavy cables. The blocks and the endless maze of rigging wailed a protest. When the drum on the donkey-engine turned, it seemed to snarl. Twice that day we had seen little puffs of smoke roll quickly up from dead punky logs as the fast-moving main line whipped to and from across them. When underbrush broke, it cracked like a rifle.

Night came and found an almost silent forest. The bushes around camp sounded that uneven and ominous rustle that bushes give out before a thunder-storm. Now and again an unseen, unfelt wind gave our stovepipes an eery rattle as it sighed northward to Queen Charlotte Sound. It was fire-time in the British Columbia timber. Loggers and wild animals sniffed the air. But supper passed and nothing had happened.

The camp itself was strangely quiet. Talk in the bunk-houses was hushed, as if by some sort of unspoken but mutual agreement. Even the poker game was mechanical. Puppet players saw and raised in low tones. The beloved accordions of the Finns were silent. Two hundred raw loggers huddled together in twenty little shacks, and hardly a sound! When one of the younger boys let a calked boot drop from an upper bunk and strike the floor, he was softly yet fervently cursed.

So subdued was everything that I recall how strident seemed the chatter of the foreman's wife that came to us in a torturing staccato from the fancy two-room shack in which they lived, somewhat apart from the rest of us. We could hear her sharp voice laughing at something her husband had said or done. She was always that way, talking and laughing. Just now she was telling her man what a fool he was for staying in the bush. Other men could make a living in town; why couldn't he? I heard her ask him that. We moved restlessly in our bunks and on the deacon-seats. All of us felt sorry for the foreman.

The wind rose and fell in short gusts. Not a crow could be heard from their favorite place near the pig-pen. No fox barked in the timber. The half-blind old camp dog, usually sleeping his feeble days away on the steps of the filer's shack, was uneasy. To-night he limped up and down . . . up and down . . . and sniffing.

✎✎✎

About half-past seven it happened. A short wail from the woods, turning in a flash from a wail to a long piercing scream that chilled the spine and made the hair stand. It was the yarder's whistle, held down by the watchman. Never was fire-siren like the uncanny shriek of a donkey-engine breaking through a silent forest night . . . And it shook us to life.

A rush for the flat-cars lined up on the side-track in camp—every one is ready—the locomotive sounds a warning blast—the donkey's screech is still cutting through our heads—hearts and ear-drums are pounding—the foreman gives the "highball"; we're off to the bush.

Back a mile in the timber even now we can see a great billow of smoke—a nasty red flame whips in and out of the cloud—it's got a quick start. The donkey's scream is dying away in a long-drawn gasp. I picture the donkey surrounded by fire, slowly succumbing . . . the gasp fades to a whisper . . . the train pounds on . . . *clickety-click* . . . and a crash as we cross the switches.

Here we are at the scene. The fire is near the loading-works; not a big fire yet, but growing fast . . . "Hit the dirt, boys," says the foreman. He quickly places his troops. A crew to dig fire-trenches, well back from the blaze but in its path; others, the fallers, get to work felling old dry snags, for these tinder posts will send fire over our heads, should they once begin to burn; hose-lines from the tank-car already are playing streams of water. The fire hisses at the water—and roars again.

Axes, picks, and shovels . . . the fire-trenches . . . stop it at the trenches . . . got to . . . Sweating cursing men work like mad giants. The fire is getting close to the trench; to us it seems a frenzied monster, striking this way and that with deadly puffs of red and black. The weaklings drop picks and shovels and run backward, choking. The foreman stalks along the line; he pleads, praises, curses . . . "Hold her, damn her, hold her!" . . . The seasoned fire-eaters stick fast to the line; the monster roars louder as it nears our trench—gathering strength for a leap, we think. It hurries faster to smother us.

At several places along the line the fire has reached the trench. In spots it seems dying; we hear a cheer from some of the young boys: "We've got her by the ears!" The old-timers don't cheer; they keep digging—and sweating—

and cursing. Throats are raw from smoke and fire . . . God! for some water, air and water.

Suddenly the monster closes in around an old snag just inside the line. It hesitates a moment, as if throttling its prey. Fascinated, we watch it. Like a streak of light we see fire flash upward the entire side of the old dry trunk—and here burn a moment. We watch it, helpless. The wind lifts live embers of punk and sends them far over our heads, away off into the timber.

In an instant new fires are springing up back of us, springing up out of the night as if an unseen devil were hurrying through the woods with an invisible torch. The old fire is burning itself out along the trench . . . but we see mocking faces in the smoke.

Tactics are changed. Crews run from one blaze to another, smothering them with dirt . . . we smother one and two new ones appear. The air is full of sparks, and brands, and burning branches—and noise . . . cracking, hissing, roaring noise . . . noise of battle . . . sometimes I think I hear the boom of far-away cannon; it is the crash and thud of great trees falling.

A dozen blazes are growing into big fires—fire on all sides, in front of us, back of us—fire half-way up the mountain . . . it snarls and bites . . . it leaps at great tall trees, devours their life, and leaves silhouettes stark against the red background . . . then leaps onward, hissing, snapping.

A human cry breaks through the roar—some one hurt. It is one of the fallers; a tree got him. . . . I see a limp form being carried to the railroad track and placed on the speeder. . . . This is my job, first aid. . . . I go—I look at the crushed thing on the speeder. First aid won't do—need a box.

Over the crooked and warped rails we run with the light car, four men and a corpse. The ties are gone; rails are loose—off the track. We lift the car, push it, *cram* it somehow over the bad spots. Fire is close to the rails. Eyeballs swell and seem bursting. God! Is fire everywhere in the whole world? . . . At last the opening . . . fresh air—we breathe it, taste it, *eat* it. . . . Here's the camp . . . seems uncanny that the camp can be so peaceful when there's battle less than a mile away.

We put the broken body on a bunk and throw a canvas over it. . . . Some one says its spirit is in Valhalla and not worrying about any damned forest-fire.

A new danger appears. The fire has been slowly creeping down through the opening toward camp, creeping, creeping through underbrush and old logs, till now it rears its head close by the filer's shack. Hardly have our glazed eyes taken in what is happening when the roof of the wash-house breaks into flame. Almost at the same time shingles on the camp office are smoldering. . . . The whole works are hay-wire! We call the cook and flunkies to help . . . pails, buckets, dish-pans of water from the brook. The pigs strike a new note with their crying when the fire gains the bushes near the pen; it is terror, terror told as plainly as ever human voiced it. With a grand squeal of triumph they mass and break through the cedar bars. Once out of their pen they wander foolishly through the camp, lost and grunting with resentment.

The fat sweating cook curses as he waddles up the camp street with two pails half full of muddy water: "Can't these damned, snuff-chewing, oary-eyed loggers have a fire without burnin' up the jeasly, cock-eyed old hay-wire camp?" His soft hands are blistered and bleeding from contact with many water-buckets. His eyes are bleary, and great drops of perspiration cling to his nose; tobacco-juice oozes from the corners of his mouth and runs in little rivers down his chin. His usually fine, sweeping mustache is frayed and drooping. He has worked hard for an old man. And his able and continued profanity has helped all of us who must conserve our breath. He beats the flunkies with a bucket to make them hurry with more water. . . . Gradually, as we get control of the roof fires, the motif of his profanity changes from shocking blasts to gentle and caressing curses.

At last we are sure the camp is safe. The roof of one shack has gone, and the sides of others are scorched a deep brown. The little house in the pig-pen is burned flat with the ground. But that is all. Small fires are burning in the old logs around camp, but they can hurt nothing now that the brush has gone.

The cook takes a fresh bite of plug and repairs to the cook-house.

✎✎✎

Back in the timber a hazy blistering dawn lays the breeze. The fire keeps close to the ground. It is traveling on its belly, dozing sullenly in the morning quiet. Half-dead men, silent, driven, haggard, lean on shovels. They barely move—like meaningless figures in the background of a dream.

"Go to camp," the word is passed around. Shovels, axes, saws are dropped; no one speaks.

Down through acres of stark black specters the loggers plod, two by two and in small groups, tired, sagging, red-eyed. They walk through hot ashes and stumble over smoldering logs, stumble drunkenly on to what seems a heaven . . . Camp.

Once here, they drop on benches, bunks, anywhere. They tell us the fire has gone over the hump, the mountain—gone to hell-an'-gone.

Food, food and drink, that's what—and sleep.

From the kitchen come clattering noises. The old cook, stiff from his unusual efforts and moving painfully, is mixing coffee in a wash-boiler—strong black coffee that curls your hair. And he has a flunky making toast, great thick slices of scorched bread. He calls toast a city fancy, and he wants to do his best. We hear him singing a hymn of thanks as he stirs the coffee. It is a ribald doggerel from Maine, "The Red Light Saloon"—the only song he knows.

The steaming brew is ready. Ah-h-h! something like! She's jake now . . . The loggers eat and drink. Things look better. Nervous laughs greet time-worn sallies. Snuff-boxes appear; pipes are filled. Sleep is forgotten when tired men feel the letdown. A few seek bunks, but no one goes into the shack where a canvas covers the hulk on a iron bed . . . We can't move it till next boat comes . . . Saturday is freight-day.

The last man from the woods is the foreman. The worries of an entire company are traced in his haggard face. He stops to talk with us a moment. "Get some sleep," he says . . . He goes to his little house.

We haven't seen his wife since the fire started. The cook says he saw her, and she was playing the phonograph in the front room, and singing.

✎ ✎ ✎

The camp is again silent. One by one the loggers have gone to their bunks. The pigs have found their way back to the pen and have returned to the rich black mud and cedar roots, where they grunt softly, happy . . . A smokey blue haze hangs over everything, barely admitting the vague rays of a red ball suspended overhead. Wispy dead embers, white like fireweed, fall listlessly . . . Faintly I hear crows trying out their voices, as if afraid of the noise they make . . . A big Dolly Varden leaps clear of the pool below camp and catches a bluebottle . . . The fire has passed on.

The sleepy quiet makes me feel dreamy . . . soft grunting of happy pigs . . . languorous splashes in the pool . . . far-away caw of crows . . . thin blue mist.

Something grates my ear. It is the voice of the foreman's wife, so long still. "Now that your funny old woods is gone, we can go to town, can't we?" It is a demand, not a question . . . "For God's sake let me sleep.". . . "Tell me we'll go to Vancouver next boat sure." Her voice is sharp. "An' anyway, if you had any guts we'd live in town all the time.". . . Again the weary voice: "For God's sake let me sleep."

From where I loll in front of my shack I see one of the pigs lift up his head at this disturbing sound. He considers a moment, cocks his ear, and subsides with a short grunt. The grunt means something, perhaps disgust.

And since that time I have often wondered if old Elizear wasn't right. Elizear always fed the pigs, and he talked to them by the hour. He said that pigs understood perfectly all human beings. He claimed they had an uncanny knack of human values. I know I felt just the way that pig's grunt sounded.

The Century Magazine (1926)

The Three Sirens of Portland

None of the three was particularly fair to look upon, yet they came to be called the Three Sirens and doubtless earned the title at their respective places of business in the Oregon city of Portland. Customers and police knew them as Liverpool Liz, Mary Cook and Nancy Boggs; and on occasion they were called by other names, though they seemed not to mind.

Of the trio Liz, who was born Elizabeth Smith in Liverpool, England, about 1850, was the best business woman. Nancy Boggs, an American, was the toughest. Mary Cook was unique in that she did her own bouncing—this in a day when bouncing was no genteel matter.

The time was from the late 1870s until a little after 1900. Portland was already old, as age goes in the Far West, but it was easily the liveliest port on the Northwest coast. Grain came here in a flood from the inland counties for shipment to the world. Eighteen big sawmills along the waterfront whined and clattered night and day. Windjammers were always in the harbor waiting to pick up cargo, while their crews cavorted on shore. Loggers arrived in droves to have their dental work done. It was a rich claim for any progressive business woman to work. The Three Sirens were progressive and they were hard workers.

Where Mary Cook was born or even where she died is regrettably not known. But she was, certainly, an able and hardy character, a behemoth of a girl weighing more than two hundred pounds and standing, in her red morocco slippers, a full six feet. She had a consuming urge to be dainty, and veterans of the time and place tell me she was indeed graceful, except perhaps when she was throwing around the crockery and bar glasses.

Mary's establishment was named the Ivy Green, and though a few disgruntled customers said a prefix, namely "Poison," should be added, it was no worse than any combination saloon-brothel, and perhaps considerably better. The Ivy Green catered to sailors and lumberjacks, but it was not exclusive, and most any male with a few dollars was tolerated.

Mary was an excellent greeter. She liked to stand just inside the swinging doors, and smoke big, black cigars while she welcomed the boys. As a blower of smoke-rings she had no equal, male or female, and if you held out a forefinger toward her, she would blow three neat rings around it, for good luck. If urged, Mary put on her Scotchman-smoking act. She'd blow a single ring, let it drift some three or four feet away, then go after it with her mouth wide open, and swallow it. This amused the customers no end and Mary never tired of it.

Although Mary was good-natured, even jolly, she was a stickler for keeping what she said was good order in the Ivy Green. I should like to have been in her establishment on that gorgeous evening in 1896 when Mary took in hand a celebrated local character by name of John P. Sullivan. This fellow was a part-time logger and a part-time fighter who claimed to be a nephew of the great Boston Strong Boy. He came into Mary's one night and took on a few. When the bar was well filled he announced himself. "I can," he said, "lick any son of a bitch in the place."

Nobody said anything. Mary herself had just blown a neat ring, but now she let it drift. All was quiet for a moment. John P. Sullivan glared at the crowd. "I can," he repeated in a loud voice, "lick any son of a bitch in the place."

Now Mary Cook spoke. "Does that apply to women too?" The voice was soprano, rather musical, but anybody short of a drunk could have detected an edge to it.

"I am talking about anybody—man, woman or devil," said John P. Sullivan, large as life.

Veterans among the barflies watched with anticipation approaching agony as Mary threw away her half-smoked cheroot. She dusted her hands a bit, then ambled toward the great John P. Sullivan like a monstrous female moose. A friend of mine, the late Edward (Spider) Johnson, was among those present. "This Sullivan," he told me, "claimed to have wrestled with a shorthorn bull and to have broken the animal's neck. But the poor man—he did not know what was coming now."

John P. stood his ground as Mary approached, planning no doubt to slap the woman's face should she be so foolish as to attack him.

Walking up close to the big fighting-man, Mary put her face near his. "Listen," she said, and her voice was like unto jasper, "listen, you mug, have I gotta make an example of you?"

John P. Sullivan started to say something, what no one ever will know, for at that instant the cyclone that was Mary Cook struck him. She grabbed him by his two prominent ears and twirled him around like a top. Next, she applied one heavy hand to Sullivan's coat collar, the other to the seat of his pants. She picked him up bodily from the floor. She turned and heaved, and John P. flew almost the length of the room, hitting the floor just short of the swinging doors.

"Not so good," Mary remarked with a deep sigh. With four long strides she was standing over the fallen man. Again she applied the Ivy Green hold, only this time she picked him up and held him aloft, as if offering a supplication. "Open the doors, some of you dingbats," she commanded. Wide swung the doors, and then with a truly mighty heave Mary sent John P. Sullivan skidding along the sidewalk, a thing composed of two-inch Douglas fir and abristle with long splinters caused by the calked books of hundreds of loggers. I have heard that no less than three hundred pieces of wood were extracted from the rear and flanks of John P. Sullivan, who never again made unseemly remarks in the Ivy Green.

"I hated to do it," Mary moaned, in reference to the incident, "I hated to do it, but I just gotta keep my refectory a decent place for gentlemen."

II

Liverpool Liz was no amazon, but she was husky enough for her height, which was about five feet two inches. She was well known for the necklace she wore upon almost all occasions. It was a rugged hunk of jewelry, so large and heavy that nobody ever thought of it as a bauble; and at the end of the enormous golden links hung a cluster of great diamonds. Her limey accent was rich and heavy, and she was a favorite with seamen, the majority of whom in that era were British.

Liz called her place the Senate saloon. The street level part was actually a saloon. Upstairs she kept her stable of female entertainers, whose number varied according to conditions in the harbor and in the logging woods. At the back of the bar were a couple of steps that led up to a small platform. In the ceiling was a hole. When drinks were wanted upstairs, the order would be shouted down, and one of the barkeeps would mix the order and hand the drinks up through the aperture. Why Liz, who was progressive in other respects, never installed a dumbwaiter is beyond knowing. Bartenders disliked the system and complained, but it was never changed.

There was, however, a modern bell system at the bar which Liz found useful on occasion. Say that a customer came in, feeling happy, and saw there were only four or five men at the bar. He'd tell the barkeep to set 'em up for everybody. "Yes sir," the barkeep would reply, meanwhile pressing a button that rang a buzzer upstairs. Within a few seconds anywhere from six to a dozen girls, often with escorts, would troop down the back stairs and into the barroom, laughing, shouting for drinks, including champagne, which Liz kept especially for the gag. The poor sucker who had originally figured that "drinks for everybody" would run to not more than a dollar, thus found himself paying anywhere from five to twenty-five dollars. Liz said that it helped pay the rent.

Yet Liverpool Liz was a pretty decent sort and probably more honest than her customers had a right to expect. She never, it is said, permitted a drunk to be rolled in her place, upstairs or down. She had an enormous safe—with an oil painting of Niagara Falls on the outside door—in which she kept the cash and valuables of her customers. This wasn't a racket. The logger or seaman who was overburdened with money and who hoped to make it last for a week or two, turned over such surplus as he wished to Liz. She put it in a manila envelope, sealed it and wrote the man's name on the cover. It was then put into the safe. Even if her place did get most of it in the end, the customer was grateful. He had not been rolled, and the system, moreover, did tend to make his stake last longer. Hundreds of loggers and seamen went away to tout the honesty of Liverpool Liz, and to return to her place when opportunity offered.

Although the record is far from clear, talk has it that Liz was married two or three times. If so, none of them could have lasted, for she appears to have run her place pretty much with a lone hand. One of her noted bouncers was a character called Tatoo Kelly. He had blue and red eagles tattooed all over his body and had once been an inmate of a sideshow. He had also been a sailor, an English sailor; and had done a little fighting. He got enough of the latter in the Senate saloon to keep him in trim; but eventually he murdered a man and was sent to the penitentiary.

If Liz had been content with her Senate she might have died a wealthy old harlot. But when the bicycle craze came along somebody talked her into buying a piece of suburban property and making it into a bicycle track, which she called Evergreen park. Right in the middle of her property she set up a saloon. This was probably an error of judgment, for parents of young cyclists did not approve of saloons in conjunction with playgrounds. Then the bicycle craze passed, and Liz was left holding property into which she had put much of her savings.

Finally, the Senate, on which her small fortune was founded, began to know days and nights when scarcely a seaman showed up for entertainment. The winged ships were passing, and the steam vessels carried fewer men into Portland.

And so at last the Senate closed its doors, and Liz herself died not long after, of pneumonia. She was given decent Christian burial in Portland's Lone Fir cemetery, in a grave not far from that of Jim Turk, who had made a business of shanghaiing men, and who had often coordinated his activities with those of Liverpool Liz and Nancy Boggs.

III

It was said of Nancy Boggs that she invented the whiskey-scow. This is probably a debatable subject, in which I am not especially interested, but it is a fact that in 1880 Miss Boggs was the owner and proprietor of a floating hellhole that was anchored in the Willamette River, which is Portland's harbor. At that time there were two cities, Portland and East Portland, with the river between them, each seeking to outdo the other. The lovely and alert Miss Boggs, learning that there was some doubt as to who should administer the law in the harbor, sought to make capital of the situation.

Dredging up sufficient cash to purchase an old sawdust scow, she had erected on its deck a two-story house. The lower section provided for the devotees of Bacchus and Terpsichore, the upper was devoted wholly to Venus. She painted it bright green and stationed it in the middle of the river. In the meantime she had stocked it with the best she could find of what came in bottles and corsets.

Miss Boggs' floating palace of sin was a success from the night it opened. On both east and west shores she stationed boatmen-pimps charged with seducing, then rowing customers to the middle of the stream, where Nancy and her girls took care of the rest. Now and then, some drunk would fall into the water, on occasion to drown; but on the whole the thing worked out very well. If the East Portland cops, in a moment of virtue, set out to raid the place, Miss Boggs, always forewarned, simply upped anchor and moved the scow nearer the Portland shore and thus into the jurisdiction of that city. It also worked in reverse order.

Then, in 1882, came one of those great moral waves that sweep over American cities every decade or so. Egged on by reformers, the police of both Portland and East Portland made a combined raid on the scow. Do not for a moment believe Miss Boggs was not ready. She herself in person met the combined police forces with hose in hand, and out of the hose issued terrific blasts of steam straight from the scow's heating plant. Cursing and screaming like all the Harpies alive, Nancy poured live steam over the bluecoats, who got out of there quickly.

Returning to their respective stations, the policemen applied grease to their burns while their superiors considered what to do. Eventually they got an idea. Along in the dark of the next morning, some unnamed policeman in a rowboat very quietly cut the manila ropes midway between the deck and anchor, and Miss Boggs' scow started on a wild trip downstream. The river was high, just then, and filled with eddies and whirlpools. Miss Boggs was aroused to find her houseboat spinning slowing in mid-river, heading straight out toward the Pacific ocean.

A woman of decision and quick action, Miss Boggs first attempted to wake the one man on board. But he was still heavy in his cups. So, bidding her frightened girls be calm, Nancy lowered away a small rowboat, got into it, and rowed as for dear life to the shore at Albina, an East Portland suburb. There, with great speed, she awoke a stern-wheeler captain and talked him into immediate action. He roused his crew and, with Nancy aboard, they set out to get lines to the heaving scow. Then, with Nancy standing staunch and bold as a figurehead at the head of her scow, it was towed back upstream and anchored at its accustomed and proper place in the middle to Portland harbor. I doubt that it was gone long enough to have lost a dollar in trade.

Miss Boggs continued in business until conditions warranted a move to dry land, and even there she did very well, it is said, but with less gusto than in her scow days.

The Burnside Street bridge across the Willamette bears a marker telling how the Messrs. Lewis & Clark, explorers, reached that point in their voyage up the Willamette. I think a small footnote could well grace the plaque. It would relate that here was anchored for several years what was doubtless the first whisky scow in all the Far West, operated for the refreshment of travelers and the benefit of Miss Nancy Boggs, able mariner and a notable grower of fine roses in the city whose slogan is: "For you a rose in Portland grows."

The American Mercury (1948)

The Cattle King

Of the several notable figures of the Old West, that of the Cattle King was perhaps the most romantic, or at least has been made so by the tireless labors of thousands of writers. Maybe he *was* the most romantic. It is certain that uncounted tons of pulp paper are required annually for the imprint of Westerns; and tons more both of slick and of book papers are needed to tell the identical story; while the film footage devoted to the Cattle King and his minions, the cowboys, and his enemies, the rustlers, is probably greater than that used for all other kinds of movies combined.

Why this should be so is a matter for psychologists, or possibly psychiatrists. Perhaps it is based on the ancient appeal of the man on horseback, the old plumed-knight-and-charger combination. In any case the Cattle King survives as a glorified symbol long after his kind has disappeared, at least in the Northwest. The annual celebration at Pendleton, Oregon, called the Roundup, is devoted to perpetuating the symbol. This is quite proper, for eastern Oregon, rather than any other part of the Northwest, was our great cattle country.

One has no difficulty naming the Northwest's most eminent cattle king. He was Peter French of Harney County, Oregon, and he easily stands first in the legend as he did once in fact. When he died, in his boots, in 1897, the twilight of the Northwest cattle kings set in. For a quarter of a century he had successfully held at bay all of the natural enemies of the cattle kings, including the United States Government, rustlers, Indians, competing cattlemen and, worst of all, the homesteaders. When he died, there was none of his kind left with the strength and ruthlessness necessary to hold out against encroaching civilization.

Not too much is known of Peter French's early years. He was born on his father's modest ranch near Red Bluff, California, in 1849. He ran away from home while still a youth, and went to work for Dr. Hugh Glenn, a wheat-and-cattle rancher of Chico. He must have shown great abilities, for Dr. Glenn advanced him steadily, and soon he married the doctor's daughter.

In the early seventies California sought to curb its powerful cattle kings and other large owners of land by a succession of fence laws. Dr. Glenn, who by then was one of the largest landowners in the Sacramento Valley, and was quick to note a trend, had heard tales of a vast range country in eastern Oregon. He had also seen some prime beef cattle from that region. In 1873 he sent his son-in-law, Peter French, to scout the land, and to buy, if it looked good.

Young French, twenty-four years old, ranged on horseback into eastern Oregon, crossing deserts marked by shallow shimmering lakes, great marshes of tule, buttes, and sagebrush. He did not find what he sought until he came to the Donner and Blitzen River in what is now Harney County. The Blitzen Valley enchanted him. There the river tumbled down the rocky slopes of grim Steens Mountain to thread a valley that for seventy miles was a fine wild meadow. The nearest railroad was at Winnemucca, 250 miles by horseback. There, in an area approximately that of the State of Maine, a scattering few ranchers ran cattle undisturbed, and were as yet largely unknown to the rest of Oregon.

In the Blitzen Valley French found an old prospector who also raised a few cattle, and used a P-brand. French bought him out. The P-Ranch was to become headquarters for the most stupendous cattle outfit in the Oregon country, the French-Glenn empire. No matter its name, Peter French himself built it—built it first with Dr. Glenn's backing, and after the doctor was presently murdered by his bookkeeper, without it.

Peter French would scarcely have fitted the pulp-paper and Hollywood conception of a cattle king. He was a mere five feet six inches tall, or nigh a foot under the standard for fiction. He was wiry, dark-haired, and wore the usual big mustaches of the period. Although he was usually genial and even-tempered, he was no mixer. There was something aloof in his character. He took his own place in any company, but never slapped backs. There was little of heartiness in him. His hospitality was openhanded, but that was in the tradition of range country, and could not be said to be a personal characteristic.

It seems generally agreed that he drove his men pretty hard, and drove himself more. He came in time to be the most feared and respected man in eastern Oregon. Perhaps he was loved, too, though I cannot find evidence of it. All accounts of him are singularly free of anything indicating devotion to Peter French. Certainly he was ruthless, yet ruthlessness in that time and period was held to be less a sin than a virtue.

With the comparatively small P-Ranch underfoot, French lost no time in acquiring the rest of the Blitzen Valley, and went on from there by various means to add to his holdings until they embraced some 200,000 acres. Meanwhile, he made his headquarters ranch into an outstanding spot in southeastern Oregon. First he built a great White House. Every stick of lumber for it came 150 miles overland by twelve-mule team from the Blue Mountains. He erected barns, cookhouses, bunkhouses, and established a store for his help. His corrals were the best in the region; they were founded on clusters of posts lashed together with rawhide. His fences were of juniper stakes bored to carry the unbarbed wire. He built everything to last. In time his fences came to enclose 120,000 acres.

Then, as now, there was a great deal of marsh land in Harney County. French set his men to draining it. One of his canals, said Julian Boyd, who knew French, ran a good fifteen miles and cost one dollar a lineal yard. At times the number of men on French's payroll was as high as two hundred.

He kept adding land all the time. It is likely that no little of this acreage was acquired though the help of a character known as the Oregon Swamp Rat, who said he had been christened Henry Owen. Hen Owen made his living from a law entitled the Swamp and Overflow Act, which permitted the purchase of marsh land at $1.25 an acre. The purpose of the Act, of course, was to cause the buyer to drain and otherwise improve the land. Peter French actually did drain much land. He also bought considerable land, at swamp-law prices, that was far from swampy. Everybody did so. It was a custom of the time.

Hen Owen's specialty was in "locating" good sound lands which, because of their remoteness from the likelihood of inspection by government agents, could be bought as Swamp and Overflow without great danger of detection. Stories are told of how Hen Owen and other locators often rode over a tract in a rowboat hauled by a team of horses; then they could swear, on any stack of Bibles, that they had covered the area in a boat. This was thought to be pretty cute business, not admirable, perhaps, but quite in accord with business ethics of the latter nineteenth century. These inspired land grabbers were known by the generic term of swamp angels.

Only once did French have to defend his empire against those who morally owned it. In 1878 the Bannocks, Paiutes, and Snakes made a determined raid into Nevada, southern Idaho, and eastern Oregon. They killed a number of settlers, burned houses, and ran off cattle and horses. A large party of them came rather suddenly over Steens Mountain to catch French and sixteen of his men at work on the Diamond ranch of the French-Glenn holdings.

French saw them coming. He ordered his men to ride for home, the P-Ranch, while he covered their getaway. This he did in a manner that would have made a nice film. Taking position on the roof of a hog house, French used a rifle to good effect, slowing the Indian advance until his men got safely away, though one of them, the Chinese cook, fell from his horse and was taken and killed. French himself managed to get away unscathed, and rode to meet his men at P-Ranch. He led his entire crew to Fort Harney, where they joined with other volunteers, and a bit later accompanied regular Army troops of General O. O. Howard's command to defeat the Indians at the battle of Silver Creek.

The next and worst danger to threaten the French empire came from homesteaders, when a government land office was opened at Lakeview, and the lands of Harney, Malheur, and Lake counties were thrown open to settlement. Swamp angels and homestead locators, who followed land booms as other men followed gold strikes, were well in the van. Homesteaders arrived in force during 1880. Sheepmen were coming in too. Something would have to be done, so Peter French sent his employees, one after another, to file homestead claims, which they sold later at token prices to the cattle king of P-Ranch.

At about this period, Mrs. Peter French decided she had had enough of life on Oregon's greatest ranch. She went back to California, never to return. There seems to be no record, or even a scrap of folklore, as to why Mrs. French went away, or as to how Peter French took her departure. His whole life, indeed, is pretty much undocumented. Probably nobody in Harney County gave any thought to French as possibly a historic character. He was less a fabulous person to them than he was a hard and immediate fact, something you accepted, like Steens Mountain, or perhaps as you did rattlesnakes. He was just *there.* You didn't write anything about him.

A few of the new homesteaders, however, tried to do something about Peter French; they took potshots at him from well concealed positions. He was never hit. Two or three of his ranch employees were less fortunate; they died from shots fired by unknown hands.

Then there were the French dams. Some of these had been built purposely to flood land, thus making it swamp, so that it could readily, and more or less legally, be filed on under the Swamp and Overflow Act. Once the land had been acquired at the $1.25-per-acre price, the dam could be taken out, and the land would revert to its pristine soundness.

But now, with homesteaders around, the French dams began going out before their time. Sometimes dynamite was used; at others, portions of dams were dug out by hand, sufficient for water to flow out.

Wherever homesteaders had managed to settle on a quarter-section within the French empire, Peter French tried to buy them out, and off. He had to keep his bounds intact; you couldn't run cattle where homesteads interfered. For the most part French managed to buy off the new settlers within the bounds of his domain, but one of them, Ed Oliver, did not care to sell. Said he liked the country. Good healthy place. He ran a few cattle. He was getting along all right. Thought he would stay. And stay he did.

Such was the condition of things on December 26, 1897, a day when Pete French chose to work with one of his crews at the division of his ranch called Sodhouse. Ed Oliver was presently seen in the neighborhood. What happened next has been so much in dispute for half a century that no writer in his right mind would think of citing his account as accurate. It is certain, of course, that there was bad blood between the ruthless French and the obstinate Oliver. Folklore has it, too, that French had warned Oliver to keep off French land. This seems likely.

Well, on this 26th day of December, French rode off a short distance from his crew to meet Oliver. The crew saw the two men parley a moment. One story has it that French struck Oliver with a whip, then turned to ride away, and was shot and killed by the homesteader. Whatever happened, Pete French died in his boots, and Ed Oliver admittedly killed him.

And now David Crow becomes something of the hero of the affair. Crow was one of French's employees. Promptly on the death of the cattle king, Crow mounted horse and started for Winnemucca, Nevada. It was one of the great rides in Oregon annals. Crow was in the saddle forty-eight hours, and changed mounts nine times. He tore into the Nevada town with the news, and from there the wires spread it all over the West.

Ed Oliver does not seem to have attempted to flee after the shooting. He stood trial on a charge of murder, and was acquitted by a jury that found him not guilty by reason of self-defense. Incidentally, folklore has it that French commonly did not carry firearms.

The one thing about the passing of Peter French with which all parties seem in agreement is that the era of the cattle king began passing with him. He was the last, as well as the greatest, in Oregon of the old school, the kind who felt and believed and acted like the crowned heads of old Europe, and who ruled by the right of God Almighty.

Yet the homesteaders who put an end to the cattle king did not remain. Harney County is more of a wilderness today than it was when Pete French died. Only six thousand persons inhabit its 10,132 square miles, and of these more than half live in the cattle-and-lumber city of Burns, in the northern part of the county. Harney County is larger than the states of Massachusetts and Rhode Island combined. Its density of population works out at something like one person for each one and one-half square miles. Nowhere else in the Northwest are the open spaces so wide, or so uncluttered with the works of man. But in the old domain of Peter French are more wildfowl than you would believe unless you had seen what is officially the Malheur National Wildlife Refuge.

The Malheur project was established by executive order of President Theodore Roosevelt in 1908, when the Government set aside 95,155 acres around Lakes Harney and Malheur. Pete French's favorite Blitzen River empties into the latter. In 1935, and again later, the Government added more of French's old range, until the whole now runs to 174,000 acres. The refuge is almost identical with the

French empire. It runs from near what is now Frenchglen, a hamlet with a hotel on the old P-Ranch, along both sides of the Blitzen to the two lakes, and around them, with bulges here and there.

Here to the refuge come wild birds by the millions, to nest and rear their young, then to take off, either north or south, for their other haunts. It is reputed, at least in Oregon, to be the greatest migratory bird refuge in the United States. It harbors virtually all Western species of ducks, as well as egrets, pelicans, terns, ibis, bitterns, and the rare whooping cranes.

Peter French's old White House has been torn down, though some of his stout fences still stand; and his empire, on which he cut ten thousand tons of hay annually, and over which he ran twenty thousand head of cattle, has now reverted to a state as primitive as it was before the first cattleman, or even the first white man, saw it. There is perhaps no greater area of complete and savage solitude in the Northwest than the old P-Ranch of Peter French.

The Far Corner (1952)

See Giles French, *Cattle Country of Peter French*, Binfords and Mort (1964), for a biography of the "cattle king."

The Original Nature Man

On sultry July 20,1914, newspapers up and down the Pacific Coast announced in blaring headlines: EYES OF WORLD ON TEST OF MAN VS. NATURE. Reading on, Western he-men learned that Joe Knowles, the Nature Man of Maine, was about to plunge, unarmed and naked as a snake, into the untamed, cougar-infested wilds of the Siskiyou Mountains of Oregon.

Next day, the *Examiner* of San Francisco, sponsor of this one-man scientific expedition, gave over a goodly part of its front page to telling who Joe Knowles was, what he proposed to do, and the conditions of this test of Man vs. Nature. The *Oregonian* of Portland did likewise, and lesser papers of the Coast region broke out with syndicated articles signed by Knowles at his jumping-off place, Grants Pass.

To assure the public there was no fakery, the *Examiner* announced it had secured two eminent naturalists as special investigators. They were Dr. Charles Lincoln Edwards, B.S., Ph.D., head of the Nature Study Department of the Los Angeles school system, and Prof. T. T. Waterman of the University of California. The two savants would be turned loose in the same wild district where Knowles was to perform and there circulate at will, picking up messages that the Nature Man might write and leave at agreed points. Also they were to set down their own impressions of the experiment and generally act as "guardians of the public interest" in the affair.

Two days later the story was still front-page stuff and getting bigger and better all the time. Wearing a breechclout and nothing else, with no implement of any kind, Joe Knowles had shaken hands with professors and reporters, posed for Mr. Hearst's cameraman, and vanished into the Siskiyou jungle. There he was to remain for sixty days, unarmed, unaided in any way, living on nuts and berries, or on game if he could snare it with his bare hands; clothing himself as he could from the forest; and pitting his naked body against the enemies of nature, which ranged all the way from clouds of vicious insects to mean mountain lions. WILD BEASTS ROAR INVITATION TO JOE KNOWLES bellowed the *Examiner* in a banner, and there were echoes all the way from Los Angeles to Seattle.

There hadn't been such a local story since the San Francisco "Fire," and it was going great guns as July crept into its last week. Joe was doing well and sitting pretty, he reported in messages written in charcoal on bark and left for the two professors to pick up. He was living on fish and small game, taken in primitive fashion, and he was about to snare a deer from whose skin he would make himself more durable clothes than those he was wearing. Red-blooded he-men, with whom the West Coast has ever been infested, could scarcely wait for their morning papers to read—pop-eyed and envious—what the Nature Man of Maine had done the day before. It even got into the comic strips and editorial cartoons.

Then came that sinister 28th of July, when all Europe started blowing up. AUSTRIA DECLARES WAR ON SERBIA screamed headlines from coast to coast and on around the world. Twelve hours later the Russian mobilization was under way, and the Kaiser had declared war on the Czar. France rose to arms. On August 2, Germany demanded free passage through Belgium. Next day, von Kluck's Big Berthas were bombarding Liége. And on August 4, Great Britain went whole hog into the riot.

It was a sad day for Joe Knowles. And you can guess what it did to the *Examiner's* great experiment of Man vs. Nature. The Naked Thoreau news from Grants Pass went into the back pages next to the classified ads, and many a

Californian doesn't know to this day whether Joe Knowles *ever* got out of the woods.

Joe was annoyed, and with considerable reason. What a lousy time to start a world war! Here he was, exposing his hide to the gnats and cougars, fighting a single-handed battle against all the natural enemies of Man—and Europe had to go and blow him off the front page . . . .

II

This, however, wasn't the first time that Joe Knowles had ventured alone into the primeval forest to prove that atavism is not only easy and pleasant, but good for newspaper circulation as well; nor was it his last trip of the kind. It was simply the one when all the breaks were against him.

The time that Joe really knocked them out of their seats was in 1913, a year before the Siskiyou affair. The setting was the woods of Northern Maine, the paper was the Boston *Post,* and the public included almost all the newspaper readers in New England and Eastern Canada. The story was handled with beautiful showmanship. When Joe went into the Maine woods in August, 1913, he was an unknown artist, a struggling portrait painter. Two months later he was a national figure, known alike to adults and schoolboys, and the center of a controversy that was second in noise only to that between the friends of Admiral Peary and the friends of Dr. Cook.

His Big Idea came out of a dream. "Not much of a dream," Joe said, "but a damned real one. I dreamt I was lost in the woods, alone and *naked,* with no hope ever of getting out. When I woke up I got to thinking if and how a civilized man should get along in such a situation. A day or so later I related my dream at a small hotel dinner. How a New York newspaperman happened to be present I have forgotten, but there was one; and next day the *Tribune* carried an interview with me, telling of my claims. In a day or two mail started flooding me."

The correspondence started a train of thought in Joe's mind. Some of the letters agreed that a naked and unarmed man could survive in the forest. Others said Joe was a fool who didn't know what he was talking about. And then, almost simultaneously, came letters from the Boston *American,* a Hearst paper, and the Boston *Post.* Both said they would like to have Joe call on them when he was in Boston . . . . The Big Idea was a-dawning.

First off, but in greatest secrecy lest the Vermonters have him clapped into jail on disorderly conduct charges, Joe conducted an undress rehearsal. Naked except for a G-string, and taking nothing with him, he went into the wooded hills back of Bradford and remained there a week. It was July. Berries were plentiful. So were flies and mosquitoes. But the dawning Nature Man rubbed his hide with wild spearmint and the pests passed him by. He cornered trout in a small pool and caught them with his hands. Fire was easy, for Joe had learned the secret years before from Indians. All in all, he put in a pleasant and interesting week. When he emerged from the Bradford woods he packed his grip and went to Boston.

For reasons not at all clear today, the editor of the Boston *American* hemmed and hawed. "You're losing the chance of a lifetime," Joe told him as he walked out, and how true he spoke any Boston newspaperman will tell you now.

So Joe went over to the *Post.* Even in 1913, the *Post* was an old paper, but it wasn't doing well. The loud *American,* still young and rowdy, was giving New England a sample of Hearst at his best, or worst, and it had seemed to Knowles that the Hearst sheet was the logical medium for his experiment. At the moribund *Post,* however, Joe found a real welcome. Charles E. L. Wingate, late general manager of the Boston *Journal,* had just taken hold of the Sunday edition, and he was open to new ideas. He also had some of his own. And so, late in July, Editor Wingate wheeled up his heavy guns and fired a double-truck barrage that startled the natives as they hadn't been startled since Paul Revere rode through Middlesex.

A man, a naked man, a man used to all the comforts of civilization, was about to plunge into the Maine wilderness to learn whether the human race had become so sissified that it could no longer combat the rigors and dangers which beset Primitive Man. It was a highly dangerous test, the *Post* took pains to point out, for fierce animals stalked silently through the forest lanes, and there was ever the specter of starvation.

But Joe Knowles was a fine physical specimen. Harvard College said so. Called in by the *Post,* Dr. Dudley Allen Sargent, physical director of the university, looked Joe over carefully and told the world:

> Sandow was perfect in strength and development.
> Knowles is perfect in strength and development. Further,
> Knowles has probably the staying power of three
> Sandows.

Now all was in readiness for the great test. The *Post* thoughtfully invited newspapers of other cities to the remote point in Maine where the Nature Man was to take off. The New York *Sun* thought well enough of the story to send its ace feature writer, Frank Ward O'Malley; and there were a score of lesser lights from various dailies. On August 4, 1913, Joe bid them all goodby and walked into the silence of the Dead River country, attired only in a breechclout.

For the next sixty-one days, New England, New York, and other parts of the country served by the *Post's* special syndication, were agog at the swellest feature story in a generation. It was Steve Brodie, Nellie Bly, and Stanley-and-Livingstone all rolled into one great juicy series. The reporters wrote their heads off, and every day or so they would come across a birchbark message, left in a forked sapling by the Nature Man; Joe had been living on roots and berries—he had caught and cooked some fine trout—he had made rude sandals of bark—he was digging a pit in which to catch a bear—he had caught a bear and was enjoying bear steak—he had got some hemlock bark and was tanning the bear's skin—he would soon have a robe— he had caught a deer with his hands, and he was now wearing hide moccasins.

At this, the game wardens of towns round about let out a howl. It was agin' the law to kill deer out of season, gun or no gun, and they were a-goin' to take this crazy man into custody. The wardens hoisted their badges and rifles and struck into the woods to arrest the Nature Man—and newspaper circulation soared again. Tipped off about the wardens by his contact man, Joe headed northward and crossed the Canadian border late in September.

The Canucks left him alone. Free once more from the harassments of civilization, Joe turned out some neat sketches in charcoal which the *Post* reproduced for a public that couldn't get enough of its Nature Man. Circulation had jumped by now to 400,000 copies, or about double the normal figure.

The nights were getting chilly up in Quebec, Joe reported via birchbark, but he was sleeping warm in his bearskin robe. Time was beginning to hang heavy on his hands, too, for reporters came across a painting—not a sketch—that Joe had made, using the juice of roots and berries for his colors and a well-chewed twig for a brush. Of course, there weren't messages from him every day, but his terse dispatches were so expertly timed and spaced that they kept the newspaper reading public on edge. The *Post*'s circulation mounted to 436,585, and there must have been a deal of groaning over in the offices of the Boston *American.*

III

On October 10, Joe emerged from the woods at Megantic, Quebec. He was the picture of health, rugged, tanned, and bearded; and he was met, you may be sure, by a small army of newspapermen, both Canadian and American. Even a movie outfit was present.

"My only regret at the time," Joe recalled in telling of it, "is that I didn't manage to catch a cub bear alive. I thought it would be a fine idea to come out of the woods leading a small and tamed bear behind me on a leash of willow."

Escorted to Boston on a special train, Joe was distinctly the man of the hour. Big shots of Boston flocked to the Copley-Plaza for a banquet tendered the Nature Man. Newsreel men dogged his steps, while low comedians at the Old Howard staged a Kno Jowles burlesque. Vaudeville booking agents from New York fought to offer a contract, and a janitor swept out Tremont Temple for Joe's first lecture before highbrows. But now, amidst the big whoopee, crept in that sour and envious note that so often attends success in any form. The *American* told its readers that on the morrow it would bring forth a "complete exposé" of the Nature Man. Its announcement hinted at gigantic skulduggery on the part of Knowles and the *Post,* and it promised shocking revelations.

The *Post* had got wind of the coming blast even before it was announced. It also got a court injunction prohibiting the *American* from publishing a story which it held was a gross libel. Things happened rapidly in the *American* office, once the injunction was served. The story was already out, in the early bulldog edition, and men were sent forth to bring in all copies of this edition. The front page was broken up, the exposé story killed, and there was no mention of Joe in the regular city edition. That is, no mention except for a striking full-page advertisement announcing publication of "*Alone in the Wilderness,* by Joe Knowles, the Nature Man." It was neatly timed: the book sold more than 300,000 copies.

The *American* said nothing more about Knowles. It didn't even mention a suit for $50,000 which Joe had brought against the paper for printing the "slanderous story" in the early edition, copies of which had pretty well permeated New England outside of Boston. But, in any event, a magnificent controversy had been loosed. Was it true, as an investigating reporter of the *American* had averred, that the Nature Man had spent most of two months lolling around in a deserted but comfortable logging camp? Had Joe been living like a backwoods potentate, attended by innumerable stooges in the form of guides, hunters, and bull cooks? Was it so that no less than four small holes, suspiciously like bullet holes, had appeared in the bear robe? Had a leather expert of Boston vowed that the little deerskin had been tanned by a commercial process? And was young Billy Lavaway lying when he told a backcounty Maine paper that he had been sent out of the woods by Joe to get some cigarets; and that when the kid had returned with Piedmonts, Joe had angrily roared he had ordered Sweet Caps? Did the *American* in short, have it right when it termed Joe Knowles the "Doc Cook of the Maine Woods"?

Those were fighting words in those days, and Joe and the *Post* fought back. They fought with heavy ammunition in the shape of affidavits of Maine guides, opinions of nationally known naturalists, and of at least one United States senator. Joe took the platform in Boston's Tremont Temple and challenged his detractors to come forward. They came not, but the thing had become a *cause célèbre* and New England was in turmoil. It was great for circulation, too.

With the booming of charges and countercharges ringing in his ears, Joe took to the Keith Vaudeville Circuit for twenty weeks with 24-sheet billing and $1,200 a week.

IV

Knowles later declared that because of the "exposé" incident, seven employees of the *American* were fired. In any case, the hatchet was buried, for *Hearst's International,* a slick-paper monthly magazine, came out with an editorial, done in brisbanal style, paying high compliments to Joe:

We thank Knowles for his experiment. It is a noble piece
of poetry. A naked man against the tooth and claw of
Nature, and coming out victor—clothed, fed, healthy; it is
a deal more comforting to our proper human pride than
the erection of a Woolworth building.

Less than a year later, Joe took into the wild Siskiyous
for Hearst's *Examiner* of San Francisco, as related. Despite
the unseasonable breaking out of the World War, Mr. Hearst
had seen what a Nature Man could do for circulation, if but
given a chance. So he had Joe go to New York, and there, in
the summer of 1916, the *Journal* prepared to make up for
what its sister paper in Boston had muffed.

This time the stunt was to be—appropriately enough,
considering the sponsor—a double-barreled affair. There
would be a Dawn Man, *and* a Dawn Woman, both of them
naked and both of them out in the Great Silence, but *not*
together. (Remember, this was in 1916.) The general routine was to be about the same as that used by Joe in his
Maine and Oregon-California adventures. It was also announced that Knowles would give the Dawn Woman a week
of serious woodcraft instruction before she went out on her
own.

The Dawn Woman soon appeared, in the columns of
the palpitating *Journal,* in the form of Elaine Hammerstein,
said by the *Journal* to be "the beautiful society leader and
well-known actress." Joe, of course, knew he was to play
second fiddle in this experiment.

The country selected for the Dawn Woman's commune
with Nature was the timbered region near Old Forge, in
Essex County, New York, and the "special investigator" for
the newspaper was no less than the eminent Dr. Woods
Hutchinson. Joe took Elaine in tow (her mother was along
as chaperon) and for a week or so he gave her intensive
instruction in firemaking, weaving and fishing without
tackle; and he showed her edible herbs, roots and berries
native to the country. As Joe told it afterward, Elaine's

enthusiasm for a Dawn life seemed perceptibly to lessen day by day during the instruction period.

But Elaine told the reporters that she was Ready and would Conquer. Boozy cameramen shot the pretty girl in all sorts of semi-Dawn attire; and they also snapped Joe in all his Cro-Magnon nakedness.

And then, on a blistering Sunday, the *Journal* double-trucked a spread that would make editors of today's tabloids sit up in envy. KNOWLES HURLS DEFY AT GRIM NATURE, said one banner; while another, somewhat leeringly, told how DAWN GIRL SLIPS NAKED INTO DARK FOREST. Young men decided to take up woodcraft. Goatish old males simply drooled.

The Dawn Woman lasted long enough to send out a few pathetic notes on birchbark. "Tango teas, Broadway, and matinees are a far cry from the absolute silence of the great woods," she wrote. At the end of seven days she came out of the absolute silence, and undoubtedly returned to her swell Riverside Drive home of which the reporters had made so much. "She just couldn't take it," was Joe's only comment.

With the Dawn Woman back in her sissy boudoir, there wasn't any use sticking around, so Joe came out of the woods himself and put on his pants.

V

For twenty years Joe Knowles made his home at Seaview on a remote shore of the Washington coast.* The wild Pacific breakers pounded his dooryard and high tides surrounded his studio, where he painted and did etchings. At the age of sixty-nine he was hearty and jovial. He held no animosity toward those who sought to "expose" him,

---

*Joe died there October 21, 1942, in the strange house he had put together, at odd times over two decades, of the flotsam of and from wrecked ships. Outside the gate, the last time I was there, still hung the sign, "Stranger, Pause a While, Joe Knowles."

not even the guy who called him the "Doc Cook of the Maine Woods." But he made it emphatically clear that he would not answer letters or other queries about his Back-to-Nature experiments.

"I'm still sorry I didn't manage to catch a bear cub, up there in Maine," he said wistfully. "It would have been a knockout—parading out of that timber a-leading a bear like a Scottie. It's just about the only regret I have . . . . That and that goddam war breaking out when it did."

The American Mercury (1936)

For Joe Knowles's later life in Seaview, Washington, see "Joseph Knowles, The Story of the Hotel Monticello Murals," *Cowlitz Historical Quarterly*, Vol. 33 No. 4 (1991).

The Wobblies Come

The shadow of whiskered old Karl Marx did not fall athwart the lumber industry until late in 1905. On the evening of December 30 that year, snow covered the ground of southern Idaho. The village of Caldwell lay under a blanket of it, marking the steps of Frank Steunenberg, ex-governor of the state, as he made his way homeward the short distance from his law office in the town.

There was a picket fence around the house. Steunenberg opened the gate, passed through, and turned to close it. At that instant a terrific explosion shattered the quiet dark of the night, and the former governor of Idaho lay dead on the reddening snow.

So great had been the explosive charge, whatever it was, that the blast was heard by farmers ten miles outside town and the windows on the front of the Steunenberg home were blown into jagged bits of glass that were found protruding from interior walls.

The blast was to have other reverberations. It brought into the national spotlight a young Idaho attorney, the present Senator William E. Borah. It brought fame to Clarence Darrow. And it produced a new antichrist in the hulking form of William Dudley (Big Bill) Haywood, ebullient genius of the brand-new Industrial Workers of the World—the Wobblies—soon to be much feared and hated and loved in the lumber industry and elsewhere.

Almost a year previous to the Steunenberg murder the I. W. W. had been organized in Chicago, and Haywood elected general secretary. "Fellow workers," Big Bill had roared at the first meeting of the order, "the aims and objects of this organization shall be to put the working class in possession of the economic power, the means of life, in control of the machinery of production and distribution, without regard to capitalist masters." There had been no loggers at this first meeting, but there would be plenty at others, and the Wobblies were to raise more hell in the timber than booze, hurricanes, forest fires, and Acts of Congress.

Where the Wobblies were, there was always turmoil and alarums, and in Big Bill Haywood they had an able leader. He was well over six feet tall, every line in his body proclaiming the strength of an ox. He could roar louder than any of them, he loved the smell of frying capitalists, and he was as clever a publicist as Barnum. Moreover, he was a first-class organizer.

Following close on the murder of Steunenberg, Idaho police arrested one Harry Orchard on suspicion. In jail at Caldwell he denied any knowledge of the set bomb hitched to the Steunenberg gate. Moved to the Boise jail Orchard had a long interview with James McParland, the Pinkerton sleuth who had run down the Molly Maguire terrorists back in Pennsylvania of the seventies. To McParland Orchard confessed a series of bombings and shootings that covered several years and numbered at least thirty victims. In his confession Orchard specifically charged three men with paying him for the "jobs," including the murder of Steunenberg. They were Charles Moyer, president of the Western Federation of Miners; George A. Pettibone, who seems to have been a sort of unofficial big shot in the union; and William D. Haywood, general organizer of the Miners' Union and head of the new Wobblies.

Kidnapped in Colorado and brought to Idaho without authority, Moyer, Pettibone, and Haywood were charged with the murder of Steunenberg. The reason implied for the murder was that the miners "had it in" for Steunenberg because of the manner in which he acted in a miners' strike in the Coeur d'Alenes, years before.

Haywood and Pettibone were tried and found not guilty. The charges against Moyer were dropped. Orchard was sentenced to imprisonment for life in the Idaho penitentiary.

The trial of Haywood became a national *cause célèbre.* Even before the case came to trial it had created wide interest and more bitter feeling than anything since the Haymarket affair in the eighties. There was no sitting on the fence. Either you were for Haywood and the others, or you were against them. The President of the United States, even, wasn't immune to the hysteria. In a letter that was made public Theodore Roosevelt wrote that whether or not the three men were guilty, they were "undesirable citizens."

This letter made a terrible noise. Writing in his paper, *The Appeal to Reason,* Eugene Debs, then a big figure in the land, made a vitriolic attack on Roosevelt. Loggers in Northwest camps went to work wearing buttons on which was printed "I am an Undesirable Citizen." Labor unions staged monster parades in protest. The letters "I. W. W." went into newspaper headlines, and by July 28, 1907, when he was found not guilty, Big Bill Haywood was more of a national character than the brilliant prosecutor, Mr. Borah, or the brilliant and sardonic counsel for defense, Mr. Darrow. The Wobblies were off to a good start.

Even before Big Bill's acquittal, Wobbly halls were opening in Portland, Seattle, Tacoma, and Spokane, and loggers and sawmill workers were the object of a big organization drive. The fir and pine forests fairly swarmed with lads who were "packing the rigging" in the form of Red Cards and other I. W. W. supplies and propaganda booklets. In March of 1907, when Haywood's trial was in full swing, they felt they were strong enough to challenge the timber barons.

They struck first in Portland, where all except one of an even dozen large sawmills were forced to close. It was scandalous, an unheard-of thing in the lumber industry of the Pacific Northwest; and retaliation was prompt. Police arrested scores of Wobs and clapped them into jail on charges ranging from disorderly conduct to attempted arson. The strike was soon broken, but lumbermen were jittery at this first attempt to organize their notoriously unorganized employees.

The Portland strike was a mild enough beginning. Over in Spokane presently occurred the first of a long series of "free-speech" battles staged by the Wobblies. When a police magistrate forbade them to soapbox on street corners, there deluged on unhappy Spokane a thousand or more wild and footloose "Rebels," attracted by black headlines in the Wobbly press proclaiming SPOKANE TOWN CLOWNS STOP WOB SPEAKERS.

Among the converging radicals was a woman. She was Elizabeth Gurley Flynn, young, handsome—with a Western hat turned up in front, and a flaming red tie around her pretty throat—and she was a hellion that breathed reddish flame; fairly sober reporters affirmed that a flash from the girl's blue-gray eyes would serve to light a Sweet Caporal.

The Flynn promptly entered the fight, shouting on a Trent Avenue corner for the workers to rise up, shake off their chains, and do battle for free speech. In what must have been an unreflective moment, the idiotic police arrested the beauteous firebrand and threw her into jail. TOOLS OF TIMBER BARONS JAIL REBEL GIRL howled the Wobbly press in studhorse headlines that even illiterates found inflaming.

Now it seemed—and they still remember it in Spokane—that every hobo West of the Mississippi had come to town to protest against this inhuman treatment of Beauty and Womanhood. They marched the streets, taking over whole blocks, and they sang rude songs. Logging crews of pine camps deserted in a body to go to Spokane where their calked boots pitted the soft asphalt and their nightly howls frightened little children and all capitalists. The city jail was overflowing for weeks. Citizens who were taxpayers began protesting against this feeding of hordes of itinerants out of the public funds.

The ganging-up was too much for Spokane. All prisoners were released, and henceforth, as the Wob press gloated, Spokane was safe for I. W. W. street speakers. Gurley Flynn returned East to start the Lawrence, Massachusetts, "revolution," and to cause employers in Paterson, New Jersey, to lie awake nights.

The Wobs were now on the upswing. For the next decade they kept the lumber industry of the Northwest in a state bordering on insanity. Indeed, even now when violence on the labor front is common, white hairs curl and blood is pumped faster through the hardening arteries of members of conservative clubs in Portland, Seattle, and Spokane, when by chance some younger member asks who was this Bill Haywood, anyway, who wrote a book and died in Russia.

Outstanding characteristic of the I. W. W. was the amazing rapidity with which they got around the country. When iron miners on the Mesaba Range went on strike, Wobbly loggers of Oregon flooded Minnesota. Dirt movers of Montana construction camps appeared as by magic on the picket lines around California hop fields. In 1908 when Wobbly ranks were torn by factions warring over dogma, what was known as the "overall brigade" and was composed chiefly of loggers, jumped freights heading East out of Seattle and Portland, and captured and dominated the I. W. W. convention in Chicago that year. The overall boys voted, and their vote became a part of the organization's policy, that Wobblies should pay no attention to political activity, which was a snare and a delusion; they should concentrate on bringing the Revolution by means of strikes, sabotage, and the eventual taking over of the sources of production by the workers—who, of course, would all be good Wobs.

The results of the 1908 convention were soon apparent. Strikes broke out suddenly in all sawmilling and logging centers. They were sporadic, never lasted long, and were accompanied by riots, sabotage, and other violence.

A celebrated Wobbly affair was the "Everett Massacre." Denied the exercise of free speech in the big sawmill city of Everett, Washington, the Wobblies on the afternoon of Sunday, November 5, 1916, chartered a steamer, packed her with approximately four hundred determined members, and left Seattle harbor. Two hours later, as the ill-fated *S. S.*

Verona nosed the Everett dock, shooting began, and when the smoke had cleared seven men were dead and sixty-eight lay wounded. The affair created a lengthy trial, in which nobody was found guilty of anything, and was chronicled in a Wobbly book. At least two Wobbly songs were written about it.

Wobbly leaders used the riot at Everett for organizing purposes, and when, a few months later the World War came to America, they were ready.

In 1917 the I. W. W. staged the greatest strike the lumber industry has known anywhere. Eighty-five per cent of camps and sawmills went out of production. Spikes allegedly appeared in logs at mills that continued operations. Logging trains were derailed. Mysterious fires broke out in timber and mill. Stickers showing horribly grinning black cats—symbol of sabotage—were found glued to the windows of camp and sawmill offices. Boss loggers and mill operators became vexed, then worried. BIG BOSSES GET WOBBLY HORRORS said banner headlines in the I. W. W. press.

There were riots on the log drives of Idaho and eastern Washington, where river crews fought against Wob pickets. Tough mill foremen threw Wob organizers into mill log ponds. Even tougher camp foremen beat them up. Genuine Wobblies were gluttons for punishment; it took nerve to be one in 1917.

The United States Army wanted lumber in a hurry to build its cantonments and it wanted spruce for airplanes—but little lumber was being produced. The wheels had all but stopped.

The Wobs shouted back that *they* wanted an eight-hour day, better wages and working conditions, and white sheets on the bunks in logging camps.

Finally, the government intervened. It formed the Spruce Production Division to log and mill timber. It formed the Loyal Legion of Loggers and Lumbermen, the 4L, of civilian and army employees and employers, and forced boss loggers and lumbermen to grant the shorter workday. Upon this, the I. W. W. voted to "return the strike to the job." That is, to return to work but to continue tactics of slowing work, and other sabotage. Wobbly stickers now showed a big clock on whose hands hung a pair of wooden shoes—sabots— and the admonition "Time to Slow Down."

But the government and the 4L prevailed, and the Wobs went into hiding or into jail for the duration of the war. Bill Haywood fled to Russia, not to return, and Leavenworth prison was filled with Wobbly leaders, many of them to remain until pardoned in 1923 by President Harding.

Once the war was over, the I. W. W. again came into the limelight, this time as the motive power behind the Seattle general strike in 1919. The various services of the city ceased to function, while armored cars patrolled the streets. Fighting broke out in the shipyards, along streetcar lines, and around the yards of local sawmills, and finally grew into the somewhat preposterous "Ole Hanson Revolution," so called from the mayor's name. It was broken with no serious bloodshed.

But the Wobblies were to appear once more in a most dramatic scene. On November 11, 1919, in small Centralia, Washington, the American Legion held a parade. When directly in front of the Centralia I. W. W. hall, the local contingent of the marching Legionnaires halted. Whether by design or because of a gap in the marchers and an effort to close ranks, will never be proved. In any case, the Centralia Legion halted in front of the Wobbly hall. What happened in the next split second has been hopelessly in dispute for the past eighteen years.

What is assuredly and horribly known is that shouts and cries and the dry, sinister crackle of gunfire broke out almost simultaneously, and that parade watchers saw three Legionnaires go down in welters of blood. Then, there was a rush on the I. W. W. hall, and Wesley Everest, Wobbly, went out the rear door, firing as he ran. Chased to the brink of a near-by river, the Wob turned and shot his nearest pursuer dead.

Wesley Everest was taken and put in the city jail, and early that grim evening every light in Centralia flicked out without warning. A group of men moved into the jail, took Everest, and departed. The city lights glowed again. Next morning Everest's bullet-riddled body was found hanging from a near-by bridge.

Whether the Legionnaires had planned to raid the I. W. W. hall, as defense attorneys claimed, or whether, as prosecution held, the Wobblies had committed downright murder, has been discussed in print thousands of times and is the "Tom Mooney Case" of the Northwest. Four Legionnaires were dead, anyway, and so was one Wobbly. Eight I. W. W. members were sent to prison for varying sentences. The affair was the beginning of the end of the Wobblies as a power, and a terror, in the timber of the Northwest.

The Wobbly press was as colorful and as noisy as its membership. Its editors never troubled themselves about facts, just so long as a news story was loaded in every paragraph with dynamite against the Ruling Classes. They were paid four dollars a day, in good times, and served but six months at a stretch. Most of them took a leaf from the book of Hearst and kept a rousing good "menace" on tap at all times. If no Wobbly hall had been wrecked for a fortnight, or no Wob organizer beaten up by police, the editor would hitch up his galluses and come out with a stirring piece scare-headed TIMBER BARONS HIRE JESUS-BILLY TO QUIET SLAVES, the "Jesus-Billy" being the late Reverend Billy Sunday, considered by many operators a good sedative for employees who had begun to grumble about the wages.

A nice thing about working on a Wobbly paper was that it was no more confined to English than is the theatrical weekly *Variety* today. The Wobs had a lingo all their own. To start with, there is the word *Wobbly* itself. Its origin is somewhat hazy. Many Wob neologists say it was conceived unconsciously by a Chinaman, a member, whose heathen tongue was not equal to the letter "w." When the Chinese wanted to tell the boys that he was a good I. W. W. man, the best he could do was "Me likee Eye Wobbly Wobbly." It proved enough.

Wobbly spread from man to man, as such things will, and by mysterious, unseen jungle-news channels, from camp to camp, until it was picked up by the Wobbly press and later became a part of everyday speech in all Western states, Wob and layman alike.

And Wobbly editors were quick to appreciate other terms used by the boys out at the "points of production." A worker who was not filled with revolutionary spirit was labeled a *scissorbill.* The Wobs wanted logging concerns to furnish employees with blankets and sheets, so the ancient practice of carrying one's own blankets from camp to camp was made ludicrous by *carrying a balloon,* with appropriate front-page cartoons. A *sab cat*—from *sabotage*—might be merely an organizer or he might be one well versed in the safest methods of wrecking machinery. A *hoosier* was a working stiff who didn't know his job; to *hoosier up* was to slow work purposely. *Pie in the sky* was a cynical reference to the bourgeois heaven. *Gyppo* was any sort of work done by contract and was much frowned upon. A town policeman was a *clown.* The prosecuting attorney was the *cutor.* The Wob press used *hijack*—"Hi, jack!" a command to throw up the arms—long before it came into general usage. A *red card* was evidence of membership. A detective, company guard, or stool pigeon was a *fink,* by all odds the dirtiest word in the Wobbly thesaurus. There were many others, fully as pointed and all of them founded on sound etymological grounds and most of them containing humor.

Reading an I. W. W. newspaper in the heyday of the order was an exciting and an interesting experience. Its star columnist was one T-Bone Slim, who liked to razz a great colleague in the pay of Hearst and referred to his stuff as *brisbanalities.* Slim rode the rods all over western Canada and United States and took time out to write a blistering column every week.

And many of the footloose correspondents were good reporters. Consider this from *The Industrial Worker,* printed in 1923 under the heading of "Job News":

> Aberdeen, Wash.—Coates-Fordney Camp—High-lead lay-out; two sides, rig-up crew and steel gang. Wages: gandy dancers, $3.75; rigging, $4.25 to $6.50. Garbage, $1.45 per day. Mattress furnished, but carry your own balloon. Slaves dissatisfied with conditions, but talk nothing but dehorn and world's series. Two of us Fellow Workers just started to line up a few of the boys when the push hit us on the behind with paychecks. He has the Wobbly horrors bad. Fellow Workers coming this way should lay off the bull-bucker here. He is a fink. Pretends to favor the One Big Union but when you ask him to stamp-up, he turns you in.

That would be good clear reporting on any man's newspaper.

From its membership peak of around one hundred thousand in the 1917 period, the I. W. W. has faded to a mere shadow. There are probably not five hundred of them in the Northwest woods, and probably not five thousand of them in the United States. What caused their decline and fall is something that is occasionally argued around bunk-house stoves by a few old-timers who don't care for the C. I. O., the A. F. of L., or the Communist Party. It would appear there were several reasons.

First were the big federal raids on Wobbly halls in 1917 and the arrests, convictions, and incarceration of members. These discouraged all but the most stout-hearted. The Centralia affair, referred to, made several Wobbly martyrs but brought a loss rather than gain in membership. Then, in 1924, came a serious split in the very ranks of I. W. W. officials. They first resorted to slugging each other for possession of I. W. W. General Headquarters in Chicago. The strife was finally taken into the courts—capitalist courts—for injunctions and other mumbo-jumbo of the Ruling Class with which old-time Wobs would have no truck whatsoever. The result of this split was two distinct groups, each claiming to be the original, blown-in-the-bottle I. W. W. Chicago, New York, San Francisco, Portland, Seattle, and Spokane each had two halls carrying the I. W. W. trademark. Two papers appeared with I. W. W. on their mastheads. It was all very demoralizing. They called each other bad names in their schismatic newspapers, and organizers were embarrassed when they approached workers, for the purpose of collecting dues, to find that a delegate of the "other" I. W. W. had been there first. The effect on simple, dues-paying members can readily be imagined.

Moreover, the Communists—"comicals" to the Wobblies—bagged a number of Wobbly editors and speakers. The Communists also continue to promise a lot more to the downtrodden than the Wobs ever did. Although the Wobblies still spend as much or more effort in fighting the Communists, the C. I. O., and the A. F. of L. than they do in reducing capitalism to pulp, their ranks have been greatly thinned by desertions to Browder, Lewis, and Green.

The two Wobbly newspapers that survive in 1938 seem mild, genteel, and even reactionary when compared to the screaming headlines in red and black ink which, as late as ten years ago, called upon the slaves to arise, unite, and shake off their chains in six different languages. There is little in them to pack a Spokane full of bellowing pickets or to cause a Judge Gary to toss fitfully in his sleep.

During the summer of 1936 the Wobblies stirred in the logging camps of North Idaho, but they stirred feebly and to small purpose. Only one man was killed in the rioting, and the principal result of the whole upheaval was to halt work, for a few days, on the filming of a log-driving scene in what Hollywood has since announced is "an Epic of the Big Timber."

Holy Old Mackinaw (1938)

The Great Tillamook Fire

It started a little after one o'clock on the hot and dry afternoon of August 14, 1933. Up to that hour the lookout forester perched on top of Saddle Mountain in western Oregon looked down on a world as handsome as man ever saw. Below him there were thousands upon thousands of acres of trees, taller than masts, greener than the sea, thick, straight, and old with the centuries—the fir named for David Douglas.

He loved this world beneath him, did the lookout, and guarded it with all of his faculties of sight, sound and smell. On this particular afternoon he was unusually alert, for the weather was bad. He scanned the hills, the valleys and the flats with a keen eye, looking for only one thing; and at a quarter past one on this August day he saw it. At that moment, as his eyes swept a wide arc to the north, a billow of white smoke came rolling up out of Gales Creek Canyon. He sighted along his fire finder a moment to make certain of the location, then picked up the telephone at his elbow and called his warden at Forest Grove, reporting in his usual laconic way and in the proper manner for lookouts, the section, township and range of what he said looked to be quite a smoke.

That was how fast word of what was to be Oregon's greatest forest fire, indeed the greatest forest fire North America has ever known, came out of the woods. A moment before the lookout got on the phone, a logger on a crew working deep in Gales Creek Canyon had watched while a length of wire rope used in yarding timber sawed across a wind-felled tree. An instant later a thin puff of smoke curled up. In another instant it was white still, but not so thin, and the watching logger shouted. "Fire!" he cried. Fire it was, fire to burn up four centuries of trees, fire to remove an immense natural resource from the face of northwestern Oregon.

That was how it began, and this tiny beginning, so uncalled for that the gods must have wept, was what the Pacific Northwest will remember for many a year as the Tillamook Fire. There have been forest fires more deadly to man than this one, but never one so deadly to trees, nor yet one so certain to be remembered so long.

Hundreds of men fought valiantly all night on that August 14, and for all the good they did they might as well have remained in their camps. The fire leaped into the tops of the trees and swept on with fearful speed, making its own wind as it went. Those great trees, many of them 300 feet high, burned like tremendous torches. I saw one great body of Douglas firs, each nearly 500 years old, burn savagely like so many huge columns of fat, spitting, crackling, then roaring like flame under a bellows.

Smoke rolled and billowed above the flames. It formed, for two days, a pillar and mushroom that stood clear and white and terrible five thousand feet above the forest. Presently ashes were drifting through the screens of the windows in Portland homes, fifty miles away. The wind over the fire rose at last to a hurricane and the noise was greater than the sea pounding the Oregon shore. It rumbled and thundered and was marked by the deep booming of ancient trees uprooted by the gale and crashing down.

Five hundred more men, then a thousand more, then two thousand were hurried to the lines that now formed a front along a hundred miles, and mariners far at sea saw dead embers fall on the decks of their ships, while the tides piled debris two feet deep along the Oregon beaches. Tillamook County, Oregon's great timbered pride, was going up in flame and smoke. I saw it burn and I never expect to see another sight like it.

Logging camps and the homes of stump ranches went up. Time after time, when the great blaze suddenly lashed out at the fire fighters like an angry snake, the crews had to turn and flee for their lives, leaving their trucks and bull-dozers and pumps and hose and axes and shovels to burn on the spot.

Throughout the region deer in small herds and alone, frantic and confused, moved westward ahead of the flames, but many were caught and killed in their tracks. Cougars, the great cats of the woods, ranged with fear and uncertainty through the heavy smoke, coughing like humans and paying no heed to humans or deer. In a hundred streams, till then cool and clear, pools were soon white with the bellies of trout, dead from charcoal stomachs. (Fish leap at bits of charcoal, thinking them flies, and die from their lunch.) One could only guess, by the pitiful balls of naked flesh found after the fire had passed over, how the myriads of grouse and pheasants had fared.

A sudden shift of the wind, on the tenth day of the conflagration, brought immediate danger to Camp McGregor, logging headquarters of the Oregon-American Lumber Company. An hour later the main body of the fire was only half a mile from the camp, and spot fires were springing up within a few yards of the buildings. Men fought these near fires, a rear-guard action, while wives and children were loaded aboard a logging train. The train pulled out just as the camp itself started to burn fiercely. It pounded down the mountain, rocked around curves and crossed dizzily high trestles that were beginning to smoulder, while back on the mountain the camp was going up in smoke.

The little hamlet of Elsie, set almost in the middle of this gigantic destruction, was soon surrounded by the fire, and for twenty-four hours it was believed that Elsie and all it contained had been wiped away. But through some quirk in the wind, Elsie survived. Not so another hamlet, Lukarilla. Settlers watched while Lukarilla, with its homes and barns and fences and one store, disappeared entirely. Strangely enough there was no loss of life here. Only one person died in all the fire, Frank Palmer, a CCC boy from Illinois, who was killed instantly when a big fir, uprooted by the wind, crushed him to earth.

The blaze burned itself out on August 24, after a fog blanket drifted in from the coast to smother it. In ten days it had killed twelve and one-half billion feet of fine timber. It burned over some 310,000 acres. How can one described twelve and one-half billion feet of timber? There is no use piling it up, in Sunday-supplement style beside the Empire State Building, which it would put in shadow many times over. But perhaps it will mean something to know that during the year 1932, twelve and one-half billion feet of logs was enough to supply the needs of all the sawmills, lath mills, shingle mills and pulpwood mills in the forty-eight states.

II

Desolation is the word to fit the scene in Tillamook County following the fire—the Tillamook Burn, as it is called, covers an area half as large as Rhode Island. No man who has stumbled through the thick ashes and over the blackened windfalls will forget it; the stark silhouettes of trees; the stumps and snags like sable tombstones; the acres as far as the eye can reach, all barren; the desolate silence, as though a cosmic hush has fallen over the stricken forest.

This terrible quiet, as though all nature were brooding over the tragedy, will induce a mood hard for a man to shake off, especially so for a man who loves the forest, because he knows very well that a forest in its natural state is never quiet, never completely hushed. In summer the noises, though often muted, are obvious to the ear—the noises of countless beasts and birds going about their daily or nightly work of making a living. In winter, winds and frost add their bit of noise to that of the fauna still active, such as the squeak of a wood mouse under the snow or the soft *whissh* of a hunting owl.

That is why the utter silence of a burned forest fastens melancholy on a man—he knows that nothing lives in this stark area, no tree, no beast, no bird, and often no fish. Gibbon sat amid the ruins of Rome and pondered the decline and fall of an entire civilization. Many a woodsman has sat on a blackened stump and pondered the destruction of an empire of forest with all it contained, wondering how many of its denizens escaped, how many tragedies of nest and burrow occurred. Were the young grouse able to follow their frantic mother out of the strange danger? Did some doe warn its mottled fawn in time—and did they run in the right direction? Did any fire department of the woods run a ladder up to the fourteenth story of an old snag where some flickers were nesting? And what happened to the sly, lone fox, a-mousing in the swamp, when suddenly he found fire on all sides?

III

Man was responsible for this devastation of an empire of timber. And promptly man set out to salvage what he could. Before the 1933 blaze had ceased to smolder, timber owners had formed a cooperative logging concern, and in the next dozen years had salvaged about one-third of the killed timber.

It is perhaps necessary to explain that fire does not burn up completely such gigantic trees as those in the Tillamook forest; what it does is kill them, whereupon hordes of parasites immediately set to work to eat up or rot the dead but still standing timber.

During the dozen years when salvage operations were going forward, nature was also taking a hand, trying to rectify the damage. The seed sources were many and they proved wonderfully fruitful; new growth sprang up and started to cover the ghastly scars, clothing the hills and valleys with new green. By the middle of 1945 on many thousands of acres there was timber, new timber, as tall as a small house.

I went over much of the Burn early in 1945 and was cheered by what I saw. The forest already was tall and thick enough for a man to get lost in. Birds had returned to the area. So had animals, and the elk and deer were numerous.

Again the streams were clear and cold. Many trout leaped in them. Indeed, all was going well until a year ago, in 1945.

What happened then compounded tragedy on tragedy, and a part of this new disaster probably stemmed from the war in the Pacific. This was the manner of its coming:

Early in the morning of July 9, 1945, a watchman on the Salmonberry River, in Tillamook County, roused to find the canyon beneath his station filled with smoke. The sight gave him the creeps, and with good reason, for forest fires do not ordinarily start at such an hour, when humidity is high and the dew is heavy on trees and underbrush. The smoke appeared to have its source in an almost inaccessible spot, a high bluff across the canyon. Many woodsmen thought then, and still think, that this fire was touched off by one of the Japanese incendiary balloons which had been falling in the Pacific Northwest since late in 1944.

In any case it was fire. The weather was ripe; humidity quickly fell as a wind like the breath of an open-hearth furnace swept down the Columbia River gorge and so on into Tillamook County. Inside of two hours a great pillar of smoke, something like the one that rose here in 1933, had risen about four thousand feet. I stood on a ridge twenty miles away that afternoon and watched the cloud grow dreadfully fast. That night the whole horizon had a fitful red base.

The fire burned on. Two days later, as if planned by some horrible and efficient coordinator of forest fires, a second blaze broke out in Tillamook County, this time at Wilson River. This one was not set by an incendiary balloon from across the Pacific but (probably) by the cigarette of an employee of a logging concern. Twelve hundred men went to fight both fires. Their efforts, like those of twelve years before, were as nothing. The Salmonberry blaze and the one at Wilson River grew swiftly, and then, merging blew up into one great holocaust.

It was 1933 all over again, only this time it was for the most part a new forest that was being destroyed; and this time it burned longer, for no heavy fog blanket came in from the coast to stop it. The second Tillamook fire roared on through July, August, September and into October, covering an area of more than 150,000 acres, nearly all of it burned once before.

What makes the Tillamook Burn so deeply tragic is that so much of the area has undergone fire at least twice. A once-burned forest will recover, for seed sources are left from the older trees. But there is no hope for a forest burned a second time as thoroughly as this one was. The second time the flames took everything, including such seeds as were stored in the forest floor, and virtually all of the trees from which seeds might be expected to blow on the devastated acres. Unless man were to take hold in a big way, nothing but weeds would grow here and even weeds would have a hard time of it in the burned-out soil.

It is fortunate that Oregon has for its state forester a man who grew up in the Tillamook woods, a man who is more often in the woods than in his office. Nelson Rogers is now facing the most gigantic job of reforestation any man has ever faced, for this vast and desolate region must be planted by hand, either with seeds or with young trees, or with both. Rogers is equal to the task, and long since he has had his young men at work, planting thousands of seedlings every day, making firebreaks and roads for protection and telling the state of Oregon he must have $750,000 a year for the next six years if the job is really to get going as it should. His young men have invented two new tools that will speed the planting fivefold, and his entire department, loathing the Tillamook Burn as only foresters can, is working enthusiastically.

But it will be many years before the Tillamook Burn will be anything more than a horrible example of what forest fires can do.

The American Mercury (1946)

Saloon in the Timber

The most interesting place I ever drank hard liquor in was Big Fred Hewlett's Humboldt Saloon, back in the very tall timber of Western Washington. There were bigger saloons than the Humboldt and many that boasted more brass and mirrors, but not one of them had the Humboldt's flavor. It was unique, and so was Big Fred Hewlett.

Big Fred was a State-of-Mainer. He came to Aberdeen, in the Grays Harbor country on the Washington coast, in the late nineties. He looked the situation over and decided that the hustling raw village was destined to become another Bangor or Saginaw, two of the most famous lumberjack towns on earth. He was correct. Within a few years Aberdeen, and nearby Hoquiam, were cutting a billion feet of lumber every year.

Holbrook with Big Fred Hewlett in 1941

A billion feet of lumber calls for an ungodly lot of logging, and an army of loggers. Big Fred, as they say, drove his stakes, and his stakes comprised the Humboldt Saloon, which he built in that part of town lumberjacks designate as the skidroad. By the turn of the century the Humboldt was well established as headquarters for the fifteen thousand wild jacks who were cutting the cloud-crashing Douglas fir and bringing it down to Aberdeen's sawmills. It continued to be a loggers' Mecca until 1920 and Prohibition. I will come to its subsequent history a little later on.

When the Humboldt was opened, Aberdeen fairly swarmed with cutthroats and harpies, bent on taking easy and lots of dough from the loggers on their periodic busts in town. If a cashladen lumberjack didn't "roll" easily, his body might be found in the Floater Fleet for which the murky waters of Grays Harbor soon became notorious. During a period of approximately twenty years, there just was not any law in Aberdeen to protect the lads who blew their rolls there.

In this den of skulduggery the Humboldt was uniquely honest. Big Fred had a rule that no woman, good or bad, was ever to cross the threshold. So far as is known, none ever did. Nor were any sort of fancy men, card sharps or hangers-on allowed in the place. And when you bought a drink of whiskey in the Humboldt you had no need to fear knockout drops. The whiskey, too, was whiskey, and not alcohol colored with tea and flavored with prune juice, which was the concoction commonly served to lumberjacks. Big Fred had his own brand, "Double Stamp" in strength as he called it, or 100 proof, and none other. On every bottle appeared a pleasing likeness of Fred, done in colors, and the same picture graced the cover of the Humboldt's boxes of cigars. Fred was a man who stood solidly behind his wares.

Big Fred's picture hardly did him justice; there wasn't room on a bottle or box for a real likeness. He stood about six feet two inches and is best described by saying he was a moose of a man and letting it go at that. His was a strong face, decorated with an elegant mustache of medium size, black as night. He wore good clothes of sober black broadcloth, a low collar with black string tie, and across his vest was strung a watch chain that was believed to weigh exactly eight ounces. He was a peaceful man, for the time and place, and never looked for trouble, but if he saw trouble coming, he met it head on.

In Aberdeen at the time was a heavyweight who had once stayed six rounds with John L. Sullivan, and he was something of a local terror. It was his custom to enter a saloon, start at the near end of the bar, and one-two, one-two—he'd knock down the drinkers, one after the other, before they knew what was going on.

Well, one day this plug-ugly reached the Humboldt. Big Fred had heard of him and was ready. As the bully came in, Fred stepped briskly around the end of the bar and came up close. "Listen, you big bum," he said quietly, sticking out his chin, "I'm the first man you knock down in here."

The big boy looked at him, apparently very surprised, but he didn't make a move. Fred went on: "Now, I'll tell you how it is in here. I don't mean to kill you but I'm planning on breaking your arm—maybe both of them. Understand?"

Fred made no move. Neither did the tough guy. The mug who had stayed six rounds with John L. Sullivan laughed nervously, then set up drinks for all hands, and departed.

"I'm glad he acted that way," said Fred. "I don't like no brawling in my museum."

Big Fred didn't like brawling and he didn't like dudes. A dude to Fred was possibly anybody who was not a logger, a sawmill stiff or a sailor, but a dude once got into the Humboldt.

"Bartender," the dude said to Fred, "mix me a Manhattan cocktail." He couldn't have done worse. In that time and place a man who would drink a cocktail was considered on a par with a cigaret smoker, which was to say, a degenerate.

Big Fred didn't bat an eye. "What kind did you say?" he inquired politely.

"Manhattan," said the dude.

Big Fred went to work. He bit off a chew of the plug he liked and reached for a bottle. Putting one of the Humboldt's generous beer mugs on the bar, he poured a good shot of whiskey into it. To this he added a slug of gin, another of rum, a dash of real brandy, of bitters, of aqua vit', and then filled the remainder of the mug with beer. Placing this dose in front of the dude, accommodating Fred stirred it slowly with a huge forefinger.

"There, mister," he said obligingly, "is your Manhattan cocktail."

The astounded city slicker protested. "That isn't a cocktail," he began. "It's a mess of . . ."

"Drink 'er down," growled Fred, whose growl was like that of a Kodiak bear, just waking up and ornery. The dude drank to the bottom of the mug and went away.

It was one of the little things that made Fred popular.

But it was Big Fred's reputation for square shooting that got the boys coming and held them. Loggers who wouldn't think of entrusting their money to a savings bank flocked into Fred's, cashed their checks, kept what they thought they needed for the night, and turned from fifty to a thousand dollars over to Fred for safekeeping. Fred put each roll into an envelope, marked the logger's name on it, and placed it in his big safe, which had a nice oil painting of Niagara Falls on its doors.

It was common, in season, for this safe to contain as much as twenty thousand dollars, all of it the property of lumberjacks who didn't want to be rolled by the horde of pimps and bawds who infested Aberdeen. Moreover, if one of the boys returned to the Humboldt too plastered to know what he was doing, Big Fred would never allow him to draw more than five dollars. "Come back tomorrow," he'd tell the souse.

Year after year better than $600,000 in loggers' checks was cashed in the Humboldt. There is no record or rumor of a man claiming to have been shortchanged. When a man returned to the woods, he took a free bottle of liquor with him, to aid the sobering-up process. Once a week Big Fred made a visit to the Aberdeen hospital, leaving cigars—but never cigarets—to loggers who had been in woods accidents or had been beaten up in fights. It all paid dividends.

Big Fred and the Humboldt were different in other ways, too. Fred didn't go in for art. He wasn't an art lover and no fat nudes in gilt frames hung on his walls. Fred was a notable patron of the sciences, though. I spent many a happy, and fairly sober, hour in the Humboldt. Some of the boys called it the Congress of Curiosities. I liked to think of it as the Hewlettonian Institution and once told Fred so. He was immensely pleased.

In glass cases along one wall was a respectable collection of minerals from all parts of the world, labeled and classified. These specimens had come in one at a time from fellows Big Fred knew. Fred probably didn't know what "ethnology" meant but his place displayed the tribal garb, weapons and "medicine" of Indians from the Blackfeet to the Pueblo. A galaxy of ordnance included flintlocks, percussion locks, and pistols that had played parts in more or less celebrated murders and holdups. A meerschaum pipe was reputedly one that Cole Younger, the bandit, smoked to while away the long hours in the Minnesota State Prison. There was an Oregon Boot said to have been worn by Harry Tracy, Oregon's noted bad man.

Various freaks of nature were shown in bottles of alcohol. In a discreet corner was a certain part of a whale. Fred did not give this exhibit the prominence it deserved because he had become tired of hearing loggers make the same lewd or envious remarks about it. Stuffed cougars, mink, owls and snakes stared and glared at the customers. There were some pieces of huge bone, thought to have been those of a mammoth, that a lumberjack had come across in a bank of the Hoquiam River. Fred gave two quarts of his best liquor for them.

Another find was made one Sunday by two loggers returning to camp from town. Near a creek they noted a long mossy heap. It turned out to be an Indian dugout canoe. It had been there for a long time and eight inches of moss had grown over it. Nearby was the huge and ancient stump from which the dugout tree had been cut.

The two men went to Fred with the news. The stump was five hundred feet from a road. Fred gave the boys five gallons of liquor to swamp out a trail through the brush and to cut an eighteen-inch section from the stump. The markings on it looked to be those of a stone ax. Fred sent a generous slice of the stump to the Smithsonian Institution in Washington, D.C., to learn if possible what sort of a tool had been used in felling the tree, and when. The Institution could only reply that the felling had been done before 1792, when the first metal axes were brought to the Pacific Coast. Until the Humboldt's end, the stump, with the Institution's letter tacked to it, was a prized exhibit in it. Big Fred was inordinately proud of this item. "Shows what a feller could do with a stone ax when he got up a sweat," he used to say.

In time, the Humboldt museum's fame reached far places. Two men from the National Geographic Society spent several days taking pictures of Fred's collections of firearms and bows and arrows. Professors from Yale, Stanford and Cornell came to look at the old bones and other things. A number of times the Smithsonian wrote Fred about this or that. He got a big kick out of these doings for he really took a great deal of pride in his collections.

From time to time Fred spent more money in adding to the museum. From sailors he collected coins from every land on the globe. These were labeled and put into cases. Somebody toted in a hunk of meteorite from Central Oregon. Swede and Finn loggers gave him miniature ships in bottles. Fred gave a standing order to the local photographer to take a picture of every lumber schooner that docked in the harbor. He had over a hundred of them. And just before the last of the bull teams was routed from the logging woods by the coming of locomotives, Fred had the photographer go into the timber and get shots of old Cy Blackwell, the fabulous bull puncher who encouraged his oxen by leaping onto the backs of the rear team and walking the full length of ten yokes, in his calked boots, yelling like a crazed Indian. "Some day," Fred said, "these pictures will show how the boys used to do it."

It was probable that no town of Aberdeen's size could boast a museum to touch the Humboldt's. Big Fred told me he calculated he had spent some $75,000 on it, and no one of the items had cost very much. As for Fred himself, he remained a lumberjacks' saloon keeper until the end. He kept peace in his place, he served honest liquor, and he protected patrons not only from others but from themselves. And he set knowledge before them, too. Many a logger got his first interest in things outside his own narrow world from a visit to the Humboldt.

During its two decades of heyday, the Humboldt had a new floor laid twice a year. The floor was of one and one-half inch hemlock, a tough hardy wood. This floor, after each Christmas and Fourth of July, was chewed into splinters by the sharp calks in the boots of countless loggers.

It was said you could tell the state of the lumber market by the appearance of the floor. In 1907, for instance, which was a panic year everywhere in the country, Fred laid only one floor.

Prohibition, as I said, did away with the old place. Even before that awful day, Aberdeen had ripped up its plank sidewalks and put down hard concrete. Loggers come to town had to take off their calked boots—or fall and break their necks—and to wear light shoes, same as any city slicker. Then, came Volstead.

Fred kept the place open for a few years, always at a loss, out of plain sentiment. He sold only soft drinks, for he would not do any sort of bootlegging. "Selling liquor is an honest business," he said, "and by God I ain't going to run no blind tiger."

Dust gathered on the finest saloon museum in the United States. Finally, and with a sad heart, Fred closed her down. The City of Aberdeen talked of buying the collections, but the depression came on, and little by little the museum was dissipated. I have a few of the photographs, but where the rest have gone, even Big Fred doesn't know.

Perhaps it is just as well. Today's lumberjacks like fancy joints with chromium plate, where they sit on red leather stools and do their drinking—which is often cocktails. There wouldn't be any room in such a place for Big Fred's Congress of Curiosities, not even for Cole Younger's pipe or that piece of whale that was relegated to a corner.

Esquire (1940)

For a colorful history of American saloons written by a friend of Holbrook's, see Jim Marshall, *Swinging Doors*, Frank McCaffrey Publishers (1949). Marshall notes that: "Even whiskey wasn't strong enough for the boys out in the dark, dank, drippy woods of the Puget Sound and Grays Harbor countries. In towns like Aberdeen, Hoquiam, Everett and Port Angeles, the custom was for a logger to buy two quarts of liquor—at 90 cents a quart for Grade A—break off the necks with his teeth, stuff a wad of fine cut tobacco into each bottle and then make the rounds with the fortified liquor cached in hip pockets. Two bottles seldom lasted more than an hour or two."

Bunco Kelly, King of the Crimps

The business of crimping is still given notice in virtually all dictionaries, but it rightly belongs there only as an antique or obsolete reference. The great days of crimping ended when the winged ship passed from the seas. A crimp, says a recently compiled lexicon, is an agent who procures seamen by inducing, swindling, or coercing them.

A crimp used to do that, and a likely candidate for the title of King of the Crimps would certainly be the late and wonderful Joseph (Bunco) Kelly of Portland, Oregon. Kelly was something of an historical character in a minor way. His work was of such dimensions and quality that it touched off a Federal investigation of the ports of the West Coast of America, and the varied and interesting practices of keepers of sailors' boarding houses.

Bunco Kelly was born in Liverpool, England, in 1838. He went to sea at an early age, first as cabin boy, later as an able seaman. And then one day, in 1879, when his ship was lying idle in Portland harbor, he went over the side. He was destined to become an outstanding and eminently notorious citizen in that community.

Kelly was a short, squat man, constructed along the lines of a gorilla, even to his long powerful arms, and was probably almost as strong as that animal. In police and other photographs, he displays a truly gorgeous moustache of the weeping-willow sort. In Portland he fell easily into the waterfront life, and was soon procuring seamen for short-handed ships in harbor; and although from time to time he operated his own boarding house for sailors, he was mainly a sort of free-lance crimp for other outfits. He was certainly never idle, and I doubt that the term "dissolute" could be applied to him. He was too much the good businessman for that. And I am not certain but that he was also an artist, for the magnificent imagination he applied to his occupation was nothing short of creative. I like to contemplate the night from which stemmed his nickname of Bunco.

It was a night and a scene sombre enough for a Poe—a wild Sunday evening in late October. The wind howled down out of the Cascade Mountains and whipped great sheets of chilly rain across Portland harbor. Ships in the stream pulled at their anchors, and the hawsers of vessels moored at the docks creaked in protest. Few folk were about in Portland's rough waterfront district.

Yet Joseph Kelly was about. The skipper of a five-masted British ship at dock was ready to sail. He wanted one more able seaman and he had demanded that Kelly produce this commodity. So, the squat figure moved along the skidroad, the haunts of sailors and lumberjacks, looking for a possible candidate. There were none, not in Erickson's, nor in Blazier's, nor in the Ivy Green, the Senate or Larry Sullivan's boarding house.

It must have been discouraging to a man proud of his calling, a man, who claimed never to have let a skipper down. So, Kelly stood at the corner of First and Glisan Streets, wondering where to try next. Across the street was Wildman's cigar store, with the wooden Indian which Wildman had left on the sidewalk to face the elements. For a moment Kelly mused. Then he went into action.

Picking up the noble-looking cedar redman, all of six feet six inches high, he packed it away to the Mersey dock where, from a warehouse somebody had neglected to lock, he procured a piece of old tarpaulin. Kelly wrapped the figure in this, then set forth into the storm, the huge package on his shoulder. He walked up the gangplank of the British ship and straight into the forecastle. Finding an empty bunk, he managed to get the vast form into it, then covered it with blankets.

Kelly went to the skipper. "I got your man," he said with great satisfaction. "He's pretty drunk, but he's a big son-of-a-bitch, and he'll make you a good man." The skipper was highly pleased. He gave Kelly $50 and his blessing.

Two days later, the Finn salmon fishermen of Astoria, a hundred-odd miles down the Columbia from Portland, were astonished to drag in their nets and find a cedar Indian amid the struggling fish.

II

From this feat came the "Bunco" in Kelly's name. The fakery might have ruined the reputation of a lesser man, but it did not hurt Kelly. He really did produce seamen when requested, or at least persons who soon became seamen. Visiting skippers found him, on the whole, to be reliable, and came to him again and again. What made crimps possible in those days, and even necessary, was the system used by sailing ships. Vessels would come to Portland in ballast, that is, with their holds filled with sand or stones. They would empty this ballast in the Linnton district along the waterfront, and then tie up in harbor to wait for a cargo of lumber or wheat to carry abroad. Often they'd be lying there anywhere from two to five months. Rather than pay and feed their large crews all this time, the skippers let some or all of them go over the side, as the saying has it, and into Portland. By thus deserting, the crewmen lost all rights to any pay they had coming. Bunco Kelly and others would board them. When a ship was ready to sail, the skipper hired Bunco, or another man in the business, to furnish a crew. For this the crimps were paid blood-money ranging from $30 to $60 a head, plus board-and-room charges, which the skippers would deduct from the sailors' pay.

By 1882 Bunco Kelly had a boarding house of his own, but his truly great success lay in the continuous public relations campaign he carried on with the madams of assorted "hotels" and drinking places. He was never too pressed to do an errand for Liverpool Liz, owner of the Senate Saloon and a very prosperous woman to boot. And Bunco was charming and helpful to Nancy Boggs, who operated a

whisky-scow in the harbor and did very well with this floating palace of entertainment for lusty males. Both Liz and
Nancy put dozens of prospects into the competent and pre-
hensile hands of Mr. Kelly. There was also dainty Mary
Cook, weighing 200 pounds, who operated the Ivy Green,
an establishment I shall not attempt to describe, and who
did her own bouncing. On one occasion Mary supplied sixteen men, all deep in liquor, to Bunco, and when they awoke
they could look out the portholes and learn they had gone
to sea. Bunco was grateful for these courtesies and he always repaid them in some manner, usually by herding
sailors set on shore into the arms of Mary and her like.

There was, however, pretty stiff competition in the
crimping business of the eighties and nineties. One Jim Turk
had a boarding house. He carried a gold-headed cane and
was something of a ward boss in the North End, receiving
many political and police favors which did not come to
Kelly. A local prize fighter named Larry Sullivan opened
another boarding house and went to crimping in efficient
style. There was also the house operated by the Grants and
another by the Whites. Bunco Kelly had to be up and coming to hold his own. It was probably the stiff competition
that induced Kelly, in a bad moment, into the unfortunate
affair of the *Flying Prince.*

III

The time was late in 1893. The *Flying Prince,* a big
sailing ship of British register, was in Portland harbor,
loaded to the gunnals with Douglas fir lumber, and ready to
sail except for one thing; her crew, the captain figured, was
short twenty-two men. He put the matter up to Bunco Kelly.
Times were hard, he said, but he promised Kelly $30 a head
for any men he could put aboard, before morning daylight.

Bunco made the usual rounds, starting at Liverpool Liz'
place, going on to Erikson's saloon, then to Mary Cook's.
Next he started for the South End of the waterfront. It was
an evil night. The driving rain beat down upon the squat,

rather sinister figure as it moved along Front Street. Just before he reached Morrison Street, where stood the Snug Harbor saloon, he noticed an open trapdoor in the sidewalk. (Portland neither had nor has alleys such as most cities have; deliveries of merchandise and such things are often made through trap doors in the sidewalks, that lead to cellars.)

Now, doors such as this should not be left open at night. And besides, Bunco Kelly was no man to pass up an open door without investigation. Moreover, a peculiar odor emanated from this particular trapdoor. It welled up out of the the blackness beneath, pungent, powerful, strange. Bunco Kelly, whose knowledge of chemicals was limited to the ingredients of Kelly's Comforters, a knock-out mixture he had used with great success, thought he had smelled something like this aroma before, but for the life of him he couldn't say where. He sniffed carefully. He did not like the smell, but he was a curious man. He prepared to descend into the dark.

"In those days," Bunco Kelly later told Spider Johnson, who in turn told me, "in those days, I always carried a small dark lantern under my coat. I got it out and lighted, and threw a beam below. I couldn't see nothing but the little ladder disappearing into the darkness." Bunco was game, however, and he went slowly down into what he described as the damnedest reek he ever hoped to suffer. He saw at once that the room was not wholly in darkness. A candle spluttered on a keg, and the scene its dim light revealed to Bunco Kelly was one he never forgot. "My hair," he related to Spider Johnson, "was pretty thin, but the few hairs I had stood up and pushed my cap into the air."

On the floor near the ladder lay a man. He was alive but not in the best of health. He was gasping, and every little while made as if to clutch at his throat. "What's the matter?" Bunco asked him. The man seemed to hear. He lifted his head a bit, tried to say something, but couldn't.

Bunco now let his dark lantern play around the room. Propped against one of many barrels were three men—

doubtless corpses, Bunco surmised. Their mouths were open, and so were their eyes, but they were not seeing anything. Lying or dropping in odd postures all over the place were other men. Kelly counted 24 all told. Going from one to another, placing his hand on their brows and listening, he came to the conclusion, hurriedly, that at least a third of them still lived. Still, he could not be sure, for he thought that as he watched one of the men gave a deep heave and died.

"I was pretty startled at first," Kelly admitted later in something of a conservative statement. But he got his nerve back quickly. He turned his attention to one of the barrels, from the bung of which a liquid was dripping. He caught some of it in his hand. It was very cold. He sniffed it and it rocked him back on his heels. In fact, the sniff nearly floored him. He quickly went up the ladder to the street. The air soon cleared his dizziness, and his usually quick mind, "By God!" he remarked to nobody in particular, as the true significance of the business struck him, "them stiffs has been drinking undertaker's dope."

It was true enough, too. Johnson & Sons' Undertaking Parlors were just next door to the Snug Harbor saloon. These men had broken into what they thought was the saloon's cellar, which happened to be the cellar of Johnson & Sons. The embalming fluid had proved too stout even for men accustomed to the vilest booze.

Without stopping to draw a moral from the sardonic tragedy, or even to notify the police, Bunco went into sudden and efficient action. He closed the big trapdoor, lest some watchman find it open, and then tore for the North End of town as fast as his short legs could carry him against wind and rain. He went directly to The Mariners' Rest, as he chose to call the old warehouse he had converted into a boarding place for sailors. From here he sent a boy on the dead run to fetch a cab. He roused four or five old friends, bar-flies whom he permitted to sleep in his place, and bade them gird their loins. "No sleep in the house tonight boys," he said.

Back came the boy with a cab. Kelly and his crew piled into it and sped away over the cobblestones, stopping at the Fashion Livery & Feed Stable, where Bunco asked for five more cabs to hurry to Front and Morrison Streets.

It was now well after midnight. The storm was increasing, which pleased Kelly; there was not likely to be so much as a cop on the street. The rain had turned to sleet that stung, for the wind was rising steadily. It was just the right kind of night for the apex in the professional career of Bunco Kelly.

Dark lantern in hand, Kelly led his crew down the ladder, advising them to breathe as little as possible. The stench at first stopped a couple of the helpers, but Kelly threatened to toss them out of his boarding house if they didn't perform like men. "Briskly, now, lads, briskly," Kelly commanded. "We'll lift these boys up the ladder and put them into the cabs."

It was hard work, and it went all too slowly until Kelly suddenly became generous. "Five dollars in gold to each of you," he told his aides, "as soon as these sailors are aboard ship." The promise proved a fine stimulant. Heaving with a will, the Kelly men passed the dead and dying up the ladder, and into the waiting cabs. Up came Kelly. He didn't even stop to close the trap but leaped into the first cab. "Drive," he told the hackman, "as fast as you can to Ainsworth dock." And away went a procession that would have pleased Ambrose Bierce, and E. A. Poe no more than it did Joseph Kelly—sparks from hooves of wheels lighting the night, the dead rolling against the living, the wind howling across the harbor, and the hulk of the *Flying Prince,* looming darker than the night, standing there at dock, awaiting twenty-two able seamen.

By half-past one fourteen corpses and ten men who were very ill had been stowed away snugly in the *Flying Prince's* forecastle, bound out for China.

Bunco Kelly had to explain to the skipper, which he did plausibly, how he had come by his men in one batch; and to argue with the skipper that he had asked for 24, not

22, sailors. The captain was so well pleased to leave with a full crew he did not argue. "I never saw so many men drunk at one time," he remarked, but he counted out $30 each for two dozen men.

"Yes, sir," agreed Kelly genially, "they are godawful drunk, and getting them so cost me a pretty penny." Putting the cash into his pocket he bade the skipper farewell. "And don't forget, sir," he said, "Bunco Kelly is a man who always keeps his promises."

At dawn the *Flying Prince* cast off and headed down the Columbia for the open sea. Long before noon the first mate made the hideous discovery in the forecastle. The ship put in at Astoria, where the corpses were removed. Astoria newspapermen soon had the story on the wires.

The sensation following the discovery of the dead men made a great rumpus in Portland. Preachers remonstrated that the city was in a moral decay. They attacked the politicians and the police. There was the usual police shakeup, with a few cops being moved here and there, and the chief ordered strict regulation of sailors' boarding houses. Kelly, Sullivan and other Portland crimps were merely questioned about the load of corpses. Nobody was charged with murder or anything else. But on a different occasion Bunco Kelly was charged with murder.

Kelly's last affair started coming to light on the morning of October 5, 1894, when Patrolman Ben Branch, walking his waterfront beat in Portland, hauled a corpse out of the harbor. It was the body of George M. Sayres, long reported missing. The body showed many marks of violence. Police arrested Bunco Kelly who, naturally enough, had an alibi. But the alibi did not hold up in court. Kelly was convicted of having killed Sayres in an attempt to shanghai him. He was sent to the Oregon state penitentiary, where he spent fourteen long years before he was finally pardoned.

Kelly's trial did bring out a great deal of evidence as to the underworld of Portland's waterfront. Federal officials having to do with ships and shipping came to Portland to investigate the charges Kelly had made when he was trying to clear himself by implicating others in the crimping racket. They are said to have made recommendations that resulted in greatly improved conditions for sailors. But I doubt that any of the regulations had much to do with the disappearance of crimping. It was the steamship that put an end to the racket. When steam drove all but a few sails from the seas, around the turn of the century, the end was near. Less than half the crew of a windjammer was needed to man a steam vessel.

So, Bunco Kelly went to prison just in time. Technological displacement of sailors was something with which not even a man of Kelly's genius could have competed.

The American Mercury (1948)

Bunco Kelly's own story is recounted in his book *Thirteen Years in the Oregon Penitentiary*, Portland (1908), where he states: "I never did anyone wrong, and there are many people in Portland who can vouch for me .... I never robbed a sailor nor did I ever make money on a sailor."

Opal the Understanding Heart

When I first came to the Northwest it struck me as odd that the only writers in the region who were nationally known in a popular sense were females. One of those was Mary Carolyn Davies, the other, Opal Whiteley.

Within the region, the two writers perhaps best known were Dean Collins and Ben Hur Lampman, both of Portland, both newspapermen, both basically poets.

Where, I wondered, in this still new country, this region of the covered-wagon trains, of Tracy the Bandit, of brawling loggers and miners and fishermen, of the wild Wobblies, of sheep and cattle wars, of anti-Chinese riots, where were the hairy prose writers to chronicle these notable violences or to celebrate them in fiction?

It turned out, just a bit later, that the hairy male prose writers were here, though not quite ripe. The Northwest was in a lull between two generations of writers. The giants and pseudogiants of early and late pioneer days were either dead or had ceased to speak in full voice; and a new group had not appeared. In the early 1920s the latter, in large part, were just finishing the college courses that had been interrupted by the war, or were working in sawmills and logging camps, or on farms and ranches, or earning a living otherwise. Many of this younger generation were only beginning to inhale properly, and required only one safety-razor blade weekly. But they were busy, learning that copy should be double-spaced, that a stamped, self-addressed envelope should accompany all manuscripts, and beginning to believe that all editors were hired expressly for the purpose of keeping anything approaching literature out of their magazines and books.

As for the Messrs Lampman and Collins, they were writing unquestionably the best essays and editorials in the region, and their verse, both light and serious, was not only popular but was getting into good anthologies. But neither man was much interested in writing for a national audience.

Of the two nationally known ladies, Miss Davies was immensely successful with her light verse and short stories in the slick magazines. She was also well known as a contributor to the little or *avant-garde* periodicals that were becoming a rage. She had been born in Sprague, Washington, and lived mostly on the Oregon coast.

Miss Whiteley is not to be described so easily. She was an enigma. She was a one-book woman, too, as it turned out; but the book was actually sensational. It was entitled *The Story of Opal: The Journal of an Understanding Heart.* Nothing like it has since come out of the Northwest, or anywhere else. Nothing likely will. No less a mogul of fine letters than Ellery Sedgwick sponsored Opal's book, and printed large chunks of it in the *Atlantic Monthly. H*e wrote the Introduction to the book. How many copies of it sold I do not know, nor does it matter. No other book published in 1920, save *Main Street,* created sufficient noise to be heard in the clamor about Opal's; and twenty-five years later Mr. Sedgwick remarked that the Atlantic Monthly Press was still getting many letters about it.

Not too many facts are known about Opal Whiteley. She was a fey and illusive creature who patently existed in a world of her own making. She could no more distinguish between what actually happened from what ought to have happened than could the late Calamity Jane Blake White Dorsett Dalton Utter, who also wrote a book. Thus was Opal able to arrange an account of her life with the greatest ease, though this was of no great help simply because the "facts" of her life changed from month to month, and sometimes oftener. She was probably born, about 1898, in Colton, Washington, a shameful place that has never seen fit to honor her memory with even a modest plaque. During the next seventeen years the Whiteleys apparently moved several times, and were living at Wendling, Oregon, when Opal emerged from the obscurity of a logging camp. This occasion was a Junior Christian Endeavor convention at nearby Cottage Grove.

The editor of the Cottage Grove *Sentinel* was Elbert Bede, then, as now, one of the outstanding figures in Northwest journalism. He was present at the convention and, hearing that a seventeen-year old girl had been elected president of the group, he sought her out for an interview. So far as is known, this was the first time Opal's name appeared in print.

Editor Bede remembers Opal as a vibrant, fluttery, exotic, deeply earnest young woman, informed strangely beyond her years. She was olive-skinned, had dark hair and dark eyes, and she told the astonished Mr. Bede she was going forth among the children of Oregon to tell them of God. No gospel preaching, however. Opal said that His work could best be furthered by interesting youngsters in God's fairy creatures of the fields, the woods, the waters, and the air. She planned to give the children messages from flowers and trees, from rocks and streams, from birds and animals, from the very shells of the sea. Editor Bede duly reported as much in the columns of the *Sentinel.*

Whether or not Opal began her Christian crusade seems not to be of record. She did, however, attend the University of Oregon for a year and part of another, then took off for southern California, even then a place given over to marvels. Here, it is known, she first dedicated her life to conducting nature classes for children. The plan failed, and she sat down and composed a book. She called it "The Fairyland Around Us." It was to be bound in genuine leather and sell for $10 a copy. While trying to raise money for its publication, Opal put out a come-on in the form of a prospectus. It carried expressions of the warmest admiration for Opal from Theodore Roosevelt, Queen Elizabeth of Belgium, Nicholas Murray Butler, and the immortal Gene Stratton Porter. It is within belief that Opal herself composed these felicitations.

Yet public response to the prospectus was discouraging. Opal thereupon wrote appeals for money to Andrew

Carnegie, John D. Rockefeller, and lesser whales of capital.
Nothing happened. But the kindly woman at whose home
Opal was rooming lent her money for a trip to the Atlantic
coast.

One September day in 1919, Opal arrived in Boston,
and went direct to 8 Arlington Street, to see Editor Sedgwick
of the *Atlantic Monthly.* Mr. Sedgwick read the manuscript
of "The Fairyland Around Us," and was not amused. He
recalled later that the book was quaintly embellished with
colored pictures pasted in the text by hand, and added with
careful Bostonian understatement that about it "there
seemed little to tempt a publisher."

Opal Whiteley, however, was something else. Mr.
Sedgwick found her "very young and eager and fluttering,
like a bird in a thicket." Being an old-line Yankee he naturally assumed that Opal might have kept a diary, too. Yes,
she had, always. Then, said the *Atlantic* editor, that was
the book he wanted, Opal's diary. The bright, shining countenance clouded. "It's destroyed," Opal replied, "It's all torn
up." Tears came to the great dark eyes, as soft as those of a
doe. A moment later she cheered. Her journal of many years,
she said, was indeed torn up, the work of a jealous foster
sister; but Opal still had the fragments, every last one of
them. They were stored in Los Angeles.

Mr. Sedgwick brightened too. He had Opal telegraph
for the journal fragments, and they came, crammed into an
enormous hatbox. When this was opened, the editor estimated it to contain at least half a million pieces of paper. A
few were of notepaper size. Others were of grocers' bags
pressed carefully and sliced in two. There were wrapping-
paper fragments, backs of envelopes, anything at all that
would hold a few words of writing. As Mr. Sedgwick looked
them over, he noted that what Opal said were her earlier
efforts, at the age of five or six, were written with childish
clumsiness, but that later entries showed the adult hand
gradually forming. They were most convincing.

Now Mr. Sedgwick *was* amused. He installed Opal in
the huge Brookline mansion of his mother-in-law. She was

to live there while preparing the diary for the printer. Next to Opal's bedchamber was a large sitting room. All furniture was removed from this room, and Opal went to work. On the floor, inch by inch, she pieced and pasted together the countless scraps of her journal. They were of all colors, and so had been the pencils and crayons the young diarist had used. I doubt that the home of the Brookline Cabots ever held a gayer picture than that of this woodsprite from Oregon crawling over the Joseph's coat of her childhood labors. She was thus occupied for more than eight months.

As one by one the pages were assembled, they were typed by an editorial employee of the *Atlantic.* The cards were filed in sequence, and at last the manuscript was ready. Mr. Sedgwick has said that everything was printed just as first written, other than omissions, the addition of punctuation, and the spelling, which was "widely amended." Thus did *The Story of Opal* of the understanding heart go to the printers, and meanwhile Mr. Sedgwick was happy to run six generous installments in the famous New England monthly that still, in 1920, appeared between covers of that favorite old-time bilious hue called saffron.

The Story of Opal was a charming performance, especially so to lovers of Nature and of classic literature. At the age of six Opal was speaking to, and confiding in, a Douglas fir tree she named Raphael, a crow she called Lars Porsena, a woodrat named Brave Horatius, and many other characters who infested the tall timber country where her father—or was he her foster father?—was employed by the Booth-Kelly Lumber Company. Here and there the otherworldly tenor of the diary was broken by reference to a bottle of Castoria ("The colic had the baby today . . . but Pearl and I had drunk up the new bottle of Castoria") and other homely things.

The diary made clear that except for her communion with the creatures of her imagination, Opal's childhood had been most unhappy. Opal was—said the diary—a foster child who had been left with the Whiteleys for upbringing.

Here began the mystery, or perhaps confusion, or maybe chaos: While the real Opal Whiteley was being taken to an Oregon logging camp with her family, she fell into a stream; and the pseudo Opal, she of the understanding heart, was substituted without Mrs. Whiteley being the wiser, an occurrence without parallel, so far as I am aware, in all Oregon.

But the original Opal was not drowned; she was rescued then and there from the dark rushing waters of the mountain stream. Yet what became of her is still as great a mystery as the name of Paul Revere's horse, though I like to hope that she grew up and lived happily ever afterward as Joan Lowell.

Opal's diary is studded throughout with French expressions. Little by little the story is developed that Opal of the diary is doubtless the daughter of Prince Henry of Orléans, Bourbon heir to the nonexistent throne of France. If the influence of heredity is accepted, then it fits neatly into the narrative, for Prince Henry was a noted traveler and explorer whose published works display his constant interest in flora and fauna. Just how neatly it fits, you begin to comprehend when you come to the acrostic which little Opal set down in her diary at the age of seven: "I did sing it le chant de fleurs," wrote the naïve child of the Oregon woods, "that Angel Father did teach me to sing of Hiacinthe, Eclaire, Nenufar, Rose, Iris, et Dauphinelle et Oleandre, et Romarin, Lis, Eglantier, Anemonoe, Narcisse, et Souci." The first letters spell Angel Father's name. Not for Opal the worn and trite strawberry birthmark method of identification.

I shan't go more deeply into the book. If copies of it are not available in all libraries in the Northwest, then it is time they tossed out their shelves of self-improvement books and stocked a volume that has few peers in the field. Opal's diary carried the fantastic little Oregon girl to England, to France, and to India, where she was soon riding in an open barouche down the streets of Allahabad, with royal outriders clearing the way for H.R.H. Mlle. Françoise de Bourbon-Orléans, which was to say, Opal herself. The daydreams of a neurotic woman never congealed more purposely than this.

Within a few weeks of book publication, both author and publisher knew they were in for a highly popular success. Sales kept climbing for months. A vast circle of enthusiastic readers wrote to express their appreciation, among them foreigners such as M. Clemenceau, M. Poincaré, Lord Curzon, together with scientists, men of elegant letters, and other distinguished characters. I was unable to find the names of any notable women in this clamorous applause, and have wondered if the ladies were skeptical or merely catty.

Sir Edward, Viscount Grey of Fallodon, K.G., a confirmed birdwatcher, was so taken with Opal's book that, being in Boston, he asked to meet the author; and Mr. Sedgwick, who arranged the meeting, remarked that the two nature lovers had a gorgeous time discussing wrens, pewits, and one thing and another. Good Sir Edward also contributed a foreword to the English edition of Opal's book, published by Putnam.

There was at least one reader of T*he Story of Opal* who was both astounded and cruelly hurt. She was Mrs. Achsah Pearson Scott of Saginaw, Oregon, whom Oregonians believed to be the maternal grandmother of the diarist. As soon as she could assemble her wits, after reading her granddaughter's book, Mrs. Scott told the *Oregon Journal* that Opal "has sold her birthright and slandered the name of a good mother." She said Opal had not begun to keep a diary until she was past fourteen, and had never before that shown any liking for writing. Mrs. Scott added that Opal had been a good child until she "got in with a crew of mind readers in Los Angeles."

Of the hundreds of thousands of readers, none gave *The Story of Opal* closer attention than did Editor Bede of the Cottage Grove *Sentinel* (weekly, subscription rate, $2 per year). To him there appeared to be in it discrepancies, omissions, and *non sequiturs* beyond count. Mr. Bede knew all the Whiteleys, found them to be good, honorable people, and literate, with at least high-school education. He reflected that if Opal of the book were not a blood daughter of the Whiteleys of Wendling, Oregon, then she bore a family likeness that was a coincidence almost too great to accept. On second thought, it *was* too great. Thereupon, Mr. Bede acquired a hobby: While continuing to carry on his duties as editor of Lane County's outstanding weekly newspaper, he devoted his spare time to research.

Mr. Bede's first efforts included many talks with several of the Whiteleys, then they centered on the books Opal had borrowed or used in the several libraries she had haunted, in Oregon, in California, and in Boston. In the Boston Public Library, Mr. Bede learned with much satisfaction, was a copy of the will of Prince Henry of Orléans which, he discovered, contained no little of the intimate information that was also found in the many French acrostics in Opal's diary. He came to believe, too, that Opal must also have looked into the books written by Prince Henry himself. Whole sections of these, almost word for word, appeared in the girl's diary of her sixth and seventh year. In the Prince's volumes parallel passages on well thumbed pages were found to bear faint marks in pencil. Mr. Bede was beginning to think the trail was clearing.

Meanwhile, Opal's book sold enormously, reached its apex, then gradually disappeared from the best seller lists. Mr. Bede continued his hobby. He talked again with the Whiteleys, except for the mother, who, he remarks, was "saved by death from the embarrassment of the diary." He talked with friends of the Whiteleys of many years' standing. Both the Whiteleys and their friends said that publication of the diary was the first intimation they had had that Opal claimed to be a foster child.

Mr. Bede next took up the trail in Los Angeles. There he learned that Opal had possessed no immense box of diary fragments when she arrived, but that after almost two years' residence there she did have such a box. He learned that Opal had spent most of her time, day and night alike, writing by hand on paper. When not at this labor, she was mostly in the Los Angeles Public Library. Library attendants remembered her; she was pure glutton for work.

One of the many things about Opal that fascinated Mr. Bede was the problem of why, if she were born in a foreign land, and at the age of six exhibited a nimble familiarity with French in her diary, she was never known to use a word of that language otherwise. Nor could he, in his wildest moments, imagine a tot of seven who was on casual "speaking terms" with Elizabeth Barrett Browning, Henry James, Aristotle, and Aphrodite, to mention only a few of her shadowy companions of the Oregon woods.

When, in good time, the literary detective of Cottage Grove got around to it, he presented his wonderings, as well as his findings, in an instructive essay. His conclusions may be stated succinctly: *The Story of Opal* is composed almost equally of hoax and plagiarism.*

Getting back to Opal; shortly after her book appeared, she departed for England with letters of introduction from Sir Edward Grey and from our own Secretary of State. A little later she turned up in France. and at this point her trail grows extremely dim. But soon it is plain again, fairly blazing, as related, in India, where she was accepted as genuine Bourbon-Orléans by two of the great maharajas of the empire, and entertained regally by tiger hunts on elephants, stupendous fêtes, and attendance of the Bengal Lancers. News of her doings diminished, and presently ceased. So far as we in Oregon were concerned, Opal had disappeared in the mists of India.

In 1936, being in Boston for a visit, I interviewed Mr. Sedgwick, and took occasion to ask about Opal. "Opal Whiteley was no mountebank," said he. "She was, and is, a remarkable person, a strange person." He said he had taken the trouble to verify her reception in India. In reply to his

---

*Mr. Bede's essay appears in *History of Oregon Literature*, by Alfred Powers (Portland 1935).

queries, he had received two letters, each carrying a regal crest, informing him that the royal master bade his secretary to say it had been his great privilege to entertain Her Royal Highness Mlle. Françoise de Bourbon-Orléans. The editor also heard from a British officer who described the turning out of the Bengal Lancers, and the tiger hunt. I asked Mr. Sedgwick if he believed Opal's story. "I believe now," said he, "more than ever I did, that her diary was a genuine thing. Whether or not she is of royal descent, I do not claim to know." He added that "Opal was touched with genius."

Ten years later, when the retired editor of the *Atlantic* published his autobiography,* he seemed still certain of Opal's genius, but he was a bit equivocal as to the truth of her story. "The child who wrote Opal's diary believed in it," he stated. One should bear in mind the fact that Editor Sedgwick was subjected to much abuse because he gave Opal's diary to the public. Letters accused him of being a party, at least of the second part, in perpetrating a monstrous hoax. Proper Bostonians and proper non-Bostonians charged the heir to the editorial chair of James Russell Lowell and William Dean Howells with committing an obscene crime fit only for editors of the more lurid Sunday supplements.

So, when in his sunset years Editor Sedgwick comes in his autobiography to the subject of Opal Whiteley, one senses that his guard is up. He remarks that for those whom Nature loves, *The Story of Opal* needs no explanation. But others, says he, who are forever demanding facts and backgrounds, asking for theories and explanations—well, those people should know that of the honesty of Opal's story he is utterly convinced. And yet, and yet—he goes on to reflect on what can happen to people who have single-track minds. They brood on the single idea. They sleep with it, wake with it. Do they not come to think of themselves as apart from the rest of mankind? Is there any among us so

---

The Happy Profession (Boston, 1946).

bold as to say where runs the boundary line that separates sanity from something else?

Is it not possible that in the heart of every little girl sits Cinderella? As the child grows to womanhood, Cinderella may be relegated to the background, though always present, ready to take over the, mind for brief periods. Witness soap opera. But if the child happens to be Opal Whiteley, Cinderella is made, is for*ced,* to bring about her marvels, just as she did in the old story.

Well, then, once upon a time Prince Henry of Orléans visited Oregon, according to a letter Mr. Sedgwick received from an unnamed Oregonian. The correspondent wrote that his father had served under the prince in the Franco-Prussian War of 1870. This Oregonian of French descent informed Mr. Sedgwick that Prince Henry had paused, in his tour of Oregon, to chat with the old soldier, his comrade of the days when Napoleon III, or the Little, was Emperor of France, and when the poilus fought desperately. though vainly, to keep the Boche out of Paris.

If Prince Henry did visit his old comrade in Oregon, which Mr. Sedgwick thinks quite possible, then was it not likely that the appearance of a prince of the blood should have created a sensation, and word of it spread "through the lumber camps of Oregon?" The Whiteleys were residents of a logging camp. What is more likely than that the legend of the prince should have captivated little Opal, and to have grown until it dominated her life?

What is far less likely is that Prince Henry of Orléans should have commanded a regiment during the War of l870, when he was but three years of age.

What Mr. Sedgwick seems to be saying is that *The Story of Opal* ought to be true but probably isn't. In one place he remarks of Opal that she was a somnambulist, and that she displayed other symptoms of abnormality. Persons touched with genius, so I have read, are almost certain to be abnormal. Doubtless Mr. Sedgwick was not far from right when he observed to me that Opal was at least touched with genius.

Even the skeptical Mr. Bede grants Opal's genius. Not long ago, when he and I spent another pleasant evening in discussing Opal, he expressed his reflections of thirty years on the subject. Remarking that if Henry of Orléans, who never married, had reason for sending a "natural" daughter to the United States, Oregon had one chance in forty-eight of being the place, and because of its remoteness might well have been chosen. Or, on the death of the prince, the heirs of his estate might have contrived the same thing to rid themselves of an awkward situation. Illegitimate children have made hash of the settlements of more than one estate, and appear to be uncommonly numerous in the families of the princely.

The kindly Mr. Bede grew mellow that evening, and wondered aloud if Opal's story might not, after all, be true; if she herself had not ruined it by her elaborate pains to establish a background with embellishments that simply could not be swallowed. His mind cleared quickly, however, as he recalled one by one the results of his extended research, and he then remarked that while discussion of Opal herself was always worth while, her book was pure Cinderella.

Mr. Bede has one regret. He never thought to ask Mr. Whiteley, who he believes, as does the rest of Oregon, was Opal's real father, how he happened to name his daughter with sheer genius. "Opal the stone," Mr. Bede observed, "is both transparent and opaque. Nothing could better describe our Opal of the understanding heart."

The Far Corner (1952)

Elbert Bede's version of the Opal story can be found in his *Fabulous Opal Whiteley: From Oregon Logging Camp to Princess*, Metropolitan Press (1954). For the view that Opal's diary is authentic, see Benjamin Hoff, *The Singing Creek Where the Willows Grow—The Rediscovered Diary of Opal Whiteley*, Ticknor & Fields (1986).

The Legend of Jim Hill

Long before his death, more than forty years ago, Jim Hill had become a legend in the American West. Whether he was hero or villain matters little. He died something of a giant in the vast region where many contemporaries came often to think him less a man than an elemental force. Time has not diminished his stature; neither has it quite managed to condemn him nor to put him safely on the side of the angels.

First of all came the blizzards. Then the droughts. Then the grasshoppers, and hard on the leaping legs of the parasites came James Jerome Hill, Jim Hill, the Little Giant, the Empire Builder, the man who *made* the Northwest, or who wrecked it—Jim Hill, the barbed-wire, shaggy-headed, one-eyed old so-and-so of western railroading.

Lasting legends are seldom ready-made. They are built from inconsequential stories laid end to end, or piled one upon the other. Of two of the best remembered stories of Jim Hill, one shows him as hero, the other as villain. Once, when a crew was trying to clear track for a Great Northern passenger train stalled in a blinding snowstorm, President Hill came out to snatch a shovel from a man and send that working stiff into the president's business car for hot coffee, while Hill himself shoveled like a rotary plow. One after the other, the gandydancers were spelled off and drank fine Java in unaccustomed elegance while the Great Northern's creator faced the storm. *That* was Jim Hill for you. Again, because the mayor of a small Minnesota town objected, mildly, to all-night switching in his village, Hill swore that its people should walk. Then he had the depot torn down and set up two miles away. That, too, was Jim Hill.

The legend carries on: Hill began life with nothing. He died lord of an empire that reached from the Great Lakes to Puget Sound, from the Canadian border to Missouri and Colorado. He had staked out provinces in China and Japan. He died worth $53,000,000, won in a region so sparsely settled that it was believed by most easterners to be an intact and worthless wilderness. There is more of substance to the Hill legend than shadow.

Born in 1838 in Ontario, Upper Canada, young Hill arrived at eighteen in the raw new settlement at the head of navigation on the Mississippi that was beginning to dislike its pioneer name of Pig's Eye, and was calling itself St. Paul. The time was mid-1856. St. Paul was in its first notable boom. The prosperity was to last a little more than twelve months longer before the Panic of '57 turned the city into what a local historian described as a place of "no business, . . . no banks, . . . no courage, no hope, . . . no foundation to build on."

Twelve months, however, was all young Hill needed. Neither then nor later did panics hurt him. Like his contemporaries, Rockefeller and Carnegie, he welcomed them. Panics shook the stuffing out of insecure institutions, leaving useful fragments that able hands might pick up and make into something solid. One year in St. Paul before the debacle of 1857 was time enough. In that period young Hill's energy put down such firm roots in the city that it was to remain his base of operations for the next six decades.

His first job was on the St. Paul water front, where he clerked and made himself useful for an outfit running a line of packet steamers. He saw the first shipments of Minnesota grains go down-river. With his own hands he cut the first stencil for the first label of the first flour made in Minnesota. He noted the increasing number of immigrants, the steadily mounting tonnage of freight. By 1865 he had set up for himself as a forwarding agent. Within months a local daily paper observed that "J. J. Hill is now prepared to give shippers the lowest rates ever quoted from here to Eastern points. Mr. Hill has nearly all the important carriers of freight in his own hands." When winter closed river navigation, his big warehouse was not idle; he converted it into a hay-pressing establishment, bringing the admiring editorial comment that "this remarkable young man evidently intends to keep abreast of the times." This was not quite exact; young Hill was keeping ahead of the times. He presently organized what became the Northwestern Fuel Company—and virtually a monopoly—to supply wood for St Paul's stoves and furnaces: then, having first leased several thousand acres of Iowa coal lands, he introduced that fuel to the St. Paul & Pacific Railroad, Minnesota's chief source of revenue for corruptionists, lobbyists, and legislators.

Among the older businessmen who had been observing young Hill's career was Norman W. Kittson, Canadian-born in 1814, a fur trader from youth, who had arrived in Minnesota in the 1830's, served in the territorial and state legislatures, done well in real estate, and was acting as agent in St. Paul for the venerable Hudson's Bay Company. Before accepting this post, Kittson had acted for the independent trappers and traders. He continued to act for them. This odd arrangement satisfied nobody, and Kittson proposed to Hill that he might find it worthwhile if he could devise a way to transport the independents and their supplies from the United States to the fur and farming regions of the Canadian province soon to be called Manitoba.

The Hudson's Bay Company was operating what it considered a monopoly steamboat line on the Red River, which flowed north out of Dakota to the Bay Company's post at Fort Garry (Winnipeg). Hill put a boat of his own on the Red. He added another. He had taken care to bond his steamers, thus complying with the United States customs law which, until then, had been a dead letter. The Bay Company's vessels were suddenly barred from carrying freight; and until the Canadian firm could comply with the forgotten law, the Hill boats enjoyed a lucrative monopoly. When Donald A. Smith, governor of the Bay Company, learned of the coup, he remarked of Hill that "he must be a very able man."

Hill promptly began a rate war against the Bay Company boats so effective as to cause Donald Smith to visit St. Paul. The outcome was a coalition. What the public saw was that Norman Kittson, the Hudson's Bay agent at St. Paul, organized the Red River Transportation Company, in which Hill was a secret partner. Shipping rates on the Red went high and stayed high. It is of interest to know what "high" meant: during its first season the Kittson-Hill combine returned a net profit of 80 per cent.

Yet Hill was not content. While engaged in his now numerous activities he watched the steady decay of the St. Paul & Pacific Railroad. If they could lay hands on that streak of rust and corruption, he told Kittson, it could be made into a profitable enterprise. Soon came the Panic of 1873 to add the ripening touch. The railroad promptly went into receivership.

Hill and Kittson together could muster a few thousand dollars. To get a firm hold on the St. Paul & Pacific called for infinitely more money. Through Donald Smith and Smith's cousin, George Stephen, head of the Bank of Montreal, $6,000,000 was raised. Hill and Kittson then borrowed and mortgaged and added $780,000 to the syndicate. The four men took over the bankrupt company and reorganized it as the St. Paul, Minneapolis & Manitoba Railroad.

To get it so cheaply, Hill had guided a bondholders' committee over the road—or, as legend has it, over the most worthless stretches of it and in the most decrepit rolling stock Hill could find. While so engaged, he gently admonished them to behold their folly.

Even at $6,780,000, the bondholders' folly was something of a bargain. The new owners promptly sold the major part of the company's land grant for $13,068,887. They still owned the railroad, such as it was. Of the four partners, Smith was soon to become Lord Strathcona, Stephen was to be made Lord Mount Stephen. The others were to remain

Kittson and Hill. Hill took charge of building the Manitoba, as the line was commonly known, into a railroad that would pay its way wherever it went.

Hill was just forty when he set out to make something from the dismal remains of the bankrupt line. Directing the job in person, he drove his construction crews at a furious rate. Across Minnesota went the rails, then north to the border to meet the Canadian Pacific, which built a line south from Winnipeg, a "happy conjunction" made possible by the fact that Hill's Canadian partners were heavy stockholders and leading spirits in Canada's first transcontinental line.

Two thumping wheat harvests followed completion of the first Hill railroad; the freight traffic grew immense. What had been a trickle of immigrants from Norway and Sweden turned to a flood, and not without reason: Hill's agents had been in Scandinavia singing the glories of the Red River of the North. Homesteads could be had free, or Hill would sell them some of the land still in possession of the Manitoba railroad at $2.50 a acre.

Jim Hill's idea of a railroad was not a piece of track to connect the Twin Cities and Winnipeg. As early as 1879 he told his directors he meant to push the line across the continent to Puget Sound. Some of his colleagues were alarmed. No other concern had attempted to build a transcontinental railroad without a subsidy from the government in lands and often in loans. Hill could get no land grant other than the one the road already had in Minnesota, and that would be of no aid in building across Dakota, Montana, Idaho, and Washington. Even if by some quirk he did manage to lay rails to Puget Sound, how then could he hope to compete with the old subsidized lines, the Northern Pacific and the Union Pacific? When Hill's presumptuous plan became public, his railway inevitably was labeled "Hill's Folly."

Hill's Folly moved westward with speed, though not so fast as to preclude shorter feeder lines being built as the main rails went forward, heading for the northwest shore. Hill seemed to know just where a branch would become a profitable feeder almost as soon as it was laid. Soon the main line started the long haul across Montana, running well north of the Northern Pacific, which Hill pretended to ignore, except to set his freight and passengers rates very low in territory where he could compete with the older road.

Hill was ruthless. Near Great Falls, Montana, which Hill's Folly reached in 1887, he showed what he could do to a stubborn community. He laid his rails in a graceful arc clean around Fort Benton, whose short-sighted townsmen had rejected his demand for a right of way free of charge, and left the settlement a good mile from the tracks. Great Falls had been debating how much to charge Hill for a strip through the city, but observing what had occurred at Fort Benton, it decided to be openhanded, and presented him with a dandy right of way through the center of its city park.

Hill always protected his rear. Grain elevators went up as the main line continued west. More immigrants came to settle on what by now had become the Great Northern Railway. Hill was ready to haul a good healthy peasant from Europe halfway across the United States for $25 if he would promise to drive his stakes along Great Northern rails.

At last the Great Northern reached Puget Sound at Everett, Washington, early in 1893. It was a bad year for railroads. The Santa Fe and the Union Pacific went into receivership. And, to the great delight of Hill, so did his major competitor, the Northern Pacific. Of all the rails that reached the West Coast, only the Great Northern remained intact.

Jim Hill himself was still intact. At 55 he had long since reminded many of a grim old lion—a thickset man with massive head, gray beard and gray hair shaggy as a shorthorn's. He had immense shoulders and one good eye (he had lost the other in a childhood game of bow and arrow) which often seemed to glow in his dark, weathered countenance—said one who saw it—like a live coal at the bottom of a cinder pit.

Men often look the way they do because conditions and their own bent have forged their personality. Hill was one of these. He made people think of some craglike geologic outcropping, a neolithic fact, old Rock of Ages. Yet his was a volcanic base. His temper was such that once he tore a telephone from its moorings and heaved it the length of his office. Again, he fired an inoffensive Great Northern clerk who, when asked by Hill, replied that his name was Spittles. It *was* Spittles, too, and Hill fired him because of it.

Hill had studied the failing Northern Pacific closely; and now, with his old associate of the Bank of Montreal, Lord Mount Stephen, he made an offer to stockholders of the bankrupt line; he would take over and operate it. The deal was halted by an injunction in support of a Minnesota law prohibiting the merger of parallel and competing railroads. But there was nothing to stop Hill from buying Northern Pacific stock copiously. This Hill did. The road was reorganized with the help of J. Pierpont Morgan. Henceforth, for all practical purposes, the NP was a second track for the Great Northern. The two roads became known as the Hill lines, and for them Hill was planning further expansion; he wanted nothing less than the great midwestern property called the Chicago, Burlington & Quincy Railroad.

Hill wanted the Burlington for several reasons, among them the fact that it would give him entry to Chicago and St. Louis. That road touched the Great Northern at St. Paul, and the Northern Pacific at Billings, Montana. It operated large mileages in Iowa and adjacent states, which together comprised America's best domestic lumber market. (The far-western portions of Hill's GN and NP relied heavily on lumber for eastbound freight.) Then, too, the Burlington would give Hill connection with the cotton-hauling roads entering St. Louis and Kansas City, and with the smelters of Colorado and South Dakota, and the packing houses of Omaha. Hill and J. P. Morgan bought the Burlington from under the nose of Edward H. Harriman, who also wanted it.

Ten years younger than Hill, Harriman "looked like a bookkeeper." A rather frail man, he wore thick glasses, had a soft voice, and was both shy and silent. He was also one of the few men who did not fear Morgan. In fact, Harriman feared nobody. At 21 he had owned a seat on the New York Stock Exchange. He headed a syndicate to take over the foundering Union Pacific. (He was soon to get control of the Central Pacific and Southern Pacific as well.) Now he felt ready to begin what went into railroad history as the Hill-Harriman wars. Both men were ruthless enough. Both meant to dominate railroading in the northwestern United States from the Great Lakes to the Pacific.

The Hill-Morgan coup—getting the Burlington—occurred in March, 1901. At almost the same time Harriman, with the backing of Kuhn, Loeb & Company, New York bankers, started secretly to buy into the Northern Pacific. If he couldn't get the Burlington, then he meant to buy control of Hill's second road and be in a position to dictate to Hill. The stock buying was begun so astutely that neither Hill nor Morgan seemed to suspect what was going forward. In fact, everything looked so serene that in April Morgan sailed for Europe, where he planned to take the waters at Aix-les-Bains. That same month, Hill set out to roll westward across his own empire.

During the last week in April Hill, then in Seattle, was perturbed to note a sudden sharp rise in Northern Pacific shares. It troubled him because the Hill-Morgan crowd owned less than half of the NP stock. True, in most cases a strong minority interest was sufficient to hold control of a railroad. But not always. Hill acted promptly. In Seattle he had his car hitched to a locomotive, ordered the tracks cleared, and started a fast run to Chicago, and then on to New York. In New York he went immediately to the office of Jacob H. Schiff of Kuhn, Loeb and demanded to know if Schiff were buying NP shares for E. H. Harriman. Yes, said Schiff, he was. What was more, if the Hill-Morgan crowd would not let Harriman have the Burlington, then Harriman was going to buy the Northern Pacific from under their feet, which, said Schiff, were not planted firmly enough to hold it. Indeed, Harriman already had control. (Schiff was bragging a little; Harriman needed approximately 40,000 more shares.)

Hill went to the House of Morgan with the bad news that they had been caught napping in the Old Man's absence. The Morgan partners cabled to Aix-les-Bains, asking Morgan for permission to buy 150,000 shares of NP Common. This happened on a Friday. Next day, while the Morgan partners awaited a reply, Harriman thought to play safe by purchasing another 40,000 shares. He called Schiff's office and gave the order. It was never executed. The devout Schiff was at the synagogue.

By Monday it was too late. Trading on the Exchange had barely begun when the House of Morgan poured buying orders into the market. On Monday alone brokers bought some 127,500 shares of NP Common for the Morgan account. The price climbed from the 114 to 127½. And the buying continued. On Tuesday the price hit 149. On Thursday it rose to 1,000.

A sudden if brief panic followed the boom, and many stocks went tumbling. But Hill-Morgan reached an understanding with Harriman. In what was really no more than a partial and temporary armistice, it was agreed Harriman should have representation on the Northern Pacific board. Control of the three railroads, however, remained with the Hill-Morgan people. Hill continued to run the Northern Pacific, the Great Northern, and the Burlington as he thought best.

A business commentator once observed that "Mr. Hill's judgment has never been seriously at fault in any of his undertakings." He had noted that Hill's plans for the three Hill lines became apparent at once. Hill's agents in the Orient prevailed on Japanese industrialists to try a shipment of American cotton to mix with the short-staple article from India they were using. It proved successful; from then on the Hill lines carried an increasing tonnage of American cotton for shipment at Seattle. Minnesota flour began crossing the Pacific in huge volume. Jim Hill liked to say that if each inhabitant of a single province in China could be induced to eat an ounce of flour daily, it would require some fifty million bushels of midwest wheat annually. Hill carried the flour dirt-cheap to Seattle. In fact, his over-all policy was not to charge rates as high as the traffic would stand, but as low as the Hill lines could stand.

Hill's campaign to populate the so-called wastelands between Minnesota and the Cascade Mountains of Oregon and Washington was only too successful. The end result was bad. In the twelve years after 1910, 42 percent of Montana's great area was tentatively settled by homesteaders, a majority of them induced thither by Hill's agents and his continuous publicity efforts. They plowed this short-grass country deep; erosion followed, and Montana's topsoil was blown away. By 1919 the average yield of wheat had fallen to 2.4 bushels per acre. Abandoned homesteads became a characteristic scene in Montana. Hill's judgment, at least on this occasion, was seriously at fault.

Four years after the armistice of 1901, the Hill-Harriman wars broke out anew. Hill was nettled because Harriman, through his Union Pacific and his large interest in the Northern Pacific, considered Oregon to be his domain and may well have believed his position impregnable. Hill, however, thought differently. Before Harriman got wind of it, Hill had completed surveys down the north bank of the Columbia River to occupy a water-level route through the Cascade Mountains, which the Northern Pacific had originally planned to use but which for some reason or other it had deflected to the south bank.

No sooner had Hill's gangs started grading and laying track down the north bank than they were met up with injunctions and other legal harassments conjured up by a couple of paper-railroads hastily incorporated by Harriman. Although most of this engagement was fought in the courts, violence broke out in the field. Some of Hill's equipment was dynamited in night raids by unknown parties. Harriman's surveyors were shot at and driven off.

Hill won the north bank fight; and his new line, the Portland & Seattle, went into joint operation by the Great Northern and the Northern Pacific, with headquarters in Portland. Yet he still was not content. He had a foothold in the extreme northwest corner of Oregon. He wanted more. The outcome went into history as the last of the classic railroad battles that had shaken and often entertained the United States periodically for half a century.

Under an assumed name and posing as a wealthy sportsman, John F. Stevens, Hill's incomparable chief engineer, went into central Oregon to buy options on ranches and other property along the Deschutes River. He also purchased the charter for a nonexistent railroad, the Oregon Trunk, which had never laid a rail. Only then did Jim Hill announce he planned to "open up" central Oregon by building 165 miles of railroad up the river to a place named Bend.

The news of Hill's plan to "develop" a region given over largely to sagebrush, extinct volcanoes, and lava beds, yet hedged with a vast stand of virgin ponderosa pine, gave Harriman a start. Almost nobody lived in the region, even in Bend, its metropolis. Harriman rightly comprehended that Hill planned to build not only to Bend but right on through that town in a direct line to San Francisco, and California was a Harriman province.

To parallel Hill's Oregon Trunk, Harriman hastily moved surveyors and huge gangs of laborers into the neighborhood, and they went to work making grade and laying track up the east bank of the Deschutes River. All Oregon, and much of the Far West, watched with interest while the armies of the two railroad generals massed for an old-fashioned construction war.

In the narrow Deschutes Canyon, little more than a cleft in high, craggy cliffs of rock, the opposing crews used dynamite on each other. For close fighting the weapons were shovels, crowbars, and pick handles. In more open spaces, the factions harassed one another's right of way with fences, barricades of rock, and court orders. Armed guards occasionally lay flat on the rimrock to shoot at any mysterious movements below.

The campaign came to a head at the ranch of a man named Smith, who sold his property to Harriman. There was no other route to Bend except through this ranch. Hill decided to arbitrate. Harriman was willing. A truce was signed by which Hill agreed to build no farther south than Bend. But west of the Cascade Range the war continued, no longer with violence but with electric lines and coastwise steamships.

This struggle was still going on when Harriman died in 1909. It was not finished in 1916, when Hill died. Only by the mid-1920's, when the Great Northern at last gained entry to San Francisco, over the tracks of the Western Pacific, could the Hill-Harriman wars be said to be over. By then it was something of a hollow victory anyhow; in the very year Harriman died, Henry Ford had announced his Model T. One era was ending, a new one dawning.

What might be called Hill's private life presented no difficulties to his official biographer. There were no family skeletons to be concealed. No de-spicing was necessary. Seemingly his private affairs were as placid as his business career was stormy. His marriage, in 1867, to Mary Theresa Mehegan, daughter of Irish Catholic immigrants, was "one of those perfect unions of which the world hears little because of their completeness." Three sons and seven daughters were born to the Hills. Of her husband Mrs. Hill remarked that "he never brought his business home."

Though Hill seems never to have embraced the Catholic Church as a communicant, he first and last made it gifts of something more than one million dollars. His will also set aside a million dollars to establish the James Jerome Hill Reference Library in St. Paul, opened in 1917. His hobbies, such as raising fine cattle and swine and experimenting in the growing of grain, were closely related to his railroad interests. Yet he took no little satisfaction from his collection of paintings. He began it with a Corot, a good Millet, then added works by Daubigny, Dupre, Deschamps, T. Rousseau, and one of Delacroix's better pictures. All these artists were much admired at the time. Yet, early in the eighties, Hill was purchasing paintings by younger men like Monet and Renoir.

Thus there is little in James J. Hill at home on which to build a legend. It was Jim Hill in action who went into legendary. One of his appealing qualities was that he was not an absentee-emperor whose knowledge of his realm came solely from his agents and captains. In person he had walked on snowshoes across Minnesota in the days when the Sioux were on the warpath. He had camped on the banks of the Red River when Manitoba was still Prince Rupert's Land. By foot, horse, or rail he had been to all the limits reached by the Hill lines. When the Great Northern's Number One train, the *Empire Builder,* whistles for Sauk Centre or Fargo or Whitefish or Spokane on its way two thousand miles across the top of the United States, the echoes find scarcely a stark butte or valley that Jim Hill himself had not seen at first hand.

One who has been riding the Hill lines for many years is likely to fancy that in them he finds certain qualities of Jim Hill the man. By this I mean the land, the climate, and the very towns and flag stops of this now spectacular, now monotonous, but often handsome, harsh, desolate, wild, and bitter region. Take little Malta, Montana, an angry sun beating down, baking the false fronts, roasting the soil . . . or Havre, Montana, at night, snapping from cold, coyotes yelping within sound of the roundhouse . . . or the glittering hill that is Butte at twilight—Butte twinkling with astonishing brilliance in this thin air, seen from the Northern Pacific's limited as she comes suddenly out of the high pass of the Rockies, while away to the south stands the enormous stack marking Anaconda, spewing yellow fumes and death to vegetation . . . The Kootenai, a tumult of white water boiling over rocks, sea green in the pools . . . then the immense lushness of the Wenatchee orchards . . . and at last the long thundering bore straight through the Cascade Range and emergence into the fog-ridden silence of the towering firs, the most somber and melancholy forest on earth; then the lights of Puget Sound and the hoarse calls of ships bound for the Orient.

Jim Hill hitched these places and things together, then went on to tie them to Chicago, to Omaha, St. Louis, Kansas City, and Denver. They comprised the Hill lines. The Hill lines comprised an empire. I can think of few other Americans who had quite so much direct influence on quite so large a region.

American Heritage (1958)

For a comprehensive biography of Hill, see Albro Martin, *James J. Hill and the Opening of the Northwest*, Oxford Press (1976).

Erickson's: Elbow Bending for Giants

Once upon a time the city of Portland, Oregon, was known less for its gorgeous roses than for an institution commonly called Erickson's, a saloon patently designed for the refreshment of giants. It occupied the best part of a city block on Portland's skid road, which was and is Burnside Street, and its noble bar presented a total length of exactly six hundred and eighty-four lineal feet. Men of Gath could have lifted their schooners here in comfort.

It was founded in the early Eighties by August Erickson, from Helsinki in Finland. It grew in size and magnificence until loggers, hard-rock miners and other hearty men from all over the West and sailors from the seven seas and beyond vowed they had rather see Erickson's with its gaslights in full blow than to view Niagara Falls tumbling into the Grand Canyon of the Colorado, with Lillian Russell, nude, riding the rapids in a glass barrel, to music by John Philip Sousa. Praise could reach no greater height. Mobile young men of the West grew up with the notion that they had

Holbrook and Bernard Devoto in Erickson's Saloon

hardly reached man's estate until they had lifted a few in Erickson's on the skid road of Portland. This aura survives somewhat into the present day, though the saloon appears in dreadfully attenuated form.

Virtually every Western state used to brag of places with "a mile-long bar." These turned out, I have discovered by no little research, to have been modest bars of one hundred feet or less. Erickson's mighty total was comprised of five bars in one great room. Two of these ran from the Second Avenue side to Third Avenue. Two more connecting bars completed the vast quadrangle. And there was one other bar down the middle.

Size alone might well have brought fame to Erickson's, but the place offered much more. The bars, fixtures, and mirrors were the best money could buy. No tony twenty-five-cent place had better. There was a concert stage, on one side of which was a "$5000 Grand Pipe Organ." Around the mezzanine were small booths where ladies were permitted, though no sirens of any sort were connected with the establishment. And no female was allowed on the hallowed main floor.

Art was not forgotten. Besides numerous elegant and allegedly classical nudes, there was a thumping great oil, "The Slave Market," which depicted an auction sale of Roman captives and was highly thought of by the connoisseurs of Art who infested Erickson's. The late Spider Johnson, one-time chief bouncer for Erickson's, told me he often saw these art lovers weep into their schooners at the plight of the poor slaves.

Yet this was no place for tears. It was vital and throbbing with the surge of life, the place where men of the outdoors came to meet and to ease their tensions, a true club of working stiffs. Indeed, in time Erickson added an outside sign which designated his establishment as The Workingmen's Club. Itinerants in funds made a beeline for the place. Five minutes after the swift *Telephone* or the graceful *Harvest Queen* docked on the Willamette River, anywhere from fifty to five hundred wage slaves converged on Erickson's like so many homing pigeons. Seven minutes after arrival of a Northern Pacific or Southern Pacific train, in barged another crowd. It was said, and with some truth, that if you wanted to find a certain logger, you went to Erickson's and waited; he would be there soon or late. It was common, too, to address letters to foot-loose friends in care of Erickson's. The place often held hundreds of such missives waiting to be claimed.

Patrons of Erickson's discussed almost but not quite everything over their beverages. Jobs, wages, working conditions were popular subjects. Stupendous feats of work were bragged about. So, too, were noble stints of love-making. The characters of logging bosses and other foremen were praised and assassinated. But hot discussions of religion, economics and politics were forbidden. The mildest form of discouragement from Erickson's corps of competent bouncers was a sharp word of admonition. This was followed, if not instantly heeded, by the bum's rush.

Men might forget the Erickson paintings, or even the $5000 Grand Pipe Organ, but no man ever forgot the prodigious Erickson free lunch. On his business cards, August Erickson described this feature of his place as "A Dainty Lunch." The word was not quite exact. Erickson's free lunch centered around the roast quarter of a shorthorn steer, done to the right pink turn that permitted juices to flow as it was sliced. Bread for sandwiches was cut precisely one-and-one-half inches thick. The Swedish hardtack bread, round and almost as large and hard as grindstones, stood in towering stacks. The mustard pots each held one quart. The mustard was homemade on the spot; it would remove the fur from any tongue. Round logs of sliced sausages filled platters. So did immense hunks of Scandinavian cheeses, including *getost* (of goat's milk) and *gammelost* (meaning "old"), the latter of monstrous strength. Pickled herring swam in big buckets of brine. At Christmas, large kettles of *lutfisk* were added to the dainty lunch.

Beer was five cents and the local brew was served in generous schooners. I possess two of these veritable glasses, and they each hold sixteen ounces of liquid. Strong men used both hands to lift a filled schooner. Genuine Dublin porter was a nickel a small glass. Imported German beers cost a dime. All hard liquor was two for a quarter. Lone drinkers were looked at askance, but when one did appear, it was taken for granted he would require not one but two glasses of whiskey.

The sizable crew of bartenders ran to grenadier size. All wore beautifully roached hair. All had carefully tended mustaches. Across the broad white vest of each was a heavy watch chain. Below the vest was a spick-and-span apron. Trousers were held in place by distinctly he-man galluses, the Hercules brand, fit to stand the strain of lifting a keg and the torsion incident to heaving a bung starter. The bartenders were known for their courtesy, and were able to converse learnedly about prize fighters, cycle champions and such; to give sound advice in matters of love or money; to prescribe suitable eye openers, pick-me-ups, and for lost manhood.

All of Erickson's beverages were sound. A handsome likeness of August Erickson himself appeared on the label of the house whiskey. He was a good-looking, even a studious-looking man, blue-eyed, blond, with a neatly curled mustache. He wore, oddly enough for one of his occupation, pince-nez with a gold chain. His broadcloth suits were tailored for him. He was a man who liked order, and this applied to his saloon.

Order is what Gus Erickson kept, with rare recourse to the police, by his own staff. My friend, the aforementioned Spider Johnson, was for a period chief of these bouncers. Spider was a tall, genial and courteous man, and of many intellectual interests. He handled men well, too. But when stern necessity called, he was lightning quick and carried a punch that was rightly feared. One of his staff was a delightful person known as Jumbo Reilly. Jumbo was big, well over three hundred pounds, and though he really wasn't much of a fighter, his size and general aspect were so downright forbidding, that he had no difficulty holding his job. "Jumbo had the appearance," Spider Johnson told me, "of a gigantic and ill-natured orangutan. He also could emit a sort of laugh-snarl that sounded like a hyena. His fighting tactics were to fall bodily upon his opponent. While not fatal, this was very discouraging. Jumbo's real ability lay in his version of the bum's rush. It was swift and expert."

A favorite story around Erickson's, which had five entrances from the street, concerned a character called Halfpint Halverson, a troublesome Swede logger who liked to argue about the comparative abilities of different nationalities. On one such occasion, when Halfpint disregarded Jumbo's warning, the bouncer plucked Halverson by the collar and pants and threw him bodily out the Second Avenue entrance. Halverson presently wandered in through one of the three Burnside Street doors. Out he went again in a heap. This continued until he had been ejected through four different doors. Working his way around to the Third Avenue side, Halverson made his entry through the fifth and last door. Just inside stood the mountainous Jumbo. Halverson stopped short. "Yesus!" said he, "vas yu bouncer en every goddam saloon en Portland?"

Erickson was a man who took things as they came. His place was but two short blocks from the water front, and when what is still referred to as The Flood of Ninety-four made much of downtown Portland look like Venice, and his own and most other saloons were inundated, Gus promptly chartered a big houseboat, stocked it completely, and moored plumb in the center of Burnside Street. Towboats, rafts and catamarans, and single loggers riding big fir logs came paddling for succor to Erickson's floating saloon. Many customers never left the place during the several days of the flood.

The glory of Erickson's lasted nearly forty years. Prohibition did not close it, nor did it become a bootlegging establishment. It simply carried on halfheartedly with near beer, and added an out-and-out lunch counter, not free. The pretty, plump nudes of the paintings, and even the "The Slave Market," were sold. So was the $5000 Grand Pipe Organ. The size of the place was cut in half, then cut again, to fit the new and dreary times. August Erickson himself died in 1925, in mid-Prohibition. Repeal did not bring a return to the great days, for Oregon's liquor law then permitted the sale of beer over a bar, but not whiskey. Recently the law was amended and on May 4, 1953, the first whiskey since Prohibition was sold over Erickson's bar.

Thus does Erickson's, still The Workingmen's Club, survive as a shadow of its former self. Yet its fame has not wholly evaporated. Every little while some old-timer, filled with nostalgia, stops off in Portland for no other reason than to see if the longest bar on earth still retains its old-time polish. It does, but there is less than sixty feet of it left. Perhaps this is just as well, for within a block of the old saloon is now a manicure parlor that caters to lumberjacks and other now thoroughly tamed men. In such a civilization, there could be no place for the lusty joint that was Erickson's.

Esquire (1954)

The Gorse of Bandon

Although the tragedy of Bandon had its origin in a forest fire, and is properly included in any account of great woods conflagrations, it was the flames from Irish gorse, a so-called ornamental shrub, that laid the handsome Oregon coast town in ashes and took a toll of human life. This gorse *(Ulex europaeus)*, also called hedge and furze, that destroyed Bandon had ironically enough been imported by Lord George Bennet, an Irish peer, who wanted to beautify the new town in Oregon he named from his native place in the Old Country.

That was in the 1870s. By 1936 the shrub had long since gone wild. It lined the streets of Bandon. It infested the second-growth timber around the town, it hedged highways for many miles north and south. At times the Oregon legislature had been moved to consider its eradication, but nothing was ever done.

The leaves of the gorse are very oily, oily enough to drip when warm, and its branches are spiked. These form spiny cushions six to eight feet from the ground; and into these catch-alls fall leaves and twigs, to stay and dry.

In 1936 Bandon was a combined sawmill town and resort city. The Moore Mill & Lumber Company sawed more than one hundred thousand board feet daily, much of it from the beautiful Port Orford, or white, cedar. There was a local fishing industry. And in summer the population of the town increased from eighteen hundred to nearly three thousand, by the "summer" people who were fascinated by the wild southwest coast of Oregon, as they had every good right to be. The country was still "new"; no railroad had penetrated southwest Oregon until 1916, and twenty years later it was reckoned the most remote district in western Oregon.

The town of Bandon was bounded on the north by the Coquille River, along which was situated the main business district. On the west was the Pacific Ocean. On the east and south were stump ranches and dairy farms, interspaced with second-growth timber, and beyond them the old-growth forest of mixed Douglas fir and Port Orford cedar. Logging had been going on in this area for sixty years, but on a large scale only since about 1908.

During most of September, 1936, slashing and clearing fires had been burning slowly and more or less harmlessly along the hills bordering Bear Creek, to the south of Bandon. The morning of the 26th was hot for the seacoast town, climbing well into the seventies long before noon. Moreover, the hygrometer at a logging camp on near-by Eden Ridge showed a relative humidity reading of only eight. (Thirty and anything below is considered very dangerous.)

Twice before noon the Bandon city fire department had made runs with its modern motorized equipment to the high-school building near the town limits, where grass and small shrubbery had reared up in flames. What set these fires, nobody knew. They may have come from a cigarette, or they may have started from an ember wafted in from the hills to the east, where slashings were burning.

By noon Chief Woomer of the city fire department realized it was going to be a busy day for him and his men. They found everything as dry as powder. But the business and domestic life of the village was undisturbed. Late summer residents and local folk were downtown buying their groceries, and the job press of the *Western World* was running off some handbills.

In front of the Hartman moving picture theater a man was putting up lobby signs announcing the evening show. The title of the featured film oddly enough was "Thirty-six Hours to Live." Came noon, and Chief Woomer got a call telling him that the town's main water line was in danger from fire. He moved his men out along it, just outside the city limits. He'd have to save that line or he wouldn't have any water.

Chief Woomer found that the Bear Creek slashings fire, now fanned by a rising east wind, meant business. White dead embers were falling lightly all over town. Some of them were not quite dead, and the firemen spent the afternoon running from the water main into town to extinguish grass and shrub fires, then back again to the city's water main.

But townspeople as yet were not even uneasy. Supper passed with nothing more startling than comment that the smoke was sure getting thick. Many women and children and not a few men went into the Hartman movie to see the show.

Quite suddenly, on the southeast end of town, in the residential district, a single burst of flame shot up into the falling dark. So sudden and unexpected was this blast of fire, rising to a great height, roaring and crackling, that for a moment folks in homes along Eleventh Street thought it an apparition, or maybe some sort of explosion.

Probably it *was* an explosion—for that is about the only way to describe what happens when fire gets into a good clump of gorse.

With sirens open the city fire department roared through the falling night to East Eleventh Street. Here was a wide road, the place to stop the coming flames if stopped they could be. Hydrants and hose were coupled in a moment, but the water seemed to have absolutely no effect on the flaming gorse, unless it was to spread the fire.

Bandon firemen vowed then, as they do today, that they never faced fire so blistering-hot as those flaming clumps of gorse, and they cursed the memory of Lord George Bennet. The fire raced quickly along the south side of East Eleventh, shooting up tongues of flame fifty—some said more than one hundred—feet into the air, spitting off oily gobs that turned into balls of fire and went whirling away over the town roofs. A hose full of water was burned in two as though it had been paper.

And now, back of the firemen, fires were springing up everywhere, on Tenth, and beyond. A second hose was burned through, filled with water though it was. Roofs along Eleventh and Tenth began to smolder. A moment later they were all in flames, almost at the same instant. The whole long street with its many fine homes was doomed. From one of the homes an ambulance pulled away carrying a woman who was to give birth to a child within the hour.

The firemen fought on. Sometime between eight and nine o'clock Chief Woomer hurried to the Hartman movie. The show was stopped for a moment while he asked that all able-bodied men present report to help fight the fire. There was no panic. The women and children, and it is said a number of men who seemed to be able-bodied, remained to see how "Thirty-six Hours to Live" would come out.

The fire department was now making a sort of last stand to keep the fire from getting down into the business section. They found they were up against something that few if any fire departments had ever seen. A stray spark would fall in a green clump of gorse near a house. An instant later the gorse was flaming higher than the house. In another instant the house was wholly on fire. Time and again it happened. Many homes were all but surrounded with gorse, hedges of it, and these fairly exploded. (I saw considerable gorse burn during the Bandon fire. All I could think of was something I had never even seen: a whole barrel of celluloid collars burning at once. The gorse burns as quickly as celluloid and makes a noise much the same.)

Meanwhile men and fire equipment had come from Myrtle Point, Coquille, and Marshfield. Chub Young and his men of the Coos Forest Fire Patrol were at the Bandon reservoir, trying to save it. They kept up their battle until the fire burned their hose away. Then they kicked their pump into the waters of the reservoir and left—with no time to spare.

All of this was only the beginning. When the movie show let out at half-past nine, you could stand on the street in downtown Bandon and hardly know what was going on just over the bluff where the residence section lay. There was a dull, reddish glow to be seen, but no naked fire as yet.

The men of the United States Coast Guard were busy. They were standing by in the river with the lighthouse tender *Rose* and trying to evacuate townspeople. It was a tough job. People, especially the old folks, seemed not to understand they were in actual danger. The Coast Guard boys had to talk rough to many oldsters to get them to pick up a few personal belongings and get aboard the *Rose.*

And not all the old folks made it. Mr. and Mrs. George Williams, Coos county pioneers, died on their patch of ground, Williams at the door of their little home, his wife in the woodshed. There were nine others that night who failed in their flight.

At some time between eleven and midnight the fire had consumed nearly every home in the residence section. Now it swept up to the rim of the bluff overlooking the business district. The little Catholic church standing on the very rim went up in an instant of flame that was reflected on the plate-glass windows of stores below the hill.

At the same time a roaring wall of flame threw itself with dreadful fury down the draw that led from the bluff to the heart of Bandon's business life. Here the flames boomed like cannon, and reddened the blanched faces of hundreds of citizens who had fled from the east side. Stopped not a moment by the puny streams of water poured into it, the fire came down the draw like so much lightning and leaped upon the business blocks—the "fireproof" district.

It was a stirring if ghastly scene. Maybe a modern Dante could have etched it, but no photograph could. The single street crammed full of automobiles and people on foot, folks bent with bundles and boxes, and wide-eyed children lugging dogs and cats and birds in cages. There was no stopping the fire now. Everybody could see that. They could tell that much when the tires on parked automobiles melted and ran over the pavement in a sticky mass, and when great plate-glass windows buckled, then crashed with the heat.

There were only three ways to go now. One was across the Coquille River to the sand dunes; another, down to the jetty on the town side of the river; and the road to Coquille village was said to be open still, but hot and blazing all the way.

The Coast Guard's *Rose,* the Port of Bandon's tug, and tugs from the Moore Mill & Lumber Company were making trips from the burning side of the river over to the sand dunes, and presently the dunes took on the aspect of a tragic picnic.

But there were many who, even in a time like this, wanted to save the gadget which meant most in their lives— the automobile. In a crush of jumbled traffic they edged their way down First Street in the direction of the jetty. The fire was right on top of them. The brave firemen covered the retreat as best they could.

The fireproof banks, the stores, the city hall, and the fire station itself—they roared inside like infernos, while flames shot up from their roofs. They were proof of nothing but building mortality in the face of a fire such as this.

In the Coos & Curry telephone exchange building, cool but white-faced girls worked feverishly at the switchboards until firemen came to order them out of the place. The rooms were choky with smoke when they left.

Down First Street moved the doomed procession of a hundred or more automobiles, with fire blistering their backs, until they could move no farther. Here they piled onto the narrow beach along the bay, some of them in the tide. The last ones didn't get to the beach. They reached the end of the pavement and there they remained to melt and run into caricatures of automobiles.

Up and down First Street the buildings lighted up, one after another; and when the hundreds of people who did not cross to the sand dunes got to the end of the pavement, there was nothing ahead of them but the jetty and the Pacific Ocean.

Soon the jetty was swarming, and the refugees were to find that the rocks within the jetty walls already were warm. Red embers beat them with a hail of fire, and overhead, carried by the strange, strong wind, went flaming pieces of boards, even whole sections of roofs.

Out onto the narrow beach piled hundreds of folk, the cars they had just abandoned now smoking. There was driftwood on this little beach, some of it fair-sized logs, and the frantic, hurrying people had no more than got into shallow water when the driftwood began to blaze. That's how hot it was at the end of First Street, and one could see the marks of the heat long afterward—log upon log, once bleached white by the tides, was black as coal.

Crouching behind these barriers of near tinder, with their knees in sand and shallow water, men and women could go no farther. They had to stay there, or drown, and they must have prayed that Bandon would not take long in the burning. Again and again the driftwood logs would break into flames, and the hands of a score of women were cruelly torn by the gravel they scooped up and threw over the protective yet dangerously dry logs.

These crouching figures, with the very hair on their heads being singed, could have seen, if they were watching, the last stand of the fire department at the end of First Street. Hose after hose was burned away, and finally the tires of the fire truck melted. It was only then that Chief Woomer and his men quit the fight, and by then all of Bandon had burned to the ground.

Across the river were the hundreds who had gone over in the boats. It was cold on the dunes, despite the fierce heat on the other side of the stream, and here as in the doomed town, there were acts of kindness and even of heroism that folks said made them keep up their faith in human nature . . . It is often that way in a fire.

The eighteen miles of road to Coquille were filled with refugees, in cars and afoot, and their way was well lighted by burning trees and barns and houses, plus the spectacular destruction of a large dance hall. Everywhere the fires burned right down to the side of the highway.

But the great loss of life and property had been in Bandon. The business section of the town had burned in the brief space of an hour. The entire tragedy, from the time fire first shot up from that clump of gorse on East Eleventh, until the last business structure was gutted, occupied less than five hours.

There were eleven known dead: the Mr. and Mrs. Williams already mentioned; Mrs. Tom Hill, Nina Bottom, Daniel Kountz, Mrs. Charles McCulloch, John Reider, Jack Bailey, J. M. Baker, and a Mrs. Martin and her ward.

The total property loss in the fire ran to about $3,000,000, of which about half occurred in Bandon itself.

All great fires have their oddities. On Bandon's Eleventh Street, otherwise a mass of ruins, stood untouched a modest bungalow, material for which could not have cost more than a hundred and fifty dollars. Two small patches of corn in the district were yellowed, but not blackened nor killed. A few yards away the heat had been such as to reduce metal to blobs.

It is customary, after large fires, to laud the laddies of the fire department. Usually it is justified. The Bandon laddies deserve more than a casual pat on the back. That fight they made on First Street, backing slowly toward the ocean while Bandon burned all around them, playing water until the last hose was gone, giving a yard, holding a minute, then giving again, until the tires of their truck melted, until men lost their hair and eyebrows—this was courageous work by a determined crew, a feat to go down in any history of fire fighting.

Able work by the department from Marshfield was credited with saving the huge warehouse of a lumber concern, and a large auto camp. Bandon's sawmill and veneer plants, thanks to their advantageous location, were saved. So was the high school. The offices of the *Western World,* a much-quoted weekly, were wrecked, but the files of the paper were saved.

In terms of forest losses the fire did not amount to a great deal. True, it destroyed several thousand acres of second-growth timber, and it doubtless killed the restocking possibilities of other acres. But it never got into old-growth timber, according to E. H. Macdaniels of the United States Forest Service.

The post-mortems showed that the main fire was a merging of slash fires along Bear Creek, east of Bandon, plus a strong east wind. These factors and the many thousands of clumps of gorse imported from Bandon, Ireland, are what destroyed Bandon, Oregon.

Burning an Empire (1943)

Whistle Punks

When I first went to work in a logging camp in the Pacific Northwest and heard mention of "whistle punks" I thought the term had reference to some mythical animal like the swamp wogglers and side-hill badgers of the East, or to some fabulous character of the Oregon timber. But I soon learned that whistle punks were very real, and very, very hard-boiled.

In the West any boy is known as a "punk," just why I haven't learned. Whistle punks are officially known on camp pay rolls as signal boys. They are the youthful loggers who, with jerk wire or electric toots-ee, give the signals for starting and stopping to engineers of donkey engines that yard the big Douglas fir timber, up and down the West Coast. They are automatons, standing throughout the day in one spot and yanking the whistle wire once, twice, or in combinations, in answer to the hook tender's orders. The hook tender has a log ready. He shouts "Hi!" The punk jerks his whistle line and the whistle on the engine snorts. The engineer "opens her up," and the log is brought in to the landing.

Despite his lowly job, which compares in dignity with that of the water boy of construction gangs, the punk is a well-known character in the Northwest. In Tacoma, Washington, the "Lumber Capital of America," a newspaper used to have a daily column headed "The Whistle Punk." I hold the punk to be well worth a column.

When placed alongside the average whistle punk, the so-called tough kids of the Bowery and the gamins of Paris are like so many cherubim. Punks are the hardest kids ever; or, at least, they *want* to be. They are so tough they won't even read the *Police Gazette.* To hear one talk you would suspect that he liked for breakfast nothing so much as a keg of iron bolts soaked in gasoline, wood alcohol, and snuff.

The vizor of the punk's cap is worn smooth where it has rested over an ear. His best Sunday conversation sounds like extracts from Rabelais; and when he is going *good* he can outcurse any cockney that ever mentioned the King of England. When he spits, it is what learned men term a cosmic disturbance . . . Yes, the punk is *hard.*

The toughness of the punk is equaled only by his bellicose precocity. He is what an Englishman calls "a little bounder." Although he is but eighteen years of age, the punk often calls the camp foreman "boy" and gets away with it. When the foreman has occasion to bawl out the rigging crew, the punk adds a caustic razzing: "Who tol' you guys you was loggers?" Of an evening when some of the old-timers are doing a bit of stovelogging around the big heater in the bunkhouse, the punk horns in with some of *his* experiences. And his talk, when they will let him talk or when they cannot prevent him, is well interspersed with those short but expressive old Anglo-Saxon words of less than five letters. The subject of his logging tales is always the same: how he told the hook tender to "go to hell," or the timekeeper to "make 'er out, damn her." I have heard twenty-odd different punks tell exactly the same story in precisely the same words, and I am forced to the conclusion that the formula has been secretly published and circulated among them.

As a gambler the punk believes himself the genuine, one-hundred-proof Hoyle. He is the kind of wise youth who tells the world he knows when to play 'em and when to lay 'em down. But he seldom has enough money to interest the camp tinhorns; otherwise someone would have to write a new song about the punk who broke the bank at Monte Carlo.

The punk's literary tastes are simple. He likes *The James Boys in Missouri* and *The Life and Battles of John L. Sullivan.* In his suitcase he has a pamphlet clandestinely purchased from a news agent on a railroad train. It concerns the life and works of a frail yet beautiful lady known as Mayme, no last name given. It was never entered at the post office as second-class or other matter. He also reads the "comic books." Occasionally he will, in a blatant voice, read aloud the asininities of that popular family of morons answering to the names of "Min" and "Andy."

It is the camp cook, more often than not, who removes some of the offensive freshness of the punk.

This camp chef is the master of all he surveys. The kitchen and dining room are his precincts, and he guards them no less jealously than he does his dignity as cook. He is supreme monarch of the mulligan. Loud, boisterous talk from the crew at mealtime, to the cook's way of thinking, should be punished by no less an operation than speedy decapitation; while derogatory remarks about the fare, or in fact any sort of wisecracks around the cookhouse, call for complete annihilation. Thus it is the cookshack where the forward-looking punk often meets his Waterloo.

Once at a camp on the mighty Fraser River in British Columbia, I witnessed—and cheered on—the freshest punk that ever blew whistle being propelled suddenly, openly, and manifestly from the cookhouse door, and to a distance of some twenty feet beyond, all by the honest right boot of one Erickson, a noted camp chef of the time. The punk was not only booted clear of the hallowed precincts, but with him at the moment were at least ten million vitamins, in the form of bread dough, plastered well over his head and running down both cheeks, thrown there, as I later learned, by Chef Erickson. Inquiry brought to light that the punk, in his usual carefree way, had wandered into the kitchen where Erickson was making bread, and had asked him, brightly, why it was that Danes were so much smarter than Swedes. Erickson, it appeared, had been born in one of the Faubourgs of Stockholm.

The punk's private idea of heaven is to have a trick suit of clothes with two-toned coat, a long haircut, a chick, at least $15 in his pocket, and an old car stripped of all but its lungs and rigged up to look as the punk thinks a Mercedes racer looks. Here is paradise enow!

Whistle Punks

But he can't have heaven and his $7.00 a day at the same time, and so when in camp the punk does the best he can with cigarets, snuff, chewing-tobacco, and loud talk. This snuff is not the kind that our forefathers sniffed. It is a powerful concoction of finely ground tobacco known as Scandinavian Dynamite and is carried in the lip. It is the badge of the he-man.

Just plain snuff, however, is not enough for the punk who is really *hard.* Not at all. He first fills his lower lip with the snuff and then wads in a bite of plug-tobacco. On Sundays he does even better, when, in addition to this monumental chew, he simultaneously smokes a cig'ret. It is here he rises to heights of *he.* He blows smoke out of his nose and mouth, and if it were possible he would blow it forth from his eyes and both ears. If a punk ever succeeds in accomplishing this latter feat, he will become the greatest punk of all time.

The punk's boots always have the longest and sharpest calks in the camp. If calks were made six inches long, the punk would have them. How he loves to stagger carelessly into the bunkhouse, stand still a moment until he gets his calks well set into the floor, and then turn sharply on his heels in an effort to rip the flooring asunder. No really good punk stops short of a two-foot splinter. Some can split an inch board. Hard? . . . If they ever build bunkhouses with cement floors whistle punks will quit cold.

When a punk stags (cuts off) his pants legs, he stags them four inches higher than any one else in camp. When he paints his slicker to keep out the rain, he paints it *red!* His bunk is the dirtiest on the claim. The cuspidor besides his bunk is a keg, sawed in two.

In all these things the punk is colossally he. But there is another side to the story of this most masculine youth, for, like all red-blooded men, he has a weakness. *It is chocolate bars.* Yes, sir, a weakness for those bars of candy so popular with children and young ladies. The choc'lit bar is his one vulnerable spot. One minute he may be telling how he would like a good meal of canned heat, or making a cynical reference to the origin and forebears of the camp foreman; but expose him to a soft brown bar of chocolate, and you have taken the wind from his sail. He is half ashamed to take it, but he is helpless.

On an average it requires six choc'lit bars daily to run a punk, with ten on Sundays. It is here that he falls down in the business of being a tough guy. For whoever heard of a tough guy, a real he-logger, eating choc'lit bars? It is preposterous. And the punk feels it. But what would you? . . . Youth must be served, and no man can rise above his eighteen years.

So, when in camp I used to tire of the punk's heavy-duty stories and tough tales and loud blats and cursing and cynical jeers, why, I would just reach out right in front of the whole crowd and offer him a chocolate bar. I called it by name, so that all might see and hear: "Hey, punk, want a chocolate bar?" He would waver a moment between acceptance and scornful refusal . . . but the choc'lit bar always won. This shamed and tamed him for the evening at least; he would munch his chocolate and remain quiet.

It was worth ten cents.

The Century Magazine (1927)

Harry Tracy: "King of Western Robbers"

Of all America's long list of eminent thugs and illustrious outlaws, only the late Jesse James has been accorded more acclaim in paper-backed biographies than has Harry Tracy, the moronic yet crafty killer known variously to my generation of dime-novel readers as the Lone Bandit, the Oregon Badman, the Oregon Train Robber, and King of Western Robbers.

Those titles are merely hyperbole. Tracy never worked alone. He was a native of Wisconsin, not Oregon; he never stuck up a train of cars in his life; and the Boswell who termed him the "King of Western Robbers" must have had an uncommonly low opinion of road agents, for Tracy's biggest job of highway robbery netted him approximately $50.

Yet this murderous person inspired as many lurid volumes as did the Daltons, or did the truly eminent Senor Joaquin Murietta, who held up and cleaned out whole mining camps and seemed so fetching that a poet, Cincinatus Miller, adopted the Senor's first name and thereafter wrote under it.

Thirty-odd years ago, I sat bug-eyed in a haymow with a copy of what was doubtless the swellest of the Tracy books. It was written by one Harry Hawkeye, an author never short of adjectives or descriptive phrases; and it made the Jameses, the Youngers and Butch Cassidy's gang look like a bunch of cherubim.

No doubt many of my contemporaries got their idea of Tracy from the same volume. Later, when I came to live in Oregon, I took some pains to look closely into the Tracy record, which shows him to have been perhaps the most unsuccessful robber of record, a man who stole small change from honest bartenders. He was bad all right; and so is any half-wit who is cornered. He was forever getting caught and

237

thrown into this or that jail. No one, not even the alert Harry Hawkeye, ever heard of him until he broke from the Oregon penitentiary.

His break though, was a dandy, and so were his two "funerals," which were veritable gatherings of moronia.

Tracy's name was Henry Severn and he was born in Pittsville, Wisconsin, in 1874. A woman who went to school with him told he was a dull yahoo who stood practically at the bottom of his class, and skipped school whenever he dared. In the early nineties he left Wisconsin and drifted south, where he was soon engaged in cattle rustling. For a time he was a minor stooge in the Powder Springs or Hole-in-the-Wall gang, operating along the northern border of Colorado. Implicated in the brutal slaying of Valentine Hoye, cattleman, Tracy was captured and thrown into the tinpot jail at Aspen, Colorado. He walked out of it one day without trouble.

He went into Utah. Taken for highway robbery (this was his "big job" and netted him $50) he was put in a road gang as a sort of trusty. But he walked away again, and in the winter of 1898-1899, turned up in Portland, where he teamed with one David Merrill, the village badboy of Vancouver, Washington.

Tracy and Merrill now took to ramming their guns into the surprised faces of God-fearing bartenders when they were just opening up in the morning. Ten dollars, dimes and nickels, was a good haul at this racket. Once they held up a street car conductor. The take was $3.85.

The cops presently had Merrill, and Danny Wiener, local detective, at last sighted Tracy on Fourth Avenue. Just then Tracy hopped aboard a passing locomotive, dug his gun into the engineer's ribs, and told him to hightail.

Back on the train, a freight, the brakeman had seen what was up. He cut the air and the train stopped. Tracy jumped from the locomotive and started to run. Across the street, a witness to the event, was Albert Way, young son of a butcher who had previously been robbed of four dollars by Tracy.

The kid recognized Tracy. He dove into the meat shop and came out with a double-barreled shotgun which his old man had thoughtfully placed there and let fly with both barrels. The charge caught Tracy fair behind the ear and the badman fell, humorously enough, over a picket fence and plumb into the yard of a policeman's home. This cop, Officer Wilkinson, happened to be at home. He forthwith manacled Tracy and called for the wagon.

Merrill was sent to the pen for fifteen years. Tracy drew twenty years. Then, on the morning of June 9, 1902, Tracy and Merrill grabbed rifles out of a cupboard in the prison laundry and shot their way over the wall, killing three guards and a lifer who got in the way. And now began the sixty days that put the heretofore unheard of Tracy into the dime novels.

The hue and cry got under way with typical Oregon zest in such matters. The National Guard was called out. Bloodhounds were brought from Walla Walla. Oregon farmers and lumberjacks organized posses. All in vain. The two thugs gained the Columbia River and forced a couple of Portland citizens to row them across the stream. Before leaving the boat, the outlaws asked for their ferrrymen's money. It was a sizable haul—for Tracy and Merrill—being four dollars. Merrill took two and returned two, along with a mighty nice Elk's badge. "Here," said Merrill, "is where you can join the Elks for two dollars." Thus did Merrill formulate a wisecrack that was to be used by vaudeville performers for many years.

Out turned the Vancouver company of the Washington National Guard. It was more than rumor that said the soldier boys took along as much liquor as they did powder. Cows and calves, peacefully feeding on Clark County's incomparable grass, were hit and ran bellowing to the barn. A farmer near Kalama got a bullet through his straw hat. The hired man on a ranch near Kelso had a milk-pail shot out of his hand. The late Joe Day, Portland detective, who was in on the chase, related to me: "The whole damned country was full of militia, and many of the boys were potted. They shot at everything, and Clark and Cowlitz counties sounded like the Spanish-American war all over again. It was the most dangerous place I was ever in."

The National Guard returned empty-handed to their usual occupations.

Near the town of Napavine, on the night of June 28, Tracy shot and killed Merrill. This was not known immediately, or until Tracy told several farmers about the shooting—which he called a "duel." The motive for the killing is not known. Harry Hawkeye, of course, knew all about it, and he made it out a noble duel in the best tradition—six paces and fire. The late Dan Bush, Chehalis newspaper man who first examined Merrill's body, informed me that the man had been shot in the back. Brave guy, Tracy!

The State of Oregon had offered $2,500 each for Tracy or Merrill, dead or alive. A Mrs. Waggoner found the latter's body, and Dan Bush aided her in trying to collect the bounty. But the State of Oregon, then as now careful of the taxpayers' money, wanted to settle for $500. Mrs. Waggoner sued, and the case dribbled in and out of courts for almost a decade. In the end the woman got nothing.

Shortly after the killing of his partner, Tracy appeared on the beach near Olympia. He got the crew of a tugboat to run him to Meadow Point, outside Seattle. Puget Sound got the jitters. Hundreds of deputies were sworn in. Fresh alarms occurred daily. The outlaw was reported seen, simultaneously, in Spokane, Boise, El Paso, and Fargo, North Dakota.

And now the King of Western Robbers demonstrated his brains. He got hold of a young lad and sent him into Seattle to buy some ammunition. The lad, of course, went directly to the police and told them where the half-wit was in hiding. The law sent a posse which engaged Tracy in a gun battle near Bothell, and Tracy killed three of them.

The outlaw worked his way up through Snoqualmie Pass and emerged into the great open spaces of Eastern

Washington. Early in August the small son of a rancher near Creston saw a man on the place who looked much like newspaper pictures of Tracy. The youngster jumped on a horse and galloped into Creston village, where he had difficulty in getting anyone to listen. Five men, however, took the boy seriously. For the record, their names were Staub, Lillengren, Morrison, Lanter, and Maurice Smith. These men are largely forgotten today, but they were the boys who were to shoot it out with the great Oregon train robber.

There was no fooling with these fellows. They went directly to the ranch. The moment Tracy spotted them he ran behind a large boulder. The posse went to work nicking off hunks of the rock until Tracy could stand it no longer. He took it on the lam into a nearby wheat field, and as he ran Maurice Smith shot a leg from under him. Tracy crawled on all fours into the field, and the watching men saw the yellowing tufts wave as he moved deeper into the grain. It was near dark.

The posse now had the badman surrounded, and like the wise men they were, they sat around all night, breaking the tedium by taking pot shots into the wheat. In the morning they advanced and found the Lone Bandit now really alone, a big hole in his forehead. He had died by his own hand, although he doubtless would have bled to death from the wound in his leg.

A photographer was summoned, while the dead thug was neatly posed lying on his left side; gun in hand, finger on trigger, with the tall wheat for background, a picture to sell in postcard size by the thousand.

The affair was now to turn into macabre farce, beside which the funeral orgies over Rudolph Valentino, two decades later, were in excellent taste. Tracy's body was heaved into a cart and hauled into Davenport, Washington, where it was laid out in the village undertaker's establishment. The town was packed and overflowing with the esthetic forebears of the New York city mob who were later to storm the Valentino obsequies.

Nearly everyone in Davenport, it turned out, wanted a close look at the remains of Harry Tracy; and they wanted "souvenirs," too. The huge crowd assaulted the mortician's joint, crashing the windows, breaking down the doors, yelling and screaming like Indians on warpath. It was bedlam. In what an eyewitness, who remained strangely calm, estimated as fifteen minutes, the body of the King of Train Robbers, with rigor mortis little more than accomplished, was naked, stripped of all its clothing. Hair was torn and cut from the head until it was bald in spots.

There wasn't enough hair and clothing to go around, so the souvenir hunters fought. Harridans brawled tearing the Tracy shirt, for a strip to put on the parlor whatnot. Strong men battled to retain a piece of overall, or a shoe, or a hunk of gallus. The five possemen were fortunate indeed to get the naked body into a rough pine box and aboard a railroad train for Salem, Oregon, where they might collect the reward which had mounted to $5,000.

In Portland, where there was a long wait between trains, the possemen sat up all night guarding the cadaver; and when they arrived in Salem, another crowd of souvenir hunters rushed them. Local police could do little with the mob, which stove in the coffin to get a look at the great man. They hacked away the pine sides until there wasn't enough to kindle a fire. Extra police had to be called before the body, with long strips of skin missing, could be removed to the prison cemetery.

What little was left of Tracy and his coffin was put away in the ground on August 8, a little less than two months after the break from the pen. A passably good cigar was named for him, but it went off the market soon. Some forgiving bartender invented a Tracy cocktail—"Three Shots and You're Out." At least a dozen women appeared at newspaper offices in Spokane, Seattle, Tacoma, Portland and Los Angeles to say that they were, separately, the one and only widow of the Oregon Badman. A Seattle impresario of drama produced a quickie with Tracy as the leading and lovable, if misunderstood, hero.

Neither Mr. Lewis nor Mr. Clark achieved such distinction. Thus passed the King of Oregon Outlaws who spent nearly all of his life behind bars and whose chief business was the robbing of lone bartenders.

The Oregonian (July 23, 1947)

The story of Tracy and Merrill's breakout from the Oregon Penitentiary is told in detail in Bunco Kelly's *Thirteen Years in the Oregon Penitentiary*. Kelly claims that the body brought back with Tracy was not that of Merrill.

Disaster in June

It had been a long sweltering day, the 14th of June, 1903. The sun traveled across the Oregon sky in a steady blaze that shriveled the wheat and sent thousands of sheep to find such shade as they could in the creek bottoms. Since dawn the windmills on the ranches had stood motionless. Heat blurred the vision as it shimmered in waves up and down and across the sides of the barns.

It was even worse in the village of Heppner, county seat and trading center of a vast sheep-and-wheat region. Set in a narrow valley along tiny Willow Creek, Heppner was hemmed by stark hills. Not a breath of air moved all that interminable Sunday. Tar oozed from the seams of papered shacks. Clapboards curled on the better homes. Dogs slunk under porches and panted. The children couldn't go swimming, for there wasn't enough water in Willow Creek to cover their knees.

But four o'clock brought welcome signs of relief. The sun abruptly disappeared. A breeze came up, fitful yet strong. The sky turned gray, then black. Heppner people began to feel better. They could tell that a cooling shower was about to break the hot spell, just as hot spells had been broken time out of mind.

A few big drops of rain splattered the parched roofs. The leaves of the cottonwoods along the creek rustled nervously, and turned the rising wind. Then the sky, as black now as midnight, was split by a bolt, followed by thunder that sounded in the close valley like the crack of doom. And the rain came down.

Heppner folks were used to quick, violent storms. This one seemed to be particularly violent. Water poured down in volume such as the oldest inhabitants had never seen. Hail came intermittently, but so thickly it began to pile up in dooryards like so much snow. The valley and the village were lighted every few moments by savage flashes in the dark sky. Thunder rolled in continuous volleys. It was a wonderfully exciting time for the youngsters. They stood at windows and saw Willow Creek rising as they watched. Fathers and mothers were unworried. The creek might fill its banks. It might overflow. It had done so in the past. But there could be no danger. There were no dams upstream to give way, either on Willow Creek or on Balm Fork, which joined the creek just above town.

The cloudburst continued for perhaps twenty minutes, and with it the hail, the wind, the thunder and lightning. Then the clatter of the tormented elements was wholly lost in a new and sudden roaring. It wasn't a noise that grew. It was a noise both mighty and full-blown when it struck the ear, and it brought men up out of their chairs and women out of their kitchens.

This strange and new noise was the meeting, just above the village, of two monstrous great torrents rolling down Balm Fork and the main creek, merging into one thunderous wave of water bearing trees, ranch houses, barns, horned cattle, sheep, fences, and baled hay. The two torrents made one flood, not of Old Testament size, but sufficient to wipe out the village of Heppner.

The new steam laundry, filled with heavy machinery, held out for a few minutes, long enough to dam the waters twenty feet deep and long enough for a few people to see what was upon them and to start running. Then the dam gave way, loosing the rush of a lake into the streets. Carrying children, a few of the running men managed to get out from under; but not many of the women. Skirts were long in 1903, and the muddy water quickly made them unbearably heavy. The women sagged, stumbled, then disappeared.

George Conser, cashier of the town bank, and his wife were at home. They heard the noise. Just then the first tremendous wave struck. The windows and doors caved in. The Consers started upstairs, water at their heels. The whole house groaned. It wrenched. It reeled, and then its lower portion collapsed. Away went the Consers in their ark of an upper story.

August Lundell had an instant in which to run out of his house and to climb a big cottonwood tree, dragging two youngsters with him. Just then the Lundell house caught the full force of the wave. It left its foundations, keeled over, and came rolling past, Mrs. Lundell clinging to the top side. Her husband reached out and caught her, like a sack of mail at a way station, pulling her into the God-given tree, where the Lundell family lived it out while Heppner was being destroyed.

At the fine Palace Hotel, three stories of staunch brick, Mrs. Phil Metchan, wife of the owner, who was absent, saw her two Japanese houseboys run out of the hotel toward the flood, a block away. She couldn't tell which way the flood was going to move next, nor how fast. She picked up Dorothy, her two-year-old, and ran for the nearest hill. Back at the hotel the waters were already trickling into the cellar.

Meanwhile, the two Japanese lads were performing heroically in pulling women and children from the water and débris; and one of them gave his life in the effort.

Now the wallowing houses, the cattle, the sheep, the mud, hail, and human beings were being piled up in a hideous jam against a row of stout trees; and another dam was formed, to hold just long enough to make and loose a second lake. It struck the little hand laundry and ground it instantly into a mass of kindling, killing the seven or eight poor Chinese within. Then the wave went on to leap at the Mallory home, picking it up entire, with Gus Mallory, postmaster, bedridden in an upper story, and sent it on a careening voyage halfway across the village, to come to rest on Main Street, facing the front doors of the Belvedere saloon.

In the Belvedere a quiet poker game had been in progress; and between interest in the cards and the terrific din of the storm the players did not know that Heppner was already under water. Then the flood hit Main Street. Frank Roberts, owner of the Belvedere, ran out to look for his family. The other players left too, and old Dick Neville, Civil War veteran and bartender, waved them on their way. "I'll stay with her till she floats," he cried, and turned down another jolt.

At the Heppner railroad station Agent Kernan and family got a look at what was coming from the upper part of town. They ran for the hills. Kernan, however, had forgotten something, but whatever it was, it was scarcely worth the effort, for when he emerged from the depot this time, Time had caught up. The rush of water tore him off his legs and whirled him into the dreadful hodgepodge of bodies, timbers, and other débris.

Meanwhile, two young men of Heppner had set out on a heroic mission. They were Leslie Matlock and Bruce Kelley. They saw the first big wave when the steam laundry gave way. They knew it was too late to do much for Heppner. It might even be too late to warn the hamlet of Lexington, ten miles down Willow Creek, and the hamlet of Ione, eight miles beyond Lexington. But a man, two men, could try.

While Kelley hurried to get horses at the one livery stable not in the path of the waters, Matlock ran to Bisbee's hardware store for wire cutters. They would have to ride overland, and between Heppner and the lower villages were fence after fence of taut, well strung barbed wire. The store was locked. Matlock kicked in the door, got two pairs of cutters, then ran for the stable. He and Kelley mounted and took off, heading over the big bare hills in order to get out of the Willow Creek Valley, now running high and fast with damnation.

It was tough going, overland. All downhill or uphill, and no road. Dark, too. Every half-mile or less was a fence to be cut, a dangerous business, with the sky flashing and every strand of wire potentially an electrode, ready to burn a man to a crisp. And down came the rain, while the great hailstones beat and frightened the horses.

The animals responded well for speed, but they were hard to manage at the fences; and the cutting took time—true, only a few seconds here and a few seconds there, but they began to add up when racing a flood tearing hell-bent down Willow Creek. The two riders came in sight of Lexington to find that the waters were going to beat them by about two minutes; but no lives were lost, though several houses were destroyed. At Lexington the waters were damming up just as the two horsemen pounded past on the hillside above the settlement. "We can beat her to Ione," Matlock yelled to Kelley. On they went.

There were more fences to cut. Both animals were tiring. The riders urged, praised, cajoled, demanded, using every trick known to experienced horsemen. The animals responded, too, and presently came galloping into tiny and unsuspecting Ione. Matlock looked over his shoulder to see what Willow Creek looked like down here. It was bankfull, swift, mean-looking, but the flood hadn't come yet. It wasn't in sight.

The sudden appearance in the hamlet of two men on wind-blown horses brought people running out of their houses. "Get to the hills!" Matlock cried. Ione's total population went into action. Driving such stock as they had at home, and carrying such household treasures as they could, they moved to the hills on either side of the settlement. The flood waters hit the village within minutes after the horsemen arrived, but not a life was lost.

Back in tragic Heppner the worst had happened. Within half an hour—some said twenty minutes—after the steam-laundry dam gave way, the flood had thundered and boiled through town, and the waters had receded until they no more than filled the banks of Willow Creek. It had been as quick as that.

The worst was bad enough. When Phil Metchan rode into the stricken village early next morning, he saw a sight he recalled vividly almost fifty years later. It was a big, long two-horse farm wagon moving slowly up Main Street to one of the several emergency morgues. On it were bodies piled one upon another, twenty, thirty of them, with the long mud-matted hair of women hanging out over the wheels. All over Heppner Death was moving in somber processions, riding in wagons, carts, hayricks, even in rubber-tired buggies.

Here and there, like the Palace Hotel, a few buildings still stood—the Odd Fellows Block, the courthouse, the Fair Store, and the Belvedere saloon and its upstairs Opera House. The latter structure's two big floors were covered now with bodies laid out under blankets and pieces of canvas.

In between these few larger buildings was the ghastly débris of the deluge—the barns and houses that had become mere piles of jackstraws in which searchers looked for, and found, still more bodies. Before night two companies of Oregon militia had moved in to help.

All day and all night, by the light of flaming torches and dim farm lanterns, an army of men dug graves while another army of carpenters sawed and hammered to make coffins. Many would be needed. The death count rose steadily throughout the day: 180 at noon, then 200, and finally 225 bodies were recovered, among them that of the brave Japanese lad who had lost his life in saving others. (In 1951 his was the only Japanese grave in Heppner Cemetery, and a granite marker tells of his courageous deed.)

Two hundred and twenty-five people had died in Heppner between half-past four and five o'clock. Nearly all were killed, not by drowning but by the dreadful battering. The number of dead amounted to nearly one-quarter of the population, for Heppner's wildest booster in 1903 claimed no more than 1,100 citizens, men, women, and children. Not even the larger and far more celebrated Johnstown Flood took so proportionately great a number of inhabitants.

Heppner in mid-century is still a small place, little larger than in the times of its Deluge. Old survivors walked with me over the site of the disaster, pointing out where the Conser house had stood, and the site of the steam laundry that had held to form the first fatal dam. (Other survivors say it was a small hospital building and not the laundry which made the dam.) They showed me where the Lundell home had stood, the house that became an ark. The Mallory house yet stands. So does the stone building that contained the Belvedere saloon and the upstairs Opera House. This is now a drugstore, with apartments above. Old-timers said that neither saloon nor opera house could survive their use as morgues; the association in the minds of townspeople could be dissipated neither by alcohol nor by dramatic and musical art.

Heppner's local history naturally divides into two periods; one before, one after the Flood. Still among living survivors of that tragic day is Leslie Matlock, now a patriarch, pointed out to strangers, and most properly so, as the Heppner Paul Revere, the man who rode out the Flood on horseback. It required some persuasion to get him to tell me of the ride, about which he was modest. When walking the streets, however, the old hero is likely to be carrying a gold-headed cane, on the brightly burnished head of which is an inscription, dim but still legible: "Leslie Matlock, Presented by the People of Ione in grateful remembrance of Heroic Ride during Flood at Heppner, June 14, 1903." (The late Bruce Kelley got a cane too.)

The flood and the ride made a front-page item in the press all over the country. Young Kelley and Matlock received telegrams from two circus outfits, offering them featured jobs. They declined. Heppner went promptly to work to clear the flood damage, then to rebuild along the banks of Willow Creek as before, and to carry on as a trading center and rail-shipping point for sheep and wheat.

When I was there last, I stood and looked long at the creek where it enters the village, trying to imagine how this piddling stream could have desolated even so small a place as Heppner, and filled a graveyard. In places the water was perhaps six feet across, never more than ten feet, and very shallow. Survivor Frank Roberts was with me. "It was the damming up behind the steam laundry that did it," he said. "When she let go—well, that's all there was to it."

In June, each year, the Heppner *Gazette-Times* runs a reminder of the Flood; but the event is little remembered outside of Morrow County, whose somewhat weird courthouse stands on a hillside at Heppner. An alleged event concerning the town clock in this structure is proof of the wondrous magic worked by Time on what men like to think are their memories. It is worth setting down here in some detail, for what we are obviously dealing with is that threshold over which fact passes to turn instantly into fancy. It is the threshold of the imagination which processes some dull or meaningless item to bring it into accord with the love of the marvelous. It is the threshold to the manufacture of myths often called folklore.

No piece of folklore is more immune than that a watch or a clock stopped miraculously at some particular moment of great drama. In sober accounts of events, no less than in fiction, we have a timepiece stopping at the instant of some eminent man's death, often miles away; or stopping at the very moment of some tragic or historic event, as so many Southern clocks did when General Lee gave his sword to General Grant. It is the same romantic notion so immortally ensconced in the verses, "It stopped short—never to go again—when the Old Man died."

Well, that was exactly what happened to the town clock in the courthouse tower at Heppner, according to several residents; its hands had halted at half-past four on the afternoon of June 14, 1903. I had fully expected this piece of misinformation, for I had been exposed to a good deal of similar folklore. And so, when I came to contribute an article on the Heppner flood to the *Oregonian*, I mentioned that the stoppage could hardly have occurred, because the works of the clock had not then been installed. I got this information, I think, from the late Phil Metchan, already mentioned in this chapter.

Letters of protest and abuse rolled in from flood survivors living in all parts of the Northwest. Many were heated, several almost incoherent. The writers termed my article fiction. What the writers meant, of course, was that my account, based on careful research, did not jibe with their memories of what had happened forty-seven years previously. It is most instructive that no two letters quite agreed on the clock or anything else concerning the day of the Flood, except that there was a town clock. Two correspondents remembered that the clock stopped "at 4:15." Others held that the hands stopped at varying times from 4:45 to 5:15. Half a dozen more were just as sure that the clock did not stop at all, and of these one remembered how "it tolled the weary long hours of that terrible night." Incidentally, the courthouse then stood, and still stands, well up a hillside, far beyond the highest waters of the flood.

The Heppner *Gazette-Times* was most courteous in helping to clear up the business for me; and in good time I received a letter from Mr. O. M. Yeager, a Heppner native who has lived there for the past sixty-seven years. "There *was* a clock," Mr. Yeager was good enough to write to me, *"but it was not running.* The tower of the courthouse had settled a little, enough to stop the works. Many weeks after the flood, Judge Ayers had me take a carpenter to the tower and put in some new supports. Then a watchmaker came and got the works to running smoothly."

This would seem to correct the memories of those who had heard the weary hours of the night marked by the striking of the clock, and of those who were just as certain that the clock had stopped at the instant of disaster. I wish that I could believe that this would settle the matter. But I don't. I feel sure that in all oral tales of the flood, the clock in the Morrow County courthouse will either continue to stop, or to toll the weary long hours, so long as a survivor has the power of speech.

Yet the supporters of this and of other myths are not to be charged with fabricating. They are merely poets, poets seeking to fasten a measure of that mysterious thing we call art to an event or a thing that is graceless without it.

The Far Corner (1952)

The Aurora Communists

There was one train of covered wagons that crossed the bloody plains and mountains of the Oregon Trail in complete safety. No arrow, no bullet, nor even a theft was directed against the caravan of the German communists who took off from Bethel, Missouri, on the glad twenty-third day of May, 1855, and arrived, almost six months later, on the shore of the Pacific, unscathed and with nothing but good to say of the Indians who had been harassing and massacring other wagon trains.

The perfect immunity of the communist train was no miracle fetched by Providence. It had been achieved by bewhiskered William Keil, the communist leader, a man who in no circumstances needed a Marx or a Fourier to tell him what to do. At the head of the train of 34 great wagons, Keil, in a stroke of genius, placed a home-made hearse in which, carefully preserved in Golden Rule Whisky, was the body of his son Willie. No flanking riflemen ever awed the enemies of a column of Western pioneers half so well as the remains of little Willie. His grave in the Oregon country deserves better attention than it has been getting in recent years.

These first communists to cross the plains were not followers of Karl Marx, and, of course, they had nothing in common with any of the modern Communist movements. Nor did their philosophy stem from Charles Fourier, whose Phalanx scheme of communal life had already been tried at Brook Farm, Massachusetts, and in New Jersey, Ohio and Wisconsin. They were mostly disgruntled Rappites, whom Keil had persuaded to follow the special kind of Christian communism he had invented.

Keil was admirably equipped to weld his fellow-Germans into a tight group able to brave the many dangers of the American West and to found a colony which persevered until time had removed all need for it. He was a Prussian, born in 1812, who emigrated to the United States in 1831, well ahead of the high tide of German immigration. Six feet tall, of rugged build and great strength, he had deep-set blue eyes that took in any situation immediately, and seemed either as cool as ice or burning with heat, according to the circumstance. He wore a fringe type of beard, the kind later adopted and made famous by Horace Greeley.

His early years seem to have been rather restless. He had been reared in the Lutheran faith, but while still a youth he became enmeshed in the occult sciences, including necromancy and mesmerism. After arriving in the United States, Keil worked as a journeyman tailor and later established his own shop in New York City. In 1838 he turned up in Pittsburgh with his own small drugstore. Here he compounded drugs and experimented with various formulae supposed to ensure life everlasting. He also practiced medicine, for which he had no training.

One day a great light beat upon William Keil and he joined a church of German Methodists. He gave up his devilish brews and, in a formal and dramatic ceremony, burned a "secret book of mystic symbols and formulae written in human blood." He vowed to devote his life to evangelical Methodism. This however, did not turn out to be what he wanted. Next, he began to study the methods of Rappites, followers of George Rapp, also a German, who had founded colonies of religious immigrants at Harmony, Indiana and Economy, Pennsylvania. The Rappites, like so many sects, had undergone schisms. A part of the Economy branch of Rappites was ready for a new prophet when William Keil turned up with the idea of establishing a Christian community somewhere in the West.

II

The forties were an era of experiment in the United States. Communal living was a part of the yeasting, and many groups, religious and secular, were trying it. The Perfectionists were beginning to boil and bubble in Vermont and New York. The various Shaker villages had been successful for many years. Swedish communities were about to settle in Illinois. The Zoar Separatists—all Germans—had but recently received 500 new immigrants from the Old Country to their community in Ohio. A group of advance intellectuals were playing farmer at Brook Farm.

William Keil was an uneducated man but a dynamic speaker and person. He talked to the now-leaderless Rappites, lost and looking for a Moses, and some 200 of them joined him and his personal followers. Dr. Keil, as he was called, acted swiftly. He made a small payment on 6300 acres of land in Shelby and Adair counties in Missouri, and led the group there in 1844. He named the settlement Bethel and laid down the rules of community government. All property was communally owned, though the titles to the land were in Keil's name. Marriage was permitted, at least in the beginning. Each worked according to his abilities, and everyone had to work; the children were trained in various crafts. Keil was the one and only leader, though he often asked for counsel and sometimes even acted on it.

The Bethel colonists were thrifty and industrious. Up went their houses, up went their sawmills, gristmills, and a distillery. What they could not use they sold, and all of their products quickly gained a reputation of excellence. They seem to have been wine, not whisky, drinkers, and the large surplus of their Golden Rule corn spirits achieved a notable reputation in whisky-drinking Missouri. They set up their own schools, blacksmith shops, and a store where colonists got what they wanted without any questions. No cash exchanged hands, no charges were made. The Bethelites made fine boots and shoes which got to be in great demand. They wove woolen cloth. A few dissidents left the colony occasionally, but there were no hard feelings. Bethel—and Aurora later—was never troubled by the lawsuits which shook more than one such community to pieces.

So, Bethel worked like a beehive and prospered. The colonists kept pretty much to themselves, except for actual commerce, and they seem not to have irritated the Missourians as the Mormons did their neighbors.

Missouri in the forties was the jumping-off place for the Oregon country, and after 1848 also for the gold fields of California. The equipping of wagon trains was a big local business. The Bethel artisans went into business of making the big wagons and, like all of their merchandise, the wagons were honest goods. They were sold as fast as they could be made.

Some of the Oregon Fever must have got into the souls of the Christian communists of Bethel. At least, it attacked Dr. Keil. He had observed that Missouri was rapidly filling up; Bethel colony itself had grown to almost 1000 persons. Buying new land would be costly. In 1853, Dr. Keil felt the time had come to move a part of his flock into a New Canaan, which, he figured, could well be the Oregon country.

Keil dispatched a party of nine to scout the possibilities. They found a likely location on the Willapa River in what is now southwest Washington. Seven of the advance party remained to make a clearing and building houses. The other two scouts returned to Bethel to report to their leader.

Dr. Keil listened and made up his mind to move. The entire colony turned to in a prodigious effort to prepare for the exodus. Some 250 elected to go; the others were to remain and carry on at Bethel as before. And in May of 1855 the 34 covered wagons, packed to overflowing, were ready. Young Willie Keil, son of the prophet, was to have driven one of the teams. He died just before the time for leaving, and perhaps by dying saved many, and possibly all, of the lives of the trekking colonists.

Willie's body, as already related, was put into a metal-lined coffin, covered with the one preservative close at hand—the Golden Rule Whisky—and sealed. The coffin was placed in a long wagon, covered on top, opened at the sides and given the place at the head of the column.

The long train moved out of Bethel with the emigrants singing, accompanied for many miles by the stay-at-homes. At St. Joseph, the last outpost of civilization, the column was ferried across the Missouri. Ahead of them lay 2000 miles of desert and mountain.

III

The migrants had scarcely passed the Big Muddy when they met several wagon trains moving eastward. The colonist were advised that the Sioux and other plains tribes were out in force, determined to stop once and for all the invasion of their hunting grounds.

Whether or not the communists were given pause by these omens, they had no discernible effect on Dr. Keil. "The Lord will guide and preserve us," he said, and the column moved on, singing a none-too-happy song, *Das Grab ist tief und Stille,* which Keil had composed for the occasion of Willie's funeral.

They reached Fort Kearney on June 18, stopped briefly, then moved on. They were halted a few days later by a small party of Sioux horsemen, who had apparently come not to raid but to inspect the strange wagon at the head of the column. By a few words and many gestures the Sioux indicated their conviction that the hearse was very strong medicine indeed. They also knew about the singing and wanted to hear some of it. The colonists responded with Luther's hymn, *Ein' feste Burg ist unser Gott,* and a group of old folk songs including the rollicking *O du lieber Augustin.* The Sioux were entranced and asked for an encore, which was given. Then the Indians' leader made a gesture of thanks, and the band rode off.

When they reached Fort Laramie the commandant there strongly opposed the emigrants' going farther. He related stories of horrible massacres of whole wagon trains in recent months, and said that Keil's party should return to Bethel, or should at least camp near the fort and winter there. "The Lord," replied Dr. Keil with all the force of an Old

Testament prophet, "will watch over His own." The train moved on, singing.

Along the Laramie River, encamped for the night, the party was visited again by Sioux, this time a huge band of hunters. They appeared to know about the weird wagon with the dead man, and also about the singing. The colonists sang for them and the Indians sat silent and obviously charmed. They had never heard anything like it before, and doubtless never heard the like again. After commenting favorably on the hearse and the music, the Sioux rode away. Other bands of Indians visited the column and showed only friendship and intense interest. In the Green River country, where the trail grew dim for many miles, two Sioux hunters left their own party and spent several days with the colonists, guiding them over the difficult terrain.

As the Keil party approached the Oregon region, more tales of depredations and massacres were heard, this time in connection with the Cayuse and Yakima tribes. Something like a genuine and sustained war was being waged against the white settlers. At this period it began to look as if the party might have serious trouble, especially after one night when several of their cows disappeared. But riders were sent out the next day and they came across a band of Indians who were driving the missing cattle, not away, but patiently toward the Keil encampment. The animals had strayed and the Indians were taking them back.

In September the colonists were crossing Idaho. In October they reached the Columbia. In November they reached their goal on the Willapa River, where they found that the advance party had worked wonders in clearing the forest and putting up cabins. Dr. Keil gave thanks to the Lord. Then funeral services for Willie were held and the body interred.

Dr. Keil was not too well pleased with the new site. It rained almost every day and night. There were fogs. The place was in an immense forest of big timber, and it was isolated from Portland, the chief city of the region. The doctor immediately sent out scouts to find a better location. He himself went to Portland to practice medicine during the winter. His scouts eventually reported an ideal spot, 28 miles south of Portland in the lush Willamette Valley. Dr. Keil went to see it and he called it good, naming it Aurora for one of his daughters. In the spring the land was purchased and the colonists moved there.

IV

Aurora was to be a happy and prosperous settlement. In addition to their sawmill, gristmill and distillery, the colonists made beds, looms and other furniture to be sold; and candlesticks, spoons, gloves and woolen braid for trimming dresses. They organized two bands and made their own instruments; they also manufactured horns for sale. A colonist named Henry G. Ehlen made clarinet reeds so good that demands for them were presently coming from California and later from many eastern cities.

The two Aurora bands were the talk of Oregon. Directed by Conrad Finck, a German of sound musical education, they were in demand for concerts throughout the state. When Ben Holladay, the pioneer railroad builder, wanted music for some spike-driving or first-train festivities, he engaged an Aurora band. (The Director's son, Henry T. Finck, went to Harvard from Aurora, and later became the music critic of the New York *Post.*)

Except for music, however, the colony had little time for cultural activities. Keil did not encourage them. The little school taught elementary subjects, all in German, and little else. But the colony cooking was wonderful, and travelers made it a point to stop overnight at the Aurora hotel, which was open to all.

Keil was, of course, an autocrat. Although he fathered nine children himself, he urged celibacy. He permitted some marriages, but forbade others, and no marriage whatever was permitted except between members of the colony. Often Keil forced married couples to live for years with the parents of one or the other spouse before he would sanction the building of a separate house. Single members were more economical; they could be housed and fed in the community shelter.

Although Keil's leadership, or autocracy, was more intelligent than that of many other religious communities, it retarded intellectual progress and must have hampered the development of individual self-reliance. In the end Keil found that his powers were limited by events beyond his control. He could do nothing about the rapidly expanding railroads or the steadily increasing number of "gentiles" around Aurora.

Worse things began to happen: Now and then an Aurora maiden disappeared from the colony, to turn up a day or so later as the bride of some outside youth. Young men of the colony were running away, to work elsewhere and to marry outsiders. The English language invaded the citadel; by the mid-seventies the younger colonists were using it in preference to German. The old people fretted, but there was not much they could do. And then, on December 30, 1877, Dr. Keil proved that he had been unable to find a formula for eternal life. He died suddenly, and for a month the colony was too numbed to work.

Andrew Geisy, who had acted as Keil's deputy back in Bethel and who was generally assumed to be the crown prince, had no desire to take Keil's place at Aurora. No one, apparently, had ever been trained or even considered by Keil as his successor. The Bethel-Aurora communities, 2000 miles apart but both held in Keil's name, were liquidated in the Federal courts, and so far as any outsiders ever knew, to the satisfaction of all concerned. At least no lawsuits were brought; and the colonists presented a handsome silver bowl, suitably inscribed, to Judge Matthew P. Deady, for his wise counsel in the liquidation procedures.

There are today in Oregon a number of aging men and women who were born in Aurora while Keil lived. They speak well of the colony, although two of them told the writer the place had become an anachronism long before it was discontinued. It had simply outlived its need. The youngsters wanted to be Americans, not members of an eccentric sect of foreign-speaking "Dutchmen."

A few of the old colony houses survive, and so does the Aurora post office. German names cling to the neighborhood. But Aurora's finest legacy, perhaps, are the fine old recipes—*kartoffel klösse, zier pfannkuchen,* a special kind of *kaffeekuchen,* and some wonderful things done to cabbage and apples. It may not be much, this heritage, but I think Brook Farm left less.

The American Mercury (1948)

The *Oregon Historical Quarterly*, vol. 92 no. 4, Winter 1991-92, is devoted to the Aurora Colony and its social and cultural history.

First Bomb

If ever the government sets up a marker on a certain spot back in the hills six miles east of the remote hamlet of Brookings, on the coast of southwest Oregon, it will be with good reason. Scarcely an American outside the West Coast states appears to remember, or even to have heard of, the extraordinary event that happened there, but the fact is that is where the continental United States was bombed for the first—and thus far only—time from an enemy plane.

There is no question about the bomb or its parentage. In order to satisfy my curiosity about it, and since I live in the region anyway, I not only went to see the bomb crater [in 1942] but I held parts of the bomb in my hands. I also talked with the men of the United States Forest Service who saw the plane from which the bomb was dropped, sighted the smoke from the blazes it started, and put the fires out before they had a chance to grow to dangerous proportions.

Shortly after six-fifteen on the morning of September 9, 1942, Howard Gardner, the forest service guard stationed on Mount Emily in the Siskiyou National Forest, near Brookings, heard a plane. The exhaust, Gardner thought, seemed labored; it had a sort of delayed-action sound, something like an echo. Presently he sighted the plane. It was tiny, the smallest he had ever seen, and it had extremely short wings. It was flying eastward at a very low altitude—so low that Gardner could see its solitary occupant in the cockpit. Gardner picked up his telephone and called the forest ranger at Gold Beach, a small town north of Brookings, where there was a ranger station; it was then 6:24 A.M. "One plane, type unknown," he reported, "flying low, seen east two miles, now circling." A moment later, as he hung up, the little plane completed its circle and began flying west, toward the sea. It eventually disappeared in that direction.

That was all, just then. Gardner, who lives in a small glass-sided cabin on the top of Mount Emily, went about his daily chores. He cooked and ate his breakfast, washed the dishes, tidied up his cabin, and returned to his job of watching the hundreds of square miles of dark-green forest below him. He saw the fog banks gradually move out of the canyons and drift westward to the sea, six miles away. He took wind, temperature, and humidity readings, all part of his daily routine, and at times he wondered about the odd sound of the tiny plane.

At 12:20 P.M., six hours after Gardner had seen the plane, he noticed a plume of smoke in the east. This was not surprising. A brief but heavy thunderstorm had swept that part of Oregon the night before, and Gardner thought, not unreasonably, that the smoke was coming from a "sleeper fire." Sleepers are a common sort of forest fire. They are caused most frequently by lightning, and they smolder for several hours in the wet woods before they start to burn in earnest, as the weather clears and the sun dries out the forest. Gardner sighted the smoke on his Osborn finder, calculated its position, and again called the ranger at Gold Beach. "A smoke," he said, using the customary forest service formula, "Township 40 South, Range 12 West, Section 22. That's all."

The ranger at Gold Beach, a veteran named Ed Marshall, who was in charge of that district of the Siskiyou National Forest, immediately called another lookout and asked for what foresters call a cross shot and, now that the smoke had been sighted from two angles, he was able to locate the fire with absolute accuracy on a map by triangulation. He phoned Gardner back and told him to go to the fire. It was 12:25 P.M. Marshall then dispatched three other foresters to the fire—Keith Johnson, Bob Larson, and Freddie Flynn. Two of these men were stationed at Gold Beach; the third had a post in the forest not far from Mount Emily. They had a fairly good trail almost to the fire, but when they arrived, bringing fire-fighting equipment, Gardner was already there.

First Bomb

Gardner's trek to the fire was made with a speed that is considered remarkable even by his fellow-woodsmen. From his station on Mount Emily to the spot designated as Township 40 South, Range 12 West, Section 22, is approximately four and a half miles cross-country. This particular four and a half miles of cross-country, in this wild part of Oregon, has to be seen—and walked over—to be believed. It is a jungle, a trackless forest of Douglas fir with a ground cover of devil clubs, chinquapin, and other difficult brush. The earth goes either uphill or down, the hills are high and the canyons deep, and there was no trail of any kind that Gardner could use. Nevertheless, he made the four and a half miles in three hours and thirty minutes, which will probably stand as an all-time record for the course. At 3:55 P.M. he was at the fire. Instead of a single blaze, he found several, some of which were burning briskly.

Long before they reached the scene, Gardner and the three other men all noticed what one of them described as an "ungodly stink." It was not, they agreed, the smoke of a forest fire, which is rather pleasant in its milder forms. Larson thought it smelled like burning rubber. Johnson said that the stench made him think of the odor from a carbide lamp. Flynn just didn't care.

When Gardner arrived, he noticed an oak tree which had been splintered and broken off as if by lightning. It was not burning. However, an old fir snag, dead and punky, was burning. The other fires were all within a radius of a hundred feet from the splintered oak. Gardner went to work with ax and shovel, removing wood and brush from around the flames and throwing soil over them. Johnson, Larson, and Flynn arrived twenty minutes after Gardner and they, too, set to work. A little later Johnson came across a sizable hole in the ground. He thought it looked like a crater made by an explosion. "Hey," he called out, "somebody dropped a bomb here."

The others came over, thinking that Johnson was seeing things. The hole, however, certainly looked as if it had been made by a bomb and the stench from it was terrific. Johnson immediately hiked to the top of a nearby ridge, unslung the five pound high-frequency radio that he carried as part of his equipment, and called Ranger Marshall, back at Gold Beach. He reported the fantastic news that the fire was not a sleeper but had been caused by an incendiary bomb, and returned to the fire. Looking around, he found fragments of evil-smelling, rubberlike stuff scattered over the ground. These were shaped like pieces of pie and each one had a small hole in it. "By God," he said, "there's enough stuff here to have set the whole of Curry County on fire."

The men paused for a few moments to inspect the fragments, then went to work on the fires again. By 8:20 P.M. they had them mopped up—not out, but under control and rapidly dying. Flynn, Gardner, and Larson left. Johnson remained to watch the fires and see that the last spark was put out.

Next morning, Les Colvill, assistant supervisor of the Siskiyou National Forest, and Marshall arrived at the scene. The old fir snag was still smoking, but the other fires were out. Colvill began digging in the hole with a shovel. The depression measured three feet in diameter and was eighteen inches deep. Presently Colvill's shovel struck something hard—a piece of metal that the three men were convinced had come from the nose of a bomb. More digging uncovered a fuse head to which was attached a little fan that looked like a propeller. On the brass collar of the fuse head were some minute markings.

All told, forty pounds of fragments were removed from the crater and the area around it and taken to Brookings. An Army ballistics man examined them and said that reclaimed rubber—old American tires, perhaps—and thermite had been used in making the bomb. The propeller fan on the fuse head had activated a powder train which burned down into the bomb, firing its thermite-and-rubber center. A charge in the nose of the bomb blew it apart when it hit the earth, scattering the fragments. The Army expert said that the bomb had not been more than 40 per cent efficient, because it had been dropped from too low an altitude to permit the powder train to finish its work. The markings on the fuse head, he said, were those of a certain Japanese arsenal.

When I saw the bomb hole, it had been worked over, so I couldn't tell much about its original appearance. I could see, however, that the fires caused by the bomb had been so hot that in some places around the crater the red clay earth had been fused into lumps that looked like the flux from molten iron. The wedge-shaped fragments, which I also examined, were still smelly. After handling them, my hands retained the stench of carbide, despite two good scrubbings.

A brief Associated Press dispatch, describing the bombing, was sent from San Francisco on September 14th, five days after the event. Then, buried under an an avalanche of other and more important news, the incident was forgotten. (Perhaps "forgotten" is not the right word. I failed to find anybody outside California-Oregon-Washington, other than foresters, who ever heard of the bombing of Curry County, Oregon.)

Except for the fact that the bomb had been dropped, however, there was not much to get excited about, thanks to the prompt action of the men of the forest service. All that the Japanese did, really, was to put another feather in the forest service's cap; and to give Township 40 South, Range 12 West, Section 22 the distinction of being the only piece of continental United States to have felt the impact of a bomb dropped by an enemy plane.

The New Yorker (1944)

Nobou Fujita, the Japanese pilot who dropped the first bomb on the United States, has returned to Oregon three times in recent years to participate in the Brookings Azalea Festival. He presented the city with the family samurai sword that he carried in his plane as a symbol of peace and friendship. See the *Oregonian*, May 27, 1990.

The Great Homestead Murders

The evening of March 8, 1900, was wild. A storm howled down out of the Cascade Mountains and swept through the Columbia River gorge as Mr. Norman Williams, a homesteader, drove a two-horse team out of the Fashion Livery Stables, finest establishment of its kind in Hood River, Oregon. Beasts and man alike bowed their heads to the wind. So black was the night that H. D. Langille, one of the Fashion's proprietors, lighted a lantern a few moments after Williams had left, and followed the team. He found it in front of Thompson's boardinghouse near by.

Langille proffered the lantern to Williams, remarking that the twenty miles to his homestead was a long way to go on so dark and miserable a night. By the lantern's feeble, flickering rays the liveryman could see a young woman, who looked to be quite handsome, on the wagon seat; another and much older woman came down the steps from the boardinghouse and got into the seat beside the girl. Neither woman spoke.

Williams thanked Langille for the light, picked up the reins, and drove out of Hood River into an inky darkness from which the two women never returned. Nor were they ever seen again, dead or alive.

Hood River folk did not realize anything was amiss, that evening of the eighth of March. Next morning at about half past eight Williams, alone now, returned the team to the Fashion Stables. That was all, just then. Williams returned the team and went away. Nobody could know that two women had disappeared as completely as though they had never lived—almost.

Four years, lacking a month, passed. In the meantime President McKinley had been assassinated at Buffalo, and Theodore Roosevelt was in the White House. The Boer War was over, the Russo-Japanese affair just getting under way. Horseless carriages were making their appearance in the larger cities in increasing numbers—even Hood River had two of them—but they were yet a long way from being a threat to livery stables in backwoods Oregon. The Fashion Livery was still doing business at the old stand.

Then one day in February of 1904 an unassuming young man of about thirty got off the morning train in Hood River. He asked the station agent to direct him to a livery stable. A few minutes later he walked into the Fashion, now operated by Bert Stranahan. The stranger said he wanted to hire a horse and buggy to go to the homestead of Norman Williams, and added that he didn't know where the place was. "Can I get somebody to drive me?" he asked.

It was a mild, sunny day, much nicer out of doors than in. Bert Stranahan said he'd go, and he hitched a fine black mare into a rig. Just as they were about to get into the buggy the stranger asked if there was a spade around the stable they could take with them. "I might want to do a little prospecting," he said.

Now Bert Stranahan had lived in Hood River a long time and he had never heard of any gold being found on a valley ranch. But in 1904 livery-stable keepers were just as used to odd people and queer requests as are taxi drivers today. Stranahan wouldn't have batted an eye if the stranger had requested an electric liver pad and a stereopticon. He got a spade and shoved it under the buggy seat.

There wasn't a great deal of conversation on the twenty-mile drive. The stranger did say that his name was Jackson, and after a while he offered the information that he used to know Norman Williams "back in Iowa." Stranahan said "That so?" or its equivalent, and the horse jogged along for another mile or two.

The road became steeper on its climb to the Parkdale district. Mr. Jackson talked some more, but it was chiefly questions. He wanted to know something of how Williams stood in the community. Stranahan racked his mind to find out, and replied truthfully that Williams didn't have much of a reputation one way or the other. He was just a common everyday homesteader in homesteading country. Nothing unusual about him, far as Stranahan knew. Come to think of it, he hadn't seen Williams in a long time. Damned if he could recall when it was.

On arrival at the Williams homestead it was immediately evident that the place had been deserted for a long time. The rude shack, the disheveled barn—they had the look and the smell of disuse and neglect. Dead grass, long yellowed, grew up in front of the doors. Boards on the barn were loose. There is even a "feel" about such places—a sad, nostalgic flavor, haunting, elusive, yet profound.

The mysterious stranger lost no time. Taking the spade, he began prodding the earth, first between the house and barn, then around both buildings. Knowing nothing of these odd doings and being a man who minded his own business, Stranahan sat in the buggy listening to the stranger, who seemed too young to mutter but who audibly was doing just that. "No, not here," he mumbled, making a pass at the ground with his spade, then moving. "Not there, not there," he repeated.

Finally this Mr. Jackson disappeared into what looked to have been started as a henhouse and never quite completed. It was a jerry-built job, now badly dilapidated. In a moment Jackson came out of the hut. His manner was changed. His words came quicker. His face seemed tense. And now he addressed Stranahan direct for the first time since they arrived at the homestead. "I think I'll dig in here," he said, indicating the henhouse and speaking just as if the digging was something they had understood and discussed. "The dirt seems loose," he added. He ducked back into the shack, then out again. "You might as well unhitch the horse," he said. "We'll likely be here all day."

Stranahan, naturally mystified but still minding his own business, took the mare out of the shafts and put her in the barn. Then he went over to the henhouse. Inside, the ground was indeed loose and there was a visible depression, roughly of an oblong shape. Jackson was already digging, methodical and unhurried. But his face was tense, Stranahan noted.

In a decent while Stranahan offered to spell the man off. He took the spade and dug in, finding that the dirt came up easily. The hole—for it obviously had been a hole—was better than two feet wide, perhaps six feet long. Stranahan dug for ten minutes or so.

It was a queer business, this going out to an abandoned homestead and digging and not knowing what you were digging for; so when Jackson silently reached for the shovel, Stranahan put the matter out in the open.

"What the hell are we supposed to be digging for?" he asked.

"That I don't know," Mr. Jackson replied. (Stranahan noted that the man's eyes were sort of set and stary. Was he bughouse?) "That I don't know," he repeated. "All I know is that something tells me this is the right place."

Stranahan decided it was time to take a smoke. Leaving Jackson at his digging, he strolled out of the shack and filled his pipe. The place was in deep shadow now. Twilight was coming down from the flanks of Mount Hood. He could see a lamp glimmering in a small house half a mile away, the only light visible in the valley. He returned to the henhouse.

By now the hole was down more than four feet. Jackson was digging faster and the loose earth made quite a pile in the small enclosure. Never a man to take stock in the metaphysical, Stranahan recalls that for the first and only time in his life he felt as if he were alive and awake but playing a part in a most unreal dream. He took the spade without a word from either man and dug.

Down went the excavation, five feet, five and a half. Suddenly the spade struck something hard. Pulled out, it proved to be a length of rived cedar a foot wide, two inches thick, and five feet long. Stranahan could see Jackson's face in the twilight. It looked like chalk. "I think," Jackson said, almost in a whisper, "I think we are going to find what, what—" He broke off, then asked, "Have you a lantern?"

Stranahan said he had. He went to the buggy and brought it back, lighted. Jackson was down deep in the hole, feeling in the cool dirt of the pit with his hands. Stranahan passed the light down to him, and watched. The man had something in his hands. "Looks like burlap—sacking," he said, holding the lantern close. "Yes, it's burlap. We'd better quit now. Leave everything as it is until daylight. It's liable to be very important."

Still mystified and still minding his own business, Stranahan hitched up the horse. The two men drove to the light that blinked from across the valley. It was a rancher's place and the two men found food and lodging. Bert Stranahan finally dozed off, marveling at the odd things in the life of a livery-stable proprietor in a small back-country town.

Breakfast was at six, and long before seven the two men were back at the henhouse. In the clear light of morning they could see some pieces of badly rotted burlap at the bottom of the hole. Jackson had brought his suitcase, which he had emptied of its usual contents, and now he put it down, open, on the edge of the hole. He got into the excavation and, using the greatest care, lifted out the burlap and placed it gently in the suitcase. It was dark and moldy. Pieces of it fell away. Looking at it closely, Stranahan could see what appeared to be a dark stain—even darker than the rotten sacking—and a few small hairs matted into the stain.

Without a word Jackson closed the suitcase, and the two men walked to the buggy. Stranahan thought it was about time he knew what was afoot, and told the stranger so.

"My name isn't Jackson," the man explained. "I am George R. Nesbitt." He seemed to think that the name might convey something to Stranahan. It didn't and Stranahan said it didn't.

They got into the buggy, and as they drove down Hood River Valley toward town Jackson, or Nesbitt, opened up. He said his home was in Harlan, Iowa, and he had come to Oregon to try to find his younger sister, Alma, and their mother.

Stranahan recalled vaguely that he had known of some woman, or women, by that name who had once lived on a homestead somewhere in the region and might still be living there for all he knew. Nesbitt continued his story. In 1899, or five years before, Alma had come to Hood River, Oregon, to take up a homestead next to that of Norman Williams. This move had been urged by Williams in letters to Alma. Williams, who was thirty years older than the girl, had known her since childhood, and her family as well. He had lived near Harlan, the Nesbitts' home.

As the horse jogged along, Nesbitt continued his narrative. Alma had been an adventurous as well as a romantic girl, he said. For months, back in Iowa, she had talked of little but of how she wanted to become a "pioneer woman," one who could go into the wilderness, file a homestead claim, and tame the ground. It became almost an obsession with her, and the letters from Williams, who already had settled on his Parkdale homestead, finally fetched her West. She had filed on and secured one hundred and sixty acres next to Williams' place.

That had been early in 1899. A few months later Mrs. Nesbitt, mother of Alma and George, also came West. For the next few months letters had come to Iowa regularly from mother and sister. Things were going well with them, they wrote. They related how Williams had helped build a small house on Alma's claim, how Alma had hired men to do stump grubbing and plowing, and how Alma and her mother had worked hard with their own hands at planting apple trees. The two women appeared happy, and they wrote of further improvements they planned to make on the place in the spring of 1900.

Then, on March 8, 1900, the letters had ceased. "A letter with that date, and mailed not in Hood River but in Portland, was the last we heard of them," Nesbitt concluded.

"Well," said Stranahan, getting back to the subject that still troubled him, "what did you expect to find at Williams' place? And, by the way, what did we find?"

"I hardly know what I expected to find," Nesbitt said in a queer voice, "and I'm not sure that we have found anything. But I'm going to take the matter up with authorities."

On the long drive back to Hood River, Nesbitt was as nervously talkative as he had been moodily silent on the way out. He went into such detail as he could about his lost sister and mother.

He related how, back in Iowa, Norman Williams had been "sort of sweet" on Alma, although she was little more than a girl and he was middle-aged. Nothing serious, though. Then, in 1897, Williams had come to Oregon. His letters to Alma had been filled with the fanciful color and romance of pioneering the land in the Last Great West. The romantic Alma saw Indians behind every tree and she could hear the rumble of covered-wagon wheels. *They* were what she thought she wanted. So Alma came; then her mother came.

"That last letter we had—four years ago, come March—was written at Winters' rooming house, 60$^{1}/_{2}$ Grand Avenue, Portland, Oregon," Nesbitt said. "In it Alma and Mother said they were coming home to Iowa. Didn't give any reason. Just said they were coming home. We back there were mighty pleased."

"Haven't you tried to find them before this?" inquired the practical Stranahan.

"Of course we have," Nesbitt said; and he told how he had written letters to Williams at Hood River, asking what had become of the girl and woman. After a lapse of several weeks Williams had replied that the two women had "gone away" and he hadn't the least idea of where they went. In reply to a second letter from George Nesbitt, Williams had unburdened himself. He wrote that Alma had promised to marry him. Everything had been arranged, including the date. Then, so Williams wrote, Alma had taken to going around with an unnamed man. "A younger man than me," Williams had written, "and good-looking." He also intimated that Alma had fallen into loose ways. And the second letter concluded by repeating that both women had gone away together, without saying why or where.

"For four years we have done everything we could to find them," Nesbitt said. "We inserted notices in many newspapers throughout the West. We offered a reward. We wrote to postmasters and chiefs of police of many towns and cities. And now, after four years of waiting and hoping, I've come to Hood River."

"You must have suspected something, to start right in digging that way," Stranahan said. "How come you asked me to take the spade with us?"

"I can't tell you why. I don't know myself. I just had a feeling. It seemed to me—well"—he fumbled for words to express himself—"I guess it was just one of those strong hunches we have sometimes. I just couldn't get a shovel out of my mind. Something said to me, 'Take a shovel; take a shovel.' Sounds queer, I know, but I simply can't make it any clearer."

II

Next day George Nesbitt, toting the suitcase with its contents of rotting burlap, went to The Dalles, seat of Wasco County, and told his story to District Attorney Menefee and Deputy Fred Wilson. The men looked at the burlap. Under a reading glass—the only scientific aid in The Dalles of the time—the dark stains looked like blood or like any other nearly black substance. Matted solidly into the stain were perhaps five or six silver-gray hairs. They might have come from a dog, possibly from a fox; both were plentiful in the Hood River Valley. Fred Wilson remembers that the mildewed, moldy mass struck him as mighty poor evidence of any sort.

But Wilson also was struck by the quiet earnestness of George Nesbitt. He sent the burlap by express to Dr. Victoria Hampton, a brilliant young woman of Portland whose profession was then known as that of "chemist and microscopist." This was a daring thing to do, in 1904, for the profession was a new one, at least to Oregon, and Dr. Hampton was a woman. In 1904 Oregon was pretty much of a man's world.

Nesbitt now swore out a warrant for the arrest of Norman Williams. The man was located without much trouble. He was working in a sawmill in Bellingham, Washington, three hundred miles away, and living with a woman. "Meet my housekeeper," Williams said to the sheriff and Deputy Attorney Wilson by way of introduction.

Williams expressed surprise, seemingly sincere, that he should be wanted in connection with a betrothed who had "thrown me over to run away with another man." He readily agreed to go to The Dalles without extradition and to do what he could, which he feared wouldn't be much, to clear up the mystery, if that's what it was.

Deputy Wilson arrived at The Dalles on February 11, 1904, with Williams in custody. Williams turned out to be a tall, well-built man, rather good-looking and younger than his sixty years—the kind of man one would turn around on the street to look at. Over six feet. The tall man's face broke into smiles when he was confronted with George Nesbitt. With a clear countenance, as Fred Wilson remembers it, he denied any knowledge of what might have happened to Alma and her mother. He said he had never set eyes on the women since the morning he had driven them back to Hood River village from the homesteads at Parkdale and taken them to the railroad depot, where they had caught a westbound train.

That had been in March four years before, Williams continued, and the books at the Fashion Stables no doubt would show the exact date. (The books did; and the date was March 9, or the morning after the stormy night when

Williams had driven out of Hood River with the two women in the wagon.)

Williams went on with his story, told it in an apparently straightforward manner. He related that Alma had obviously tired of him after their engagement. He felt sure she had fallen in love with some man whose name he did not know but whom Alma had met during a short period when she worked as a domestic at The Dalles. She had "worked out" the winter of 1899-1900, Williams said, in order to get ready cash with which to buy farming tools. During this same period Williams had worked at a small sawmill in the Parkdale district. But in the spring a homestead didn't look so attractive to Alma.

"When she and I went out to the homesteads together the first time in the spring of 1900," Williams related, "I could tell that she didn't want to settle down and be a rancher's wife. She had got notions. No back-country ranch would do for her."

The man's story was convincing enough. His face and eyes seemed to soften as he spoke of Alma, and the watching attorneys fancied they detected sadness untouched by bitterness when he told of Alma's faded love. "I'd marry her today if she'd only come back," he concluded.

They locked Williams in Wasco County jail and held him in $10,000 bond, which he made no attempt to raise. "It'll all come out all right," he smiled.

III

Now began the unraveling of a mystery without any aid from professional detectives. The only sleuths in this case were George Nesbitt, a farmer from Iowa, and young Deputy District Attorney Fred Wilson, a home-town boy who had never in his life worked on a crime of any kind— much less a disappearance as mystifying as this one appeared to be. I can think of no comparable case that called for so many matched and interlocking links, let alone ones forged by two rural and strictly amateur detectives.

First thing the two back-country sleuths did was to take a train for Portland, the Oregon metropolis. Here they went to the rooming house at 60 ½ Grand Avenue operated for many years by Henry D. Winters. This was the place where Alma had written the last letter to her brother in Iowa, in March of 1900. Proprietor Winters got out his four-year-old register, now covered with dust. There in the clear, flowing hand of the days before typewriters became common were two signatures: "Alma Nesbitt, Hood River, Ore.," and "Mrs. Louisa Nesbitt," with a ditto mark.

George Nesbitt scanned the writing. He declared that both signatures were in his sister's hand. The women had registered on February 8, 1900, and had remained until March 8. The latter date, it will be remembered, was that of the last letter written by Alma to George. It was also the date Norman Williams had hired the two-horse team at Hood River.

Proprietor Winters remembered the two women well. He said that a man had called on them and the three had spent some time in the rooming-house parlor. They had talked a long time, and Winters was positive they were having some sort of argument. Concerned land, or property, he thought, for he had heard mention of a homestead. The discussion had become rather heated.

Winters' testimony was offered the two sleuths without prompting. And it was something. The next step was a lot more. Acting on what Wilson says today was nothing more than a hunch—the way a man bets on a horse sometimes—Deputy Wilson and Nesbitt went to Vancouver, Washington, just across the Columbia River from Portland. Vancouver, then as now, was a noted Gretna Green. In the Clark County recorder's office they learned that on July 25, 1899, or some six months before Alma's disappearance, she and Norman Williams had been married by a justice of the peace. This find made Williams out a liar.

In the meantime District Attorney Menefee, back in The Dalles, had learned that Williams also had married a woman in Dufur, Oregon, in 1898, and had left her without troubling about a divorce. So Williams was a liar and a bigamist, if nothing worse. The pattern was still far from clear, but something approaching a motive for murder began to take shape.

Next the amateur detectives located one J. R. Reese, a laborer in the Hood River Valley. Reese told of once doing some day labor for Norman Williams. It had consisted of cutting an immense amount of brush and scrub timber and of grubbing a good many stumps on the Williams homestead. That had been, Reese said, sometime in April of 1900, or in the month after the women disappeared.

Later that summer, Reese continued, he had occasion to visit the Williams homestead again. The brush and stump pile, which he described vividly as "the god-damnedest pile of stuff you ever see," had been burned. This, of course, had not been strange, for it is customary to burn brush and stumps.

The sleuths canvassed the scattered homesteads of the valley for someone who had known Alma Nesbitt. They found an acquaintance in a Mrs. Mary Riggs, homesteader. Mrs. Riggs said she had talked with Williams a number of times "since Alma and her mother went away" and she had always asked him about Alma. At least four times, she said, Williams had replied that he had received letters from Alma, that she and her mother were well. Mrs. Riggs, who had considered Alma and herself to be rather close friends, thought it mighty queer that the girl had left the valley without even saying good-by to her.

Detective Fred Wilson next visited Norman Williams in his cell. He showed him, for the first time, the rotting burlap that had been dug up beneath the henhouse. Williams smiled. Yes, he said, that sure was blood on that sacking. A mare of his had foaled a colt on it. It was mare's blood. Why had it been buried so deeply in the ground? Williams smiled again. The henhouse, he said, had been built over the hole of an old outhouse. Into this hole Williams had thrown the sacking. Later he had moved the outhouse, placing it nearer the barn, and had then filled the hole. He had built the henhouse on the site.

Wilson and Nesbitt made a return trip to the Williams homestead to check the man's story about the outhouse. The dilapidated remains of such a structure were, as Williams had said, near the barn. But at the small sawmill four miles away, where Williams had worked at odd times, the sleuths gathered information in conflict with what Williams had told. Mill employees recalled that Williams' mare had indeed foaled a colt, but at the sawmill and nowhere else.

Neighboring ranchers, including Mrs. Riggs, vowed that at no time had there been an outhouse where the henhouse now stood. One neighbor remembered an interesting incident. He had called at Williams' place one day. It was raining hard and had been raining for several hours. Yet Williams had a pile of several sacks of oats in the open, on the ground, in the approximate place where the henhouse had later been built. Seemed strange, this witness had thought, that a rancher should leave good oats out in the rain when a barn was handy.

The amateur detectives did much more investigating, but the results were not made known until the trial.

Despite the quiet manner in which Wilson and Nesbitt had gone about their work, the disappearance of Alma Nesbitt had by now become an Oregon sensation destined to spread as the trial progressed. It had that something about it—the man driving two women, one of them young and beautiful, out of Hood River and into a dark from which the women had not returned. And almost overnight, in the press, Alma Nesbitt became the Lone Girl Homesteader, the pioneer covered-wagon woman right down to date. It was the kind of copy to make front pages and headlines in the Far West.

Williams went on trial in the old Wasco County courthouse at The Dalles on May 24, 1904, more than four years after the two women were last seen in Hood River. Their disappearance into the night of March 8, 1900, had not made a ripple at the time. They had few acquaintances and almost no close friends in the district. Now, however, Oregon witnessed the power of the press with a good story as it hadn't been witnessed since Harry Tracy and Dave Merrill shot their way out of the Oregon penitentiary and into the paper-back dime novels in 1902.

The Dalles was packed with the biggest, liveliest crowd seen there since the eastern Oregon gold rush of the 1860s. Seattle, Spokane, Portland, even San Francisco, newspapers sent reporters and sketch artists to cover what was already "The Great Homestead Murders Case." The *Morning Oregonian*'s reporter was Leslie Scott, and he wrote that "the nodding plumes and gay ribbons show that the female contingent is out in full force." The courtroom overflowed. Fortunately the day was warm and Judge William Bradshaw, a humane man, permitted open windows, thus allowing those in the yard to see and hear. The milling crowd, that soon became very quiet, packed the yard and flowed into the street.

In his opening statement Fred Wilson, now playing the part of prosecutor instead of detective, told the jury that the State would attempt to prove: (1) that Norman Williams drove the two women to his ranch on the night of March 8, 1900, and there murdered them in cold blood; (2) that he buried their bodies in the ground, covering the hole with a pile of oats from March 8 until such time as he had gathered a great pile of brush and stumps; and (3) that this pile was used as a funeral pyre.

As a motive, prosecution said, the State would prove beyond any doubt that Williams had another wife living when he married Alma Nesbitt; that Alma may have discovered this fact, or in any case had planned to leave Williams; and that Williams wanted Alma's homestead for himself.

Important to the State was the testimony of H. D. Langille, the onetime partner with Bert Stranahan in the

Fashion Livery Stables. Langille related how Williams had hired the team and told of seeing two women in the wagon. That had been late at night. Ordinarily when he worked late, Langille said, he did not show up at the stable next morning. But on this occasion, and for reasons which now escaped him, he was on duty next morning at the stable. He testified that he had been standing at the front of the stable and had seen Williams driving into Hood River by the Parkdale road, the same road he had taken on the way out the night before. "There was no one in the wagon but Williams," Langille said on oath, "and Williams drove direct to the stable. That was about half past eight."

Prosecution now brought out a blackboard and on it Prosecutor Wilson drew a rough chalk-line map of Hood River village to show that Williams could not have driven to the Hood River railroad station without first having passed the Fashion Stables.

Next the chief train dispatcher of the Oregon Railway & Navigation Company testified that the only westbound train to pass through Hood River on the morning of March 9, 1900, had done so at five-thirty-three, or some three hours before Langille had seen Williams driving into town.

It will be recalled that Williams had claimed the last he ever saw of the two women was when he put them on a westbound train on the morning of March 9.

Prosecution next sprang what the press termed a bombshell. The bomb was in the form of John H. Hall, United States attorney of Portland. Hall told the jury how, late in 1900, a Norman Williams had brought to his office a document purportedly signed by one Alma Nesbitt in which she relinquished her homestead in favor of Williams. The transfer had been made, the federal man said. Then, he continued, a clerk in his office got to thinking. He had remembered Alma Nesbitt, a very handsome girl, at the time she herself had filed her original homestead claim. He became suspicious of the signature appearing on the relinquishment. He confided his suspicions to Mr. Hall, and Hall had then sent to Washington, D. C., for the original homestead application, on which he knew the woman's genuine signature would appear. This document proved beyond any doubt that the relinquishment was a forgery.

Hall continued his testimony. He had gone to Norman Williams, he said, and accused him of the forgery. Williams admitted having signed Alma's name, but said she had given him permission in writing to do so. Asked to produce such permission, Williams said it had been stolen from him together with letters from Alma. "At the time Williams was arrested on a charge of murder," Hall concluded, "my office was looking for him. He was under indictment for forgery."

The links in the chain were becoming tighter. Reporters at the trial noted how the prisoner, at first so calm, if morose, now moved about in his chair, changing his position every little while.

Dr. Victoria Hampton, the Portland chemist and microscopist, was called to the stand. Here was the sensation of the trial. Dr. Hampton was young and stunning. She was a scientist, but she was also a woman; and the conjunction was almost unheard of in the Oregon of 1904. The boys in the press box wrote their heads off.

Amid a silence so tense that Fred Wilson remembers it more than thirty-five years afterward, the young microscopist took the stand.

"The stains on this gunny sacking," she said in a clear, musical voice, "are of human blood."

The prisoner was seen to twitch. The jury was bug-eyed.

"Matted in the stains," Dr. Hampton went on, "I found several hairs, white in color—or nearly white. They are human hairs. They were torn from the head before death."

The hush was tomblike. Scientific testimony was new to The Dalles, Oregon. Jurors were amazed at this sort of witness, and they had a number of questions to ask Dr. Hampton. She explained, clearly and to the point, how she had arrived at her conclusions. The jury seemed satisfied, as well as highly pleased; but one of the members wanted to know just how it was that she could tell the hairs had been pulled from the head b*efore* death. Dr. Hampton explained that microscopic examination had shown the roots still clung to the hairs. If they had been pulled after death, there would be no roots adhering.

In a series of understatements the boys in the press box wrote that the testimony of Dr. Virginia Hampton had "made a profound sensation on jurors and spectators alike." One wonders how it affected Williams.

The State closed its case with Dr. Hampton.

Now Henry E. McGinn, Oregon's most noted criminal lawyer of all time, loosed his eloquence, which was very great. He called no witnesses at any time. He did not put Williams on the stand. He rested his case solely on the premise that the State had not shown a corpus delicti—which, as he explained carefully to the jury, meant that the State had not proved that a*nybody* had been murdered, much less Alma Nesbitt and her mother.

"Gentlemen," cried the dramatic McGinn, "the State of Oregon has not proved, and cannot prove, death in this case. The prosecuting attorney knows it. There are suspicions, gentlemen, grave suspicions, but nothing more. You cannot hang a man on mere suspicion, especially when there is such serious doubt of death as there is in this case."

Here McGinn went into many legally famous cases of the past. Some of his citations went to prove that neither judge nor jury would condemn a man, no matter how damning the circumstantial evidence, unless a corpus delicti—the body—were shown. Other citations showed how this or that man had been hanged for a crime of which he was later, and too much later, proved to be innocent.

"For all you and I know, gentlemen," cried McGinn in his closing, "and for all prosecution knows, Alma Nesbitt and her mother are today alive and well, living for reasons of their own in some obscure place. You can't find this man, this Norman Williams, guilty of a crime that *you don't even know has been committed."*

It was a dramatic and a forceful plea, one of the best ever heard in an Oregon courtroom but the jury could and did find Norman Williams guilty as hell. In less than four hours they brought in a first-degree verdict.

An appeal was taken to the state supreme court, but the learned judges denied a rehearing. The Oregon court's denial has been cited again and again in the intervening years and in almost every state in the Union. Said the court, in part:

> The strict rule contended for by defendant would operate completely to shield a criminal from punishment for the most atrocious crime, and afford him absolute immunity if he were cunning enough to consume or destroy the body . . . or completely hide it away or otherwise destroy its identity. But the death of the person alleged to have been killed is a distinct ingredient in the case of the prosecution for murder and must be established by direct testimony or presumptive evidence of the most cogent and irresistible kind . . . . Where, as here, the circumstances point with one accord to the death of the person alleged to have been murdered, the finding of fragments of a human body, which are identified as part of the body of the alleged victim, will be sufficient, if believed by the jury, to establish the fact of death, when this is the best evidence that can be obtained under the circumstances: *People v. Alviso,* 55 Cal. 230; *McCulloch v. State,* 48 Ind. 109; *Commonwealth v. Webster,* 5 Cush. 295 (52 Am Dec. 711); *State vs. Williams,* 52 N. C. 446 (78 Am. Dec. 248); *Gray v. Commonwealth,* 101 Pa. 380 (47 Am. Rep. 733). No universal rule can be laid down in regard to the proof of the corpus delicti . . . . The body of the crime may be proved by the best evidence which is capable of being adduced, if it is sufficient for the purpose . . . . There was sufficient evidence, without commenting on it, in the case at bar, in our opinion, to establish the death of the alleged victim within the rules of the law referred to.

More than a year after the trial The Dalles was again crowded with the curious, many of them to witness the hanging—the last public affair of its kind in Oregon. Williams made a good subject. He walked firmly to the gallows and shot through the trap promptly at 6:00 A.M. on July 21, 1905, thus ending the Great Homestead Murders case, although Norman Williams lived on in a ballad.

> Oh, Williams built a fire
> And he throwed the bodies in;
> He thought he'd covered up
> His bloody trail.
>
> But he left a couple hairs
> A-buried in the ground, and
> They hanged him at the
> Wasco County jail.

Today the case is forgotten except by Hood River oldtimers, who still mention it on wild March evenings, and by lawyers the country over, to whom this homestead drama is known only as 46 Ore. 287 (80 Pac. 655).

Murder Out Yonder (1941)

For additional information on the Homestead Murders, see Chapter 11 of *Murder Out Yonder.*

Lumberjacks' Saturday Night

A wan December sun struggled briefly against the heavy clouds, then gave up, and the winter gloom of the Pacific Northwest settled down to bring night at four o'clock. All along the single street, the pavement began to gleam in the rain as one by one the neon signs came on in the score of false-front hotels, restaurants, stores and beer joints. Sifting through the leaky sides of the joints came the music of juke boxes, played by slugs furnished by the proprietors themselves, for Saturday night was coming to Chokertown and it has long been an axiom here that the joint with the most light and the most noise gets the business.

"Business" in Chokertown means loggers, lumberjacks. Less than half a mile from the High-Lead Hotel, in the center of town, begins the vast forest that runs almost uninterrupted for a hundred miles west to the Pacific shore and fifty miles east to the top of the high Cascade Range. It is a tremendous forest and here in the rain belt it is growing fast enough, so many foresters say, to keep Chokertown's loggers busy until the Round River freezes solid and alcohol and snuff drip copiously out of hemlock bark.

There, in an opening of this forest, stands Chokertown, already fifty years a lumber town but now getting a new lease on life as a place of entertainment also, a blow-in town, a whoopee place for lumberjacks.

Tire and gas rationing first brought Chokertown its new night life. It was really a revival, for, quarter of a century ago, Chokertown made lumber and also served as a place for loggers to blow her in. Then came the automobile and the good roads. Roads led right up to camp doors in the tall timber. No longer had a lumberjack to toil for six months without going to town to get his teeth fixed—as it is euphemistically termed. He could go to town every night in the week, if he wanted to. And he did. He spent a little but not much money, and returned to camp the same night. But this new-style lumberjack seldom went to Chokertown at all; he lit out for Seattle, for Aberdeen, for Bellingham—the big towns. So, small Chokertown kept on sawing the logs into lumber and lived a rather staid life. The great whoopee days had gone, never to return—or so most people thought— even though Chokertown's mills produced millions of feet of lumber every year.

Then, in 1940, began a demand for lumber the like of which had never been seen—lumber for cantonments, for hangars, for ships, lumber without end. Pearl Harbor set loose a new and greater demand which continued unabated through the war years and after. Prices hit the ceiling and so, finally, did wages in the woods.

Along came the tire menace. At first the loggers, like other folks, gave it little thought; but as old tires gave out, the logger found he would have to stay in camp nights, or walk—usually a matter of from twenty to forty miles. So the jacks stayed in camp, listening fitfully to the radio, or boredly to old-timers who liked to do some stove-logging. The younger jacks soon tired of such doings, for they were not accustomed to six months solid of camp life, or even six weeks of camp life, without a break. They pooled the surviving travel equipment—a couple of tires here, a couple more there, and a car—and ganged up for a trip to town on Saturday night. In many cases, it was not too difficult to persuade the bull of the woods, the logging boss, to run a train to town right after Saturday's whistle. It became a habit.

Look out, Chokertown, here we come!

So, last Saturday night, just as it has done on many Saturdays recently, the Two-Spot coupled up a mulligan car and a caboose at Camp Six of the Dosewallops Logging Company. The lokey's whistle let go a blast, and inside of two minutes, one hundred and forty loggers piled aboard. The Two-Spot's bell rang and she started with the train for Chokertown, twenty miles away.

We're the blue-eyed, bandy-legged, hump-backed old mackinaw hodags from Dosewallops!

Down, down the mountain, across high trestles, over dizzy canyons rolled the two carloads of lumberjacks, while the Two-Spot moaned and chugged, letting go a blast on the curves. Inside the swaying, bounding cars, young loggers shouted pleasant obscenities to each other. The lokey rattled on.

Look out, Chokertown, here we come! Eighty feet to the nearest limb and six foot through at the butt!

The Two-Spot's bell began to ring. The whistle sounded. The train crossed a switch with a clatter and ground to a stop at the log dump beside the river and less than twenty yards from the main street. Under blinking lights, the boys from the woods could see some of their handiwork—the log pond of the big sawmill filled with sticks, big ones, the stuff they had felled and bucked and sent to the saws. Under the lights, the pond men were still working, feeding the huge logs to the bullchain that took them up the curved slip and on to the whining bandsaws. Mills can work all night. Loggers can't.

II

In half an hour Chokertown was alive. I went to the High-Lead first and found the bar lined two deep, all drinking beer, the only drink served. The overflow stamped into Joe's Tavern and the Logger's Rest, two other beer places. A few of the more serious drinkers did not stop at all until they got to the State liquor store, where the State of Washington purveys hard stuff at rather high prices.

"No Liquor to be Consumed on the Premises," says a sign.

"Who the hell wants to?" It was Dan Peters, a tall and rugged hooktender from Dosewallops. With two pints of rye in his tin coat and two chokerman pals similarly rigged, the three headed direct for the Stockholm.

The Stockholm is not the fanciest place in town, but it has that something about it which attracts young and older loggers who take their fun as seriously as their work. Its modest neon sign, looking so modern and new against the false front of weatherbeaten boards, says simply that this is "The Stockholm, Good Food, Beer, Rooms." Inside, too, the Stockholm is a mixture of periods. It is one great room with a bar down one side, booths on another, food counter at the rear. In the exact center is a gigantic barrel stove, its pipe running nearly ten feet to the high ceiling, then ranging thirty feet through haywire loops to the rear wall. The floor between stove and lunch counter is broken only by one of the biggest and gaudiest juke boxes ever to come out of Chicago. It is lighted like Borealis and it fairly gleams and leers.

Above the bar, and hiking back to five-cent-beer days, is the conventional moth-eaten deer's head. Back of the bar stands Gus himself, the only bartender left in Chokertown with an indubitable walrus mustache. The bar gleams from polish. The glasses are piled in intricate patterns. A small framed sign contains a one-dollar bill and a historic notation: "First Dollar Taken Over This Bar, August 22, 1899."

"Hallo, falers" Gus greeted the arrivals. The booths already were filled with loggers, loggers and girls, guzzling beer or beer spiked with rye. The juke was hitting "Somebody Else is Taking My Place," loud enough to be heard above the alcoholic laughter. Half a dozen couples were on the floor. Not a mackinaw on the men, but all in conventional city clothes. Dan the hooktender and his pals sat down in a booth where four half-consumed glasses of beer still sat on the table. Just then, the juke ceased for a moment and two couples came to the booth. And right here marked, better than anything else could, the change that has come over lumberjacks. The two couples were strangers to Dan and his pals. They had obviously been occupying the booth. But no roughhouse ensued.

"Guess we took your booth," Dan said, starting to rise. "Sorry."

"That's all right," one of the strangers spoke up. "We can all squeeze in." They did too. The boys from Camp Six spiked everybody's beer. Turned out the other two lads were gyppo spruce loggers from the opposite side of the river. In a little while everything was rosy. Dan danced with one of the girls, and later took her upstairs to look at the stars. One of the gyppo loggers passed out and slid under the table, very quietly. Booze and bawds, maybe, but not battle. The lumberjacks' trinity has lost its third angle.

Over at the High-Lead, loggers still lined the bar and filled the booths, they and their girls. The juke box blared endlessly. I watched while men slid under tables, girls screamed beery laughter, or wept into their glasses; and one old battle-ax with a deep bourbon contralto stood up by the juke and sang "Good-bye, Little Darlin'" in a true and musical if husky voice, while a rigging slinger from Hamma Hamma, way to hell and gone over the other side of the hump, wept great tears and told me his girl didn't love him any more.

The odd thing is that nobody hit anybody. Nobody threw a beer bottle. And those who might have looked closely at the husky contralto's hands could have seen calluses on them. For eight hours that day she had been pulling lumber—boards to you—off the chain in the mill across the river. She was but one of hundreds of women who were lumberjacks for the duration, helping lumber go to war and still working in a mill. And now a likely-looking lad rushed over to the big contralto and filled her glass with whiskey. She broke into her own song without benefit of the juke music:

> I'm a tearing old stiff full of slivers
> of Sitka,
> And I'm packing the wallop that
> went to beat Hit-la

"Amen, sister."
"Hold her, cutie, and watch that rigging."

The juke blared again and the dancers cavorted. The High-Lead was shaking and shivering in every one of its old boards and timbers. The proprietor told me it was going to be a one-thousand-dollar evening, with no breakage except for possibly a few beer glasses.

"No, sir," he told me, "loggers don't live in trees any more and they won't necessarily eat hay if you sprinkle whiskey on it."

In the Red Front Department Store across the street, a young rigging man from Camp Six was ordering a copy of *Trees and Forests of the Western United States,* by Hanzlik, a standard work on forests. In another section of the same store ("We Sell Everything") a high-climber from Hemlock Bay was buying a whole list of stuff—for his wife back in camp; thread and didies and a cord for the electric flatiron and such domestic things.

Mac's Barber Shop (four chairs) had a waiting line and many of the boys were getting the works—shampoo and all—while a Filipino lad shined their shoes, just as though they were city slickers. The talk in the shop, I noted, was not about women and automobiles, but about log production.

Across from the barber shop I could see the windows and sign of Painless Prentice, the chain dentists. Four patients were in the chairs. This was the ultimate, the incredible—loggers coming to town to "get their teeth fixed" and actually going to a dentist! It almost passed belief.

One block away, down on the river bank, a row of three shacks represented all that was left of Chokertown's one-time full two blocks of cribs. In 1920, the cribs here numbered at least a score and they housed, so old-timers say, sixty women. Tonight, half a dozen women would entertain perhaps as many as twenty loggers, possibly thirty. This doesn't mean that morals have changed, for they never change. It means that many of today's loggers have wives, either in camp or in town.

III

I went back to my room at the High-Lead and there, over a few drinks, talked with a forester who had once been a lumberjack. Now he had charge of a forty-acre tree nursery owned and operated by a group of logging concerns.

"So loggers themselves are planting trees in these incredible times?" I asked.

"We'll plant about eight million this winter," he said matter-of-factly. "Beginning next season, about ten million a year. We raise them from seed at the Nisqually nursery."

"Did I understand correctly?" I asked. "Did you say that this nursery is owned and run by the logging operators themselves, the lumbermen?"

"That's right. And we can raise enough trees at Nisqually to plant every burned-over acre in Oregon and Washington. What is more, we *are* planting them."

I reflected on the late and terrific Jigger Jones, the old woods boss who swore that he wouldn't leave a tree standing between Bangor and Seattle, nor a virgin anywhere. The times were changing even more than I had thought.

At five minutes to midnight, the Two-Spot blew a blast and I went over to the siding to see how the boys had been making out. Perhaps a score of them showed signs of alcohol—in mild doses. Two were indisputably drunk, but moving under their own power. One was drunk *and* had a black eye. Only eight were missing and five of these were married men with wives in town . . . . In my days in the woods, I recalled, the only ones who would have been ready to return to camp at midnight would have been those who were carried. I watched the boys climb aboard. The bell rang and away went the hell-roarers of Camp Six, back to the timber.

One by one, the lights went out along Chokertown's main drag until only the High-Lead showed in the dark. I went in and talked with old Bill, the night clerk and chef, about lumberjacks old and new. "No," he said, "they don't kick out windows any more. But one'll kick hell out of more timber than the two of his grandpappies could. They're high-ball these days. Don't spend so much money in town. Nowhere near. Never throw money away, like it used to be. These boys going to get their money's worth. Hardly ever get to fighting. Jes' like to drink some beer, to dance them jitter things, play pinball machines."

I asked Bill if the young loggers were different in any other ways from the old-timers. He eyed me a moment, then spoke slowly and I thought sadly. "Well," he said, "they wear rayon underwear."

"That all?"

Bill turned his bloodhound's sad eyes on me. "No," he said, then lowered his voice as one does in speaking of some terrible infirmity. "They smoke cigarets and use talcum powder after they shave."

I went up to bed. Chokertown had gone to bed, too; that is, all except for the sawmill. I could hear the faint whine of its saws through the rainy night, and down on the pond I could see men poling logs to the ever-hungry slip. Four miles up the mountain, the Two-Spot sounded a last moan on her whistle as she headed up a ravine, carrying the boys who are better loggers and far shrewder playboys than their fathers were.

The American Mercury (1943)

The Last of the Wobblies

The gloom of late winter afternoon draped and permeated all Portland. Wind whipped the harbor wildly. It flapped awnings of the joints along Burnside Street. Rain streaked the windows and glistened like rhinestones as the lights began to come on, one by one, in Erickson's, in the Valhalla, in a hundred other places known the world over to men who work outdoors with their hands. Dusk was coming down on Burnside, the most celebrated Skidroad in Oregon, or on earth.

Holbrook and Arthur Boose, the last of the Wobbly paper boys

At the corner of Third stood a figure familiar to this spot on Saturdays for two decades and more, Arthur Boose, the Wobbly paper boy, in fact the last of the Wobbly paper boys, here or elsewhere, a bundle of the *Industrial Worker* under one arm, the other supporting the husky overcoated man with a stout cane. . . . Get your copy of the *Worker,* he was saying, get your double-dose of industrial unionism hot off the griddle, learn the truth about the labor fakers, get in to the One Big Union, be a man, five cents buys a complete education for any scissorbill, get your *Worker* now. . . High wind, low rain, sunshine, sleet, or snow, or even troublesome cops, they are all the same to Arthur Boose, the Old War Horse, and the Saturdays of twenty-odd years have found him on the Skidroad in Portland doing his level damnedest to convert the dehorns, the scissorbills, the finks, the Mister Blocks, the Hoosiers, homeguards, hoboes and bums into Rebels; and the only Rebels who count with Boose are members of the Industrial Workers of the World—the Wobblies.

It is perhaps necessary, for those who came in late, to explain that the I.W.W., commonly called Wobblies, are likely the most distinctive and certainly the most American labor group the United States has ever known. Founded in 1905, militant, aggressive from the start, and as swiftly mobile as their membership which is (or was) composed of itinerant workers, the Wobblies raised more plain and particular hell in their twenty years of operations than any other union before or since. They organized the working stiffs of the woods, the mines, the harvest fields, the construction jobs, and occasionally the textile and the steel slaves. They staged strikes or riots in Lawrence, Massachusetts; in McKee's Rocks, Pennsylvania; in Calumet, Michigan; Virginia, Minnesota; Wheatland, California; Everett, Washington, and many other place. Wherever the Wobblies were, there too was battle.

The Wobblies were out for nothing short of Revolution, immediate, manifest, and complete, and to this end they bent their every energy. No voting for them, no peaceful revolution. They were lighting the fire for the Red Dawn which many of them devoutly believed would blaze up from behind the mountain at the very same moment the money palaces of Morgan and Rockefeller exploded, and turned into rubble, the result of well placed charges of 90 per cent stumping powder. World War I conditions took heavy toll of the Wobs, though they rallied and flared again in 1919 and appeared to be going pretty strong until internecine warfare ripped them into two factions. By 1925 their ranks had dreadfully thinned. Nor did the depression revive them. Their aging leaders joined the Communists, the Socialist Labor Party, Technocracy, and their rank and file went into the C.I.O., or even into the A.F.L. But not Old War Horse Boose.

II

Mellowed today, yet truculent enough in matters pertaining both to Capital and "the right kind of Unionism," Arthur Boose lives a spartan life and keeps bachelor quarters in a corner room of the Chester Rooms ("Reasonable Rates"), a venerable building along the Portland waterfront. He is a man of medium height, broad shouldered, with a fine head topped by a heavy growth of silver hair. Always clean-shaven, except for a neatly trimmed mustache, he might make you think of a banker—God save us—were it not for the man's eyes. In them smolders the light that comes not from bonds and mortgages, nor yet from Arcturus, but from some inner fire, kindled perhaps from the same coals that burned in the eyes of old Johann Most, the anarchist of demoniac intensity from whom the young Arthur Boose of long years ago learned that things were not as they should be, that peace on earth and good will to men were a delusion so long as The System prevailed.

Boose is always dressed in quiet good clothes of heavy blue serge, and wears a spanking old-fashioned watch chain across his vest. He has carried a cane since that time, early this century, when a big white pine log came whirling down a Wisconsin rollway and crushed his leg. He was born in 1878 in Milwaukee of German immigrant parents, and in his speech is yet a faint trace of accent in respect to "w" and "v."

Arthur Boose's mother died when he was six. Ten years later he quit school and home, to work in logging camps as a cantdog man, then as a teamster, in the pineries along the Chippewa and other streams. It was near Phillips where his leg was crushed, and while convalescing in Milwaukee he attended art school. Painting today is his only hobby. While recovering from his injury, too, young Boose attended lectures in the Milwaukee Freethinkers' Hall, a place of hellish reputation among the godly, and there one evening he listened spellbound while the aging Johann Most, wild eyed and wild whiskered, the very model for the cartoonists' Anarchist, told of the need for revolution by the working class; and Lucy Parsons, widow of the Haymarket Martyr, related the manner by which the rulers of creation kept the working class in their places.

"Those two lectures made a great impression on me," Boose recalls. "I talked with Mrs. Parsons afterward. She was a brilliant and altogether wonderful woman. I came away convinced that the world could be bettered, even though I myself wasn't quite ready to do anything about it."

For the next few years Boose followed, as they say, the wheat harvests and worked in logging camps. He drove team on construction jobs. And in 1909, in Minneapolis, he took out the Little Red Card that made him a Wobbly. Since that day he has never been in arrears with I.W.W. dues, nor has he ever joined another union. If there is merit in consistency, then Wobbly Boose is a man of merit. Through good times and bad, very bad, through days and weeks and months and years in jails, workhouses, penitentiaries, through days of danger and of riot, under his real and his phony names, Old War Horse Boose has never wavered. The Wobblies are *right*, and their aging stalwart would rather be right than popular.

III

Wobbly Boose came first into national prominence in 1916. The first World War was under way and two years old. Wages in most industries had been going up and the iron miners of the great Mesabi in Minnesota wanted more pay. They started a half hearted and wholly unorganized strike. Boose was in charge of the I.W.W. hall at Duluth. Quickly seeing that their strike wasn't getting anywhere, a group of Finn miners sent a telegram to the Finnish newspaper in Duluth asking for an organizer, and Boose was asked if he would go. Turning over the Wobbly hall to another, Boose went to Aurora, a Mesabi mine town, and staged a couple of hot meetings. Local police, naturally dominated by the mining companies, put Boose in jail on a charge of "inciting to riot."

The War Horse was now stabled, but there was kick in him yet. Talking through the bars of the tiny jail in Aurora, he urged the miners to spread news of the burgeoning strike to all parts of the range as rapidly as possible. Spread it like forest fire, he said. That night a young Finn, Ormi something or other, started the spreading. He had no horse, no train of cars, so out of Aurora that evening he walked until he was beyond the vision of mine police. Then he ran.

In the prime of young manhood, the Finn ran swiftly through the twilight, traveling like a shadow blown by a soft Mesabi wind. At Biwabik he roused the boys, then on to McKinley, and so on to Virginia, where he waked the secretary of the Finnish Brotherhood Lodge. Next morning few miners showed up for work anywhere along the eastern section of the range.

At the time of his arrest, Boose also managed to get word of events to I.W.W. headquarters in Chicago, and now to the range came a whole pack of able organizers, among them Sam Scarlett, Elizabeth Gurley Flynn, Frank Little, later lynched at Butte, and Carlo Tresca, whose murder at Fifth Avenue and Fifteenth Street in 1943 still mystifies Manhattan police. At almost the same time that the organizers arrived, shooting started in the mine towns. Several miners were killed, and so were a couple of mine police.

Boose was moved from Aurora and confined in the jail at Virginia, then bailed out by a saloonkeeper. He promptly mounted the platform in the Finn hall and addressed a mass meeting of strikers. He said, among other things that although the I.W.W. did not believe in the use of violence, nevertheless, workingmen must protect themselves and now that the "mine Cossacks" had begun killing "innocent workers," it was perhaps time for the workers to arm themselves. He went on to speak of rats and parasites, and wound up by saying: "Parasites should be exterminated!"

"Fine, fine!" shouted Carlo Tresca, chairman of the meeting.

"For every miner killed," Boose went on, "a mine cop must die!"

This kind of talk was a great mistake, Boose says today. Eugene Debs had made the same kind of mistake in an earlier day, and so had Bill Haywood.

Well, the clubbing and shooting continued, and also the arrests of Wobbly organizers and sympathizers. The strike committee, figuring Boose was now a man marked for the cops, sent him to Duluth, just as newspapers came out with word of an indictment for murder against him and four other Wobblies. Boose, who seldom bothered to read capitalist newspapers, knew nothing of the indictment. A friendly attorney in Duluth told him about it and advised him to get out of there. Boose hid until train time, while cops hunted him, then went to Minneapolis. It was still too warm. Wobbly Frank Little showed up with a copy of the newspaper in which Boose was quoted as saying that all of the mine cops ought to be killed. It also played up the murder indictment in a front-page box.

Now began a time of great danger for Boose. He knew he had nothing to do with the murder for which he had been indicted: it had occurred before he delivered his fiery speech in Virginia. But Little and Haywood warned him that would make no difference; he was a Wobbly organizer, hence he would be railroaded. They urged him to leave Minnesota. Boose went to Wisconsin to work a while in the woods, then to Chicago. Here he met Haywood, Gurley (The) Flynn, Joe Ettor and other Wob leaders, and they all told him he was "hot," to get going to far places and to stay until the Mesabi strike was done. Changing his name to Arthur Fritz, Boose grabbed a fast freight and landed in Oklahoma, where he went to work driving team on a railroad construction job. Early in 1917 Haywood detailed him to go into the western oil fields to organize the working stiffs. He did, then was called to Tulsa to take charge of the I.W.W. hall. He now dropped "Fritz" and became Boose again.

On September 5, 1917, the so-called Palmer Raids took place all over the country. Radicals and persons suspected of independent thought were arrested and jailed all the way from Maine to California. Oddly enough, the raiders overlooked Arthur Boose, secretary of the I. W. W. at Tulsa. But not for long. On the twenty-eighth, three large, rather grim men attended one of Boose's educational talks in the Wobbly hall, then arrested and took him to jail. "I was charged," he remembers, "not only with being a fugitive from the murder charge in Minnesota, but with almost every crime I had ever heard of, including lack of what is commonly called patriotism."

They took Boose to Chicago, and there, throughout most of 1918, he and one hundred and sixty-five other Wobblies and sympathizers were tried on five counts charging conspiracy to obstruct the war. The evidence, including tons of Wobbly papers, pamphlets, and even correspondence, much of it illegally seized, would have filled three freight cars. The correspondence was particularly damning. "Haywood was always careless of his mail," says Boose, who adds that it was matter from Haywood's correspondence, all of which tactically should have been destroyed as soon as read, that was used as evidence to convict Boose and several of the other defendants.

Ninety-three of the Wobblies were found guilty in various degrees and were sentenced to from one to twenty years in prison. (Haywood, out on bail, skipped to Russia, where he died.) Boose drew five years, and was released on expiration of his time in June of 1922.

While in prison at Leavenworth, Boose read constantly in such works of philosophy and economics as he could lay hands on. They merely confirmed his beliefs that the Wobblies had the right idea, or at least the best ideas that had so far been put forward, for a new and a better world; and when he came out of the Big House, he picked up where he had left off. The stiffs must be educated and organized. Incidentally, of his jail and prison days, Boose recalls that the Christmas of 1917, spent in what he calls the Cook County Can in Chicago, was brightened considerably by receipt of gifts of a necktie, two pairs of socks, and a handkerchief, from Helen Keller. Each of the ninety-three prisoners received like presents from the famous blind woman.

IV

In the autumn of 1922, War Horse Boose, by then one of the most celebrated of Wobblies, started west on a speaking tour which eventually took him to Portland, Oregon. He soapboxed during the longshore and all of the lumber strikes of the 1920's and 1930's. Arrests on what appear to have been trumped-up charges were a regular thing. Once, in Walla Walla, Washington, Boose had barely hit town and had not yet had time to set up his flag and soapbox when a motorcycle cop arrived and took him to jail. "Quickest pinch I ever knew," he says today. There were many other pinches, too, one on the charge of "profanity" ("I said that the Bible shouters sell Jesus Christ over the counter like so much sugar"); another on a charge of "obstructing traffic," something Boose was always careful not to do. Incidentally, he has been arrested, on one charge or another and always in connection with his work, in

Aurora, Virginia, and Minneapolis, Minnesota; in Tulsa and Drumright, Oklahoma; in Great Falls, Montana, and in Portland, and Walla Walla. Cops have slugged him. So have patriots. Judges have lectured and fined him. His meetings have been broken up with fire, with water, with stinkballs, eggs, brickbats, with shouting and rioting.

Yet Old War Horse Boose, a name applied by admiring Wobblies many years ago, is still packing the rigging, as they say of active I.W.W. organizers, and he remains a cheerful and wholly unreconstructed Wobbly. "I'd prefer anarchism," he told me one day recently, "for that is the highest and finest form of civilization possible. But we aren't ready for it yet. We aren't even ready for the kind of world the I.W.W. wants. It takes time." He considers Communists both comical and hopelessly entangled in dogma. He would as soon think of voting the Republican as the Communist ticket.

It irritates the War Horse to call him the Last Wobbly. He claims there are some 20,000 members of the I.W.W. in this country and Canada. Maybe there are, but they are not in evidence in the Pacific Northwest, the real home of the Wobs; but Arthur Boose is. Everyone familiar with Portland's Skidroad district knows him as the only Wobbly paper boy left in the Northwest, and as nearly as I can learn, the only one on earth. He peddles his papers as related, every Saturday, no matter the times nor the weather, and along with the *Worker* he sells a few copies of I.W.W. pamphlets, and the latest edition (the twenty-eighth) of the justly famous Little Red Song Book, which contains a good picture of the late Katie Phar, songbird of the Wobblies, who rallied the boys with her sweet voice from 1910 to her death three years ago. The twenty-eighth edition of the song book, like all the others since it was composed, contains Joe Hill's Last Will, "written in his death cell on the eve of his judicial murder by the authorities of the State of Utah, Nov. 18, 1915."

Oldtime Wobs, passing through Portland, usually call on Boose, who is the official, stationary delegate of the I.W.W. in that city. They often find him brewing a cup of coffee on the gas plate in his room, his table covered with brushes and water colors, at work on some forest scene, his favorite motif. For an oldtime Wobbly, Boose will put away his colors and brushes, and talk of the great days when the Wobbly brand of revolution ran like fire through the wheat, the mines, the woods of the West; when the West fairly reeked of Wobblies, and Wob organizers hung stiffly from bridges and trestles by their necks, or died on the bloody decks of the *Verona* in Everett harbor, or went down in the choking dust of Wheatland or Bisbee. . . . Aye, my lad, those were great days, days when working stiffs had nothing to lose but their chains, unless on occasion their lives. Almost alone, the Old War Horse has survived them, unchanged.

The American Mercury (1946)

Additional Reading

Checklist of the Books of Stewart H. Holbrook

Holy Old Mackinaw: A Natural History of the American Lumberjack. New York: The Macmillan Company, 1938. *New, Enlarged Edition:* New York: The Macmillan Company, 1956. *Reprint:* Sausalito, CA: Comstock Editions, Inc., 1979.

Let Them Live. New York: The Macmillan Company, 1938.

Iron Brew: A Century of American Ore and Steel. New York, The Macmillan Company, 1939.

Oregon, End of the Trail. (The American Guide Series). Oregon Writers Project. Portland: Binfords & Mort, 1940. (Stewart Holbrook, unnamed editor.)

Ethan Allen. New York: The Macmillan Company, 1940. *Illustrated Edition:* Portland: Binfords & Mort Publishing, 1958.

Tall Timber. New York: The Macmillan Company, 1941.

Murder Out Yonder: An Informal Study of Certain Classic Crimes in Back-Country America. New York: The Macmillan Company, 1941. *Reprint:* Glenwood, IL: Meyerbooks, 1989.

None More Courageous: American War Heroes of Today. New York: The Macmillan Company, 1942.

Burning an Empire: The Study of American Forest Fires. New York: The Macmillan Company, 1943.

A Narrative of Schafer Bros. Logging Company's Half Century in the Timber. Seattle: Dogwood Press, 1945.

Green Commonwealth: A Narrative of the Past and a Look at the Future of One Forest Products Community. Seattle: Dogwood Press, 1945.

Promised Land: A Collection of Northwest Writing. Edited by Stewart H. Holbrook. New York: Whittlesey House, 1945. *Reprint:* New York: Ballantine Books, 1973.

Lost Men of American History. New York: The Macmillan Company, 1946.

The Story of American Railroads. New York: Crown Publishers, 1947.

Little Annie Oakley and Other Rugged People. New York: The Macmillan Company, 1948.

Northwest Corner: Oregon and Washington, the Last Frontier. Garden City, NY: Doubleday & Company, Inc., 1948. (Photography by Henry Sheldon; Introduction and commentary by Stewart Holbrook.)

America's Ethan Allen. Boston: Houghton Mifflin Co., 1949.

The Yankee Exodus: An Account of Migration from New England. New York: The Macmillan Company, 1950. *Reprint:* Seattle, WA: University of Washington Press, 1968.

The Portland Story. Portland: Lipman Wolfe & Co., 1951.

Personalities of the Woods. n.p.: Bethlehem Pacific Coast Steel Corporation, 1950. *Expanded edition,* 1955.

The Far Corner: A Personal View of the Pacific Northwest. New York: The Macmillan Company, 1952. *Reprint:* Sausalito, CA: Comstock Editions, Inc., 1987.

Saga of the Saw Files. Portland: Armstrong Manufacturing Co., 1952.

Wild Bill Hickok Tames the West. New York: Random House, 1952.

The Age of the Moguls. Garden City, NY: Doubleday & Company, Inc., 1953. *Reprint:* Salem, N.H.: Ayer Co. Publications, Inc., 1981.

Down on the Farm, A Picture History of Country Life in America in the Good Old Days. New York: Crown Publishing, Inc., 1954. (Commentary by Stewart H. Holbrook; pictures assembled and collected by Milton Rugoff.)

James J. Hill: A Great Life in Brief. New York: Alfred A. Knopf, 1955.

Machines of Plenty: Pioneering in American Agriculture. New York: The Macmillan Company, 1955.

Davy Crockett. New York: Random House, 1955.

Wyatt Earp: U.S. Marshall. New York: Random House, 1956.

The Columbia. New York: Rinehart & Co., 1956. *Reprint:* Sausalito, CA: Comstock Editions, Inc., 1991.

The Rocky Mountain Revolution. New York: Henry Holt & Company, 1956.

Dreamers of the American Dream. Garden City, NY: Doubleday & Company, Inc., 1957.

The Swamp Fox of the Revolution. New York: Random House, 1957.

Mr. Otis. New York: The Macmillan Company, 1958.

The Golden Age of Quackery. New York: The Macmillan Company, 1959.

The Golden Age of Railroads. New York: Random House, 1960.

Yankee Logger: A Recollection of Woodsmen, Cooks and River Drivers. New York: International Paper Company, 1961.

The Old Post Road: The Story of the Boston Post Road. New York: McGraw-Hill Book Company, Inc., 1962.

The Pacific Northwest. Garden City, NY: Doubleday & Company, Inc., 1963. (Stewart Holbrook, co-author, with Nard Jones and Roderick Haig-Brown. Edited by Anthony Netboy.)

The Wonderful West. Garden City, N.Y.: Doubleday & Company, Inc., 1963.

The Columbia River. New York: Holt, Rinehart and Winston, 1965.

Selected Sources

Beebe, Lucius, "Tribute to a Friend," *The Oregon Journal,* September 24, 1964, reprinted in Lucia, Ellis, Editor, *This Land Around Us,* Garden City, NY: Doubleday & Company, Inc., 1969.

Chittick, V.L.O., Editor, *Northwest Harvest, A Regional Stock-Taking,* New York: The Macmillan Company, 1948.

Colby, R.M., "Author Stewart Holbrook Succumbs," *The Courier,* Littleton, New Hampshire, September 10, 1961.

Ficken, Robert E., "Stewart H. Holbrook" in *Historians of the American Frontier: A Bio-Bibliographical Source Book,* New York: Greenwood Press, 1988.

Hagenstein, W.D., "It's Time to Think Green," *Wood Review,* August 18, 1978.

Holbrook, Stewart H., Papers. University of Washington Libraries, University of Washington, Seattle, Washington.

Holm, Don, "There Were Giants in Those Days, or Oregon's Golden Age of Literati," *Northwest Magazine, The Oregonian*, September 2, 1973.

Holmes, Kenneth L., "Pages from our Past," Astoria, Oregon, *Astorian*, January 20, 1962.

James, David, "Tales of Simpson in Time," *The Simpson Lookout*, June 1951.

Lipman's Gallery, "The Elegant Paintings of the Celebrated Mr. Otis, Founder of the Primitive-Moderne School: Catalog and Program Notes of Original and Warranted Hand-painted Works," Portland, Oregon, June 1957.

Lucia, Ellis, Editor, *This Land Around Us*, Garden City, NY: Doubleday & Company, Inc., 1969.

Lucia, Ellis, "Just Who in the Heck Was James G. Blaine?" *Northwest Magazine, The Oregonian*, September 14, 1967.

Lucia, Ellis, "Stewart Holbrook," *The Sunday Oregonian*, March 28, 1976 and April 4, 1976.

Mahaffay, Robert E., "Erudite Logger: Holbrook Writes for all Classes," *The Sunday Oregonian Magazine*, April 20, 1947.

Mahaffay, Robert E., "This Ink-Slinger Eats Bark!" *The Weyerhaeuser News*, 1948.

Mattila, Walter, "Holbrook Lent Talent to Conservation Cause," *The Portland Reporter*, September 4, 1964.

Meier & Frank Co., "The Paintings of Mr. Otis—Catalog and Program Notes of Exhibition and Sale of Original Hand-painted Works of this Portland Artist," Portland, Oregon, April 1959.

Powers, Alfred, *History of Oregon Literature,* Portland: Metropolitan Press, 1935.

Shoemaker, Marvin, "Stewart Holbrook: Logger to Literary Light," *The Sunday Oregonian Magazine*, April 27, 1952.

Stephens, James, Papers. University of Washington Libraries, University of Washington, Seattle, Washington.

Steiner, Dr. Richard M., "Holbrook Memorial Service," September 12, 1964.

Editor's Note

During high school and college I rotated summer jobs between reporting for a daily newspaper and working in the plywood mills of southern Oregon. So it was a foregone conclusion that I would encounter the ubiquitous Stewart Holbrook.

In the 1950s, before the dominance of television, Stewart Holbrook was an almost legendary figure for anyone in the Pacific Northwest with an interest in writing, journalism, history or the area's leading industry—forest products. He was one of the few residents of the region with a national reputation in any field, and his celebrity was a matter of local pride. Holbrook linked the remote Northwest with the glamorous literary and publishing world of New York. And, as the leading spokesperson for the "Far Corner," he articulated to the rest of the country what a special place this region was, and helped convince its residents how fortunate they were to live here.

I grew up reading Holbrook's *Oregonian* articles, received my first Holbrook book as a high school graduation present, and recall getting a leave from Fort Lewis to see an exhibit of the paintings of Mr. Otis in the Meier and Frank auditorium in Portland. Years later, in 1987, when Oregon Institute of Literary Arts established its special award to honor lifetime achievement in Oregon letters, it seemed natural to me to name the award for Stewart Holbrook. However, I soon learned that today many Northwest writers and readers have little knowledge of Holbrook's work or his career. This project was undertaken to help remedy that situation.

In preparing this book, I was fortunate to have the complete cooperation of the late Sibyl Holbrook Strahl and her daughter Sibyl Holbrook. The two of them graciously met with me on numerous occasions, allowed me to review the family's scrapbooks and library, introduced me to friends of Stewart Holbrook, and cooperated in allowing the use of his work. I am greatly indebted to them.

The Stewart Holbrook Papers fill some sixty boxes in the Manuscript and University Archives Division at the University of Washington Libraries. Janet Ness and the other staff members helped guide me through the wealth of material. I extend my sincere thanks to them. I also thank the staffs at the Oregon Historical Society Library, the Special Collections Division of the Knight Library at the University of Oregon, the Oregon State Library, the Bradford Millar Library at Portland State University, as well as the Multnomah County Library that Stewart Holbrook loved so much.

Several friends of Stewart Holbrook were especially helpful in kindly sharing their experiences, insights and memories of Stewart Holbrook. They are: the late Ruth Manary, widow of lumberman Gordon Manary (one of Holbrook's favorite bulls of the woods) and a neighbor of the Holbrooks' and Mr. Otis; Reginald "Dutch" Brummer, a longtime Holbrook colleague and fellow North Country New Englander; W.D. Hagenstein, former Executive Vice President of the Industrial Forestry Association; and Albert L. McCready, retired Managing Editor of the *Oregonian*. Dutch Brummer and W.D. Hagenstein also read early drafts of the introduction. I thank them for their comments and suggestions.

Others who knew Stewart Holbrook and gave their time to tell me about Holbrook and his times included: Vivian Bretherton, Maxine Brummer, Fred Jacobson, David James, Don James, Ellis Lucia, Katharine McCanna, Connie McCready, Preston McMann and Nan Phillips. My thanks also to the following for their kind assistance given in a variety of ways: Professor Edwin Bingham, Tom Booth, Marcia Brown, Walt Curtis, Bruce Hamilton, Ed Kemp, Richard LaSasso, Thomas Lauderdale, John McClelland Jr., Eugene Snyder, Thomas B. Stoel and George Young.

I am grateful to my wife, Gwyneth Gamble Booth, for her patience and support. I know she will be glad to get the dining room table back for more normal use. My editor, Jo Alexander, of Oregon State University Press, faced with the unpleasant task of editing a lawyer, was enthusiastic, helpful and discriminating throughout the process.

With regard to all of the above, I shall repeat the words of Stewart Holbrook in *The Far Corner*: "I shall not attempt to saddle my authorities, either named or unnamed, with responsibility for the opinions, prejudices and other fallacies that may be found in this book. They are my own opinions, prejudices and fallacies."

Brian Booth

Acknowledgments

The Editor wishes to thank the copyright holders and publishers listed below for their permission to reprint the materials included in this volume. Every effort has been made to trace the ownership of copyrighted material and to make full acknowledgement of its use. Material in the public domain has been listed with the date of original publication for purposes of reference. If errors or omissions have occurred, they will be corrected in subsequent editions, provided that notification is submitted in writing to the publisher.

These pieces have been reprinted in the form in which they first appeared, except for the omission of footnotes that no longer appear relevant, the correction of obvious errors of fact or spelling, and the deletion of certain transitional paragraphs that do not seem appropriate in the present context.

In addition, the Oregon State University Press and the Editor would like to thank Sibyl Holbrook and the University of Washington Libraries for permission to quote from material and to use photographs in this book from the Stewart H. Holbrook Papers in the University of Washington Libraries, and the Oregon Historical Society for permission to use the photograph on page 10, negative number 79080.

"Death and Times of a Prophet" from *Murder Out Yonder: An Informal Study of Certain Classic Crimes in Back-Country America* (1941).

"Daylight in the Swamp" from *American Heritage*, October 1958; copyright 1958 by American Heritage Publishing Co., Inc.. Used by permission of Sibyl Holbrook and the publisher.

"The Affair at Copperfield" from *The Far Corner: A Personal View of the Pacific Northwest*, The Macmillan Company (1952); copyright 1952 by Stewart H. Holbrook; copyright renewed 1975 by Sibyl Holbrook Strahl. Used by permission of Sibyl Holbrook.

"Cargoes of Maidens" from *The Yankee Exodus: An Account of Migration from New England*, The Macmillan Company (1950); copyright 1950 by Stewart H. Holbrook; copyright renewed 1978 by Sibyl Holbrook Strahl. Used by permission of Sibyl Holbrook.

"Anarchists at Home" from *The American Scholar*, 1946; copyright 1946 by Stewart H. Holbrook; copyright renewed 1971 by Sibyl Holbrook Strahl; reprinted in *Little Annie Oakley and Other Rugged People*, The Macmillan Company (1948). Used by permission of Sibyl Holbrook and *The American Scholar*.

Acknowledgments

"Erickson's: Elbow Bending for Giants" from *Esquire*, April 1954. An earlier version included in *The Far Corner: A Personal View of the Pacific Northwest*, The Macmillan Company (1952); copyright 1952 by Stewart H. Holbrook; copyright renewed 1975 by Sibyl Holbrook Strahl. Used by permission of Sibyl Holbrook and *Esquire*.

"The Gorse of Bandon" from *Burning an Empire: The Story of American Forest Fires*, The Macmillan Company (1943); copyright 1943 by Stewart H. Holbrook; copyright renewed 1970 by Sibyl Holbrook Strahl. Used by permission of Sibyl Holbrook.

"Whistle Punks" from *The Century Magazine*, 1927; reprinted in *Little Annie Oakley and Other Rugged People*, The Macmillan Company (1948). Copyright 1948 by Stewart H. Holbrook; copyright renewed 1970 by Sibyl Holbrook Strahl. Used by permission of Sibyl Holbrook.

"Harry Tracy, King of Western Robbers," from the *Oregonian*, July 23, 1947. Reprinted by permission of the *Oregonian*.

"Disaster in June," from *The Far Corner: A Personal View of the Pacific Northwest*, The Macmillan Company (1952); copyright 1952 by Stewart H. Holbrook; copyright renewed 1975 by Sibyl Holbrook Strahl. Used by permission of Sibyl Holbrook.

"The Aurora Communists," from *The American Mercury*, July 1948. Another version included in *The Far Corner: A Personal View of the Pacific Northwest*, The Macmillan Company (1952); copyright 1952 by Stewart H. Holbrook; copyright renewed 1975 by Sibyl Holbrook Strahl. Used by permission of Sibyl Holbrook.

"First Bomb," from the *New Yorker*, October 7, 1944; copyright 1944 by the *New Yorker* Magazine, Inc.(formerly the F-R Publishing Corp.); copyright renewed 1971 by Sibyl Holbrook Strahl; reprinted in *Little Annie Oakley and Other Rugged People*, The Macmillan Company (1948). Used by permission of Sibyl Holbrook and the *New Yorker*.

"The Great Homestead Murders," from *Murder Out Yonder: An Informal Study of Certain Classic Crimes in Back-Country America* (1941).

"Lumberjacks' Saturday Night," from *The American Mercury*, March 1943; copyright 1943 by Stewart H. Holbrook; copyright renewed 1970 by Sibyl Holbrook Strahl; reprinted in *Little Annie Oakley and Other Rugged People*, The Macmillan Company (1948). Used by permission of Sibyl Holbrook.

"The Last of the Wobblies," from *The American Mercury*, April 1946; copyright 1946 by Stewart H. Holbrook; copyright renewed 1973 by Sibyl Holbrook Strahl; reprinted in *Little Annie Oakley and Other Rugged People*, The Macmillan Company (1948). Used by permission of Sibyl Holbrook.